HARDPRESS.NET
HOME OF HARD-TO-FIND BOOKS

The Beggars (Les Gueux) Or, the Founders of the Dutch Republic
by Jacob B. Liefde

Address:
HardPress
8345 NW 66TH ST #2561
MIAMI FL 33166-2626
USA
Email: info@hardpress.net

Margaret Eliza Keep
from her friend J. C.
3 August 1868

THE BEGGARS.

The Beggars:

(LES GUEUX).

OR,

The Founders of the Dutch Republic.

A TALE.

BY

J. B. DE LIEFDE.

LONDON:

HODDER AND STOUGHTON,

(LATE JACKSON, WALFORD AND HODDER),

27, PATERNOSTER ROW.

MDCCCLXVIII.

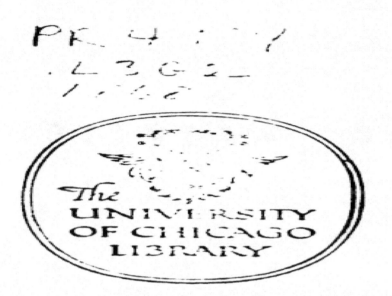
WATSON AND HAZELL,
Printers.
London & Aylesbury.

CONTENTS.

—••◆◆◆••—

CONTENTS.

CONTENTS.

CONTENTS.

THE BEGGARS.

Chapter First.

A BIRD'S-EYE VIEW.

THE market-place of Brussels presented a dismal sight, when the sun of the 5th of June, 1568, rose upon that city. Before a large, imposing edifice a scaffold was erected, upon which two of the first nobles of the country, the Counts of Egmont and Horn, were to be beheaded. They were the sacrifices, by the blood of which the soil of the Netherlands was to be consecrated as the scene of one of the noblest struggles which the history of the sixteenth century records.

It was a struggle for the holiest and most precious concerns of man—religious and political liberty. The first defenders of these costly treasures, though a mere handful of people, were animated by an indomitable spirit of freedom and strengthened by faith in the word of God which, it is said, is the "victory that overcometh the world." The adversaries whom they resisted were

B

the greatest powers of the age ; the Roman Pope, the Spanish King and the powerful instruments of both, the terrible Inquisition.   If ever priestcraft and despotism united cunning with force to crush the good cause, it was in this pertinacious contest, which lasted not less than eighty years.   But it has been shown in this contest too that even a small, weak nation can conquer the mightiest empires, if that nation united and harmonious is ready to lay down its life for the sake of liberty and truth.

The name of the Netherlands is at present only given to the kingdom of Holland.   In the sixteenth century however, that name indicated a cluster of provinces extending from the Zuiderzee and the Dollart, to the northern frontiers of France, and forming that track of fertile alluvial land, which is at present occupied by the two kingdoms of Holland and Belgium.   These provinces were at the time of our story a portion of the dominion of the king of Spain, Philip II, who ruled them under the title of count of the Netherlands, in which capacity he was named Philip III.   He had inherited this property from his father Charles V., and it undoubtedly was one of the finest portions of his extensive dominion.

By a gradual process of industry and intelligence, of bold and cautious speculation, the people of the Netherlands had at the end of the 15th century arrived at a state of prosperity second to none in the world.   They were reckoned amongst the boldest navigators of their time.   Their manufactures in velvet, in silk, in tapestry and in linen were valued wherever they were known, and strange to say, in a country for the greater part singularly destitute of romantic scenery, there was founded a school of painters inferior only to that of Rome. The prosperity of the inhabitants was proverbial. The wealth which they displayed in their houses and on their persons was so great, that a crowned visitor, when walking one day through the capital, exclaimed in astonishment that she could fancy herself surrounded by princes instead of simple burghers.

No wonder then that Philip dreaded the loss of this rich part of his possessions as a great calamity. And for this dread there was indeed some ground. It is true the Netherlanders were as loyal subjects as he could desire them to be, for, though very jealous of their privileges and ever trying to obtain freedom of self-government, yet the thought of renouncing their allegiance to the Spanish crown never occurred to them, nay, they were so far from it, that, not until Philip himself had in the most inhumane and reckless way torn asunder the ties which bound that faithful people to his throne, could they be brought to establish themselves as an independent nation.

But the light of the Reformation which had set Germany all ablaze, had also penetrated to these districts. Philip who was as bigoted a papist as he was a cruel tyrant, foresaw that a separation between his house and the Netherlands would become inevitable, if he did not in time prevent the spread of the horrible heresy in these quarters. Much to his dismay, on his visit to this part of his dominion in 1559, he found that not only had the evil already made alarming progress, but that it was also of the worst kind, for the heresy which here prevailed was the Calvinistic or Reformed, which was reported as being fraught with still stronger revolutionary and rebellious tendencies than was the Lutheran.   In his anger he resolved not to allow himself any rest until he had extirpated Protestantism root and branch.   He formed a scheme with the French king Henry II., to massacre all heretics whether high or humble, and thus to deliver the world of that " accursed vermin."

This plan was imprudently revealed to William, Prince of Orange, who was at that time a hostage at the court of the French king,   From that moment dates the resolution of this noble prince to protect the innocent people of the Netherlands, even though it should cost him his life.   This disposition of the Prince however, was not known to the king of Spain else he would most assuredly not have appointed him as governor of the four wealthiest and most powerful of the Northern provinces, namely Holland, Zealand, West-Friesland and Utrecht.

The government of the whole country was intrusted to the king's sister Margaret, Duchess of Parma who was assisted by Cardinal Granvelle and a council of the principal nobles, amongst whom, besides the Prince of Orange, the Counts of Egmont, Horn and the Baron Berlaimont were most influential.   Ere long, however, it was discovered that the king had resolved to carry on the government in his own way, and independent of the will of the country as expressed by the estates and the council of nobles.   In spite of all opposition, and in the face of all the rights and privileges possessed by the people, the Cardinal Granvelle, the real governor, introduced the Spanish Inquisition.   The persecution at once became virulent and general.   The members of the Order of Jesus crept into every family and fished out the most hidden secrets.   The officers of the Inquisition, whose diabolical cruelties were often not even masked with an assumption of piety, seized upon everyone who bowed down in anything but abject submission.   They strangled, burned and imprisoned thousands of people· And yet even then there were to be found those who were bold enough to proclaim the pure Gospel and attack the errors of the church, in the face of poverty, of life-long imprisonment, of death by hanging, by strangling, by flaying alive, by roasting alive, and by such exquisite forms of torture as kept their victims drooping and slowly dying often for the full space of thirty-six hours.

The people became uproarious.   Even the Roman Catholics could not bear this.   But popish Bulls and excommunications were showered down upon the unhappy country.   Imperial decrees were thundered forth, and were upheld and executed by troops who were paid from the wealth which the oppressor had principally screwed out of his victims.   The fleets of trading vessels, formerly carrying merchandise to every port of the world, were now freighted with the flying merchants themselves, who, settling in Germany and England, transported to these countries their capitals and their industry.   The prisons, which were numerous and large, were filled with the innocent, while their proper occupants, were allowed to go at large, provided they were poor and could repeat an "Ave Maria." . People suspected their nearest relations, their own children, their wives, their husbands.   No one dared to speak openly about religion, and only then in private, when, two or three being assembled in Jesus' name, the oppressed heart could pour itself out and be strengthened in Christian fellowship.

The nobles who had never been accustomed to restraint, and had no idea of being thus overruled, became furious. The governess (the Duchess of Parma) was overwhelmed with angry reproaches, with appeals, with threats. She was a soft-hearted woman, and she felt the invectives keenly. But she could not give them a satisfactory answer, for she could not tell these haughty nobles that the fault lay not with her but with the king, and most of all with the Cardinal. They found it out themselves however, and the Prince of Orange, who was looked up to as the first man in the country, followed by all the people, turned bitterly upon this ecclesiastical assailant of their liberties. His removal from the provinces was demanded. At first the king preserved a cold and haughty silence ; then he gave a kind but evasive answer. This however would not satisfy the nobles. They insulted and ridiculed the Cardinal, they threatened the king, they spoke of revolt. The King grew furious, hurled back their threats with increased bitterness, but gave in at last, and the Cardinal retired in the year 1564.

Great was the joy in the provinces at this event, and a golden age was now expected. It is true it was found that the Inquisition had not departed with the Cardinal. But now that he was away, the governess showed far greater leniency, and the persecution for a time almost ceased. The nobles and estates were once more convoked, the persecuted adherents of the Reformation again came forward, the fields swarmed with immense multitudes of people who often walked many miles to listen to some pious preacher, and frequently carried their clubs and swords with them to defend him against attacks. The people revived ; it was fondly hoped that freedom of religion at least would be allowed ; that peace and goodwill would return amongst men ; that happiness would once more reign amongst the loyal inhabitants of the Netherlands.

This was not to be. An event took place in August, 1566, which at once destroyed these hopes. It was that strange, and hitherto not yet sufficiently explained, outbreak of fanatical wildness which is known in the history of those days as the famous image-breaking. It seized upon the people—especially upon the lower classes—like a demon. Within four days not less than 400 churches, and everything they contained, were destroyed. The report of this riotous outrage set the king in a rage. He now *resolved* to renew the old persecutions with the utmost rigour. In August 1567 he sent the Duke of Alva, at the head of 30,000 picked troops, to replace Granvelle. And now six years of misery ensued, the history of which is written with blood and tears. If the Cardinal was a whip, the Duke was a scorpion. He was a great warrior, and a great fanatic, quick of perception, decisive in action, firm of will, and never afraid nor merciful. Philip never possessed a more devoted servant ; the Pope never a more bigoted subject ; the Jesuits never a fitter tool. Not a month elapsed before he was working at the head of the famous " Blood Council." In another month the principal nobles and commoners had been seized, imprisoned or beheaded, and as if that were only a prelude of what was to come, in six months he had passed a sentence of death upon *every inhabitant in the country.*

The people trembled. Whoever found it possible, sold his possessions and left the country, even with the greatest loss and danger. Those who could not, bowed in silence under the yoke, and turned their eyes to the only man, whom they knew to be able to help them, "THE PRINCE."

But the Prince of Orange, one of the ablest and most profound statesmen of his time, knew the character of the king of Spain and of his regent, the Duke, too well to expect any leniency from that quarter. Consequently no sooner had he heard that Alva was coming than he made his arangements and left the country five months before the Duke entered it. In vain he endeavoured to convince the other nobles of the necessity of this step. In vajn he pointed to Alva's, to Philip's character; to the threats they had already received and the secret information he had gained as to their intentions. Few believed or heeded his warnings, and, accompanied by his brothers, he retired to his German possessions to await the fulfilling of his prophesies. It came even sooner than he had expected.

In the latter days of August Alva entered Brussels. A fortnight afterwards, the Counts of Egmont and Horn were invited to dine with him and some of the principal officers. Egmont was warned on all sides not to go. Even at the dinner some one whispered into his ear, that he should fly, but he would not distrust his host. Half an hour after that warning, he and Count Horn were each imprisoned in a room guarded by soldiers ; a few weeks afterwards they were conveyed to the castle of Ghent, where they remained for nine months until they were led back to Brussels for their execution.

The consternation which the news of this arrest spread through the country baffles all description. The two counts, and especially Egmont, whose brilliant military. career in the war with France had made him the darling of the army, were much beloved and respected, and as their arrest was followed by that of many other prominent men, every one began to feel alarmed. The Prince, who was in exile, whose goods were confiscated, most of whose friends were imprisoned, could do but little against the overwhelming forces of the Duke. It is true in the beginning of 1568, and about a month before the time in which our story commences, his brother Count Louis had gained a victory over the Spaniards in Friesland, but a few days after the victory, the hired troops disappointed in their expectations of plunder, became mutinous and the battle was unattended by any good results.

Thus owing to the fanaticism verging upon madness of the King, the Prince of Orange was both by the supplications of an ill-treated people and by the dictates of his own conscience, induced to take the lead of an insurrection, which soon assumed the form of a war. At first that war was only waged against the Duke of Alva and the other Spanish officials; it was not before thirteen years of this bloody struggle had elapsed, and Philip had publicly outlawed the Prince, that the estates of the Northern provinces abjured the king himself. It may be easily imagined that the reasons which prompted the people to unite in this great contest were of a various character, for since the men who tried to extirpate the new religion at the same time tried to keep the people in political slavery, the opposition was stimulated by political as well as religious motives. Some took up arms in defence of the preaching of the Gospel, of the true service of God, of the freedom of conscience. But many too, and these probably formed the great number of the combatants, fought in defence of their political liberty and independence. And not a few were merely animated by the spirit of vengeance or by covetousness and rapacity.

Thus a great number of men, who had been deprived of all they had in this world, some of them of very good families, and, full of vengeance, had formed themselves into guerilla-bands and attacked their enemies, the Spaniards and the priests, whom they looked upon as the principal cause of all the evil. They called themselves " Beggars," or " Gueux" the origin of which name will be explained in another chapter. Often these daring, and for the greater part godless, men did nothing but plunder, rob, and murder. But often too they rendered great services to the cause of liberty by intercepting supplies and despatches destined for Alva. Some of them too were noble enough to undertake a task fraught with so many dangers and having comparatively so little reward that it is almost astonishing to read of the daring exploits of these heroes. They carried letters, writen in cypher-language or otherwise rendered unintelligible except for the initiated, between the Prince, who was in Germany, and his correspondents in the provinces. Thus to keep the Prince informed of all that passed in the Netherlands these heroes risked their lives every hour of the day.

Soon after the victory of Count Louis in Friesland, it became known that the Duke would march against Louis himself at the head of Spain's picked troops. The people began to lose all hope, when another rumour, more appalling than the first, was spread through the land. It was said that before starting, the Duke would witness the execution of the principal nobles and amongst them of the two Counts Egmont and Horn. It was but too true. After a mock trial, conducted in a manner directly opposed to every law and statute, they were sentenced to death, transported from Ghent under a strong detachment, and lodged in the Broodhuys at Brussels.

The news flew with lightning speed through the town and beyond it. The citizens seemed thunderstruck and passed each other without speaking. The political horizon seemed to grow blacker and blacker. The towns and villages half empty, their noblest, wealthiest, most intelligent inhabitants either in exile, in prison or leading a guerilla life, the people and especially those who were inclined to accept the new religion, feeling the yoke of oppression heavier each day, it seemed indeed as if God had forsaken them. But He had resolved to make them go through greater tribulations yet, in order that they might come out pure as gold, and that the beginning of their freedom should come when they had lost everything but their faith in His power.

Chapter Second.

TWO DECENT BEGGERS.

Was it a thought of these troubles which clouded the brow of a young horseman, who was riding at a sharp trot through the forest of Soignés, which extends for many miles south of Brussels ? From his appearance the contrary would have been expected, for he was dressed in the attire of a Spanish officer, and he was followed by a trooper of the army. His fair locks were covered with one of those costly and highly ornamented helmets, called *Morions,* which the Spaniards copied from the Moors during their long wars with that people, and introduced into the European armies about the 16th Century. An equally costly breastplate covered his chest and though his legs and arms were left unguarded, the brace of pistols in his saddle and the formidable sword at his side seemed sufficient to protect him in an age in which the lance and the battle-axe had long since gone out of date. His trunk hose and that part of his doublet which could be seen, were in keeping with his costly armour, and the embroidered leather scarf which hung across his shoulders, as well as the hilt of the sword attached to it, showed that he could occupy no mean place in the Spanish army.

And yet his face looked anything but that of a Spaniard. His fair locks, his blue and expressive eyes, his cheeks which had been browned neither by the sun nor by the infusion of Moorish blood, his thin and erect stature betrayed in him a child of the North. His thin and firmly-set lips gave to his face an expression of determination, and at times, when the deep thoughts, with which he seemed occupied, made him press them closer upon each other, and caused him to frown under his helmet, his features, though they spoke of scarcely more than a score of summers wore an expression of sternness which made him look ten years older than he really was. He rode his beautiful horse with perfect ease, but ever and anon he threw an anxious look at it and patted it on the neck, for it gave signs of fatigue and its blown condition was evidence of the long journey it had already made.

His companion was a man of a different stamp altogether. His short stout-body, his broad shoulders and his powerful arms would have marked him as belonging to a more common type, had not his inferior horse, the helmet or iron pot that covered his head and the cuirass of a common soldier been sufficient to show it. And yet when one looked at his face one found a different expression there from the general look of dulness or ferocity common to the soldiers of those days. He wore a beard with a point, cut close at the cheeks and revealing on the right cheek a frightful scar running from the mouth to the ear. It gave his face a weird appearance, but the smiling mouth and the gay light which danced in his black eyes redeemed its ugliness. On the whole it was a face expressive of good-humour, of fidelity and of courage, and only now and then when anger contracted his brow could it be seen that that courage might upon occasion degenerate into ferocity.

It seemed as if his armour was not so well made as that of his master, or indeed it looked as if it had been made for some one else, for his cuirass, though it had been buckled closely, could not altogether enclose his broad chest, and the helmet, which seemed heavy, was continually pushed from one side of the head to the other.

He was blowing and puffing under this restraint, and sundry coughs and small remarks which he made indicated, that he would not be in the least sorry should his master rein in his horse and somewhat slacken his speed. The youth however paid no attention to these hints, but wrapped in thought, sat erect in his saddle and heeded nothing around him.

The sun was already on its decline. Powerful though its rays still were, yet they could but seldom penetrate the thick foliage which sheltered the travellers, throwing only an occasional ray on the bad and dusty road, if such it could be called. The clatter of the horses, re-echoing through the wood startled its inhabitants the deer, the hare, the rabbit, and innumerable birds out of their resting-places, and with a shrill screech or a swift movement they fled from the two men, to whom no idea was at that moment farther than pursuit. They had ridden for some time in silence and the servant showed signs of increasing impatience when that, which he seemed unable to do, was effected by his master's horse.

Perhaps not thinking of the condition of his steed the

youth spurred it. It made a dash forwards, stumbled and but for the skill of its rider would have fallen. A gleam of pleasure passed over the servant's face.

"We have made a good way already Yonker, and they won't be fit for much more unless we spare them a bit," he said reining his horse.

"We must give them some water. Is there a place near?" asked the youth who had been addressed as Yonker, an abbreviation of "Jonkheer" the Dutch title of the descendant of a noble family. He had jumped off his horse and was examining it carefully.

"A hundred yards from here is 'the Duke,' I think," answered the servant smacking his lips in anticipation.

"Come on then," said the Yonker. Proceeding at a slow pace they soon arrived at a wretched hovel where a strange mixture of a variety of colours upon a board acquainted the passer-by that this was "the Duke," where "man and beast could get a feast." As to the beasts it seemed to be literally true, for in front of the house a happy family of pigs was holding a pic-nic under the shadow of the immense trees which surrounded the inn. Giving his horse to his servant, the youth, determined to convince himself of the truth of the first part of the inscription, stepped inside a low and ill furnished room and desired to be served with a can of beer. The weather was very warm, and the beer tolerable, so that the Yonker drank with pleasure. Suddenly however he put down the goblet, started up and ran to the door opposite to that which he had entered, and through which came the sounds of an angry conversation, and immediately following, the clash of swords.

Entering the small yard he saw his servant in the act of attacking a stranger, and he just arrived in time to prevent them from exchanging blows as both had drawn their swords.

The servant had obeyed his master's command, and, taking the two steeds to the yard at the back of the house, he was quickly engaged in refreshing the two animals, a trough and some pails having been pointed out by the host for his use. As he was feeding them and dashing the cold water over their feet, he began to sing with a low voice one of the many songs which in those days were the only literature the people possessed.

It was one of the productions of the guild of Rhetorics or Rederykes, whose members belonging to the middle classes, gave vent to their feelings and to public opinion in verses, generally of an inferior character as regards the poetry, but by their biting sarcasm and irony infinitely more popular than were the more sublime literary productions of those times. The Rhetorics had for some time been forbidden to assemble, and it was highly dangerous to sing or repeat one of their songs within the hearing of any of Alva's partisans; but many spirited men, and especially the Beggars, took a secret delight in repeating them wherever they could, and copies of them were often found stuck up at the most conspicuous parts of a street or square. To give an idea of what they were, I will write down a translation of the song which the fellow was singing by his horses :—

> Oh Alva who chills us,
> Oh Alva who kills us,

Oh, Alva who fills us
   With rage and dismay.
The Beggars will shake you,
The Prince will quake you,
The Devil shall take you
   For ever away!

The " Council" that pains us,
The King who disdains us,
The tyrant who chains us
   They can't live for aye;
For God, He will aid us,
To slay them that slayed us,
And drive them that flayed us
   For ever away!

As he was humming this song between his teeth his
eyes fell upon a horse which was tied to a second trough
in the corner of the yard. It was somewhat hidden behind
the overhanging branches of a tree, but a noise which it
made attracted his notice. He immediately saw that
it could not belong to the inn, as its saddle and accoutre-
ments showed that it was owned by a traveller, and that
that traveller was some one of tolerable wealth, if not
importance.

He involuntarily stopped singing, and glanced around
him to discover whether the owner of the horse was near,
and might perhaps have heard his tune. He took his
precaution too late, however. During the time that he
had been busy at the animal a man who stood in the
back door of the inn had regarded him with great
attention, and a smile of satisfaction seemed to steal over

C

his face when he heard the notes and words of the well known Beggars' tune.

The stranger, though he was of the same age as the servant, that is to say, some thirty-five years old, was exactly his opposite in the build of his person. He was thin, tall and sufficiently well made to promise those who intended attacking him a tough resistance. His face, though it was surrounded by the same black beard and locks as those of the other, was of quite a different cast. It was long, and bony, and decidedly striking. The high and narrow forehead, in which care had ploughed many a furrow, the deep-lying and shining cat's eyes, which flew from one object to another with lightning speed, without expressing anything but perfect coolness and composure, the hooked-nose, the high-cheek bones and the thin lips, made up an *ensemble* which could not fail to attract attention though it would have been called unpleasant by many.

It seemed at any rate to make an unfavourable impression upon the Yonker's servant, for when he had finished his survey, to which the other subjected himself with a complacent smile, he asked in a tone which was clearly meant to be insulting—

"Well, my man, you seem mightily fond of a tune, that you are thus listening to me."

"Possibly so," answered the stranger. "But I would advise thee, my good fellow, to moderate thy musical zeal somewhat, for even trees, thou knowest, have ears in these days," and he stepped out of the door and approached the trough.

The servant looked at him from under his helmet, and

his eyes shone dangerously. The words had been spoken in a calm and dignified manner, as if the speaker were accustomed to command, and were at that moment giving some reproof to his own servant. He answered nothing, however, but taking up one of the pails proceeded to throw some water over his horses. He saw that he had acted very imprudently, that probably the stranger was a Spaniard or a spy, and might bring him into trouble. His resolution was taken in a moment, and he coolly determined to pick a quarrel with the man and rid himself of the danger. Thus, as the stranger was leisurely approaching, he put down the pail with a dexterous movement before his feet, in such a manner that he must either give it a kick or stumble over it and fall. The stranger did the former and sent the pail rolling over the yard.

"As sure as my name is Hans," said the servant putting himself in front of the stranger and feigning astonishment and rage, "what mean you by this? Is it not enough that you take advantage of me in one way and must you insult me above?"

"Hold, my good Hans! I did intend no injury for thee; a timely warning is a useful thing, and sure the secret of thy Beggarship is quite as safe with me as with thyself. Nay, press not thus, I hate a needless quarrel; besides, I never fight a servant when his master can be had. Stand off."

So saying the stranger, who had remained perfectly calm, gave the servant a push. But it was evident that the latter desired to pick a quarrel, for he answered in sarcastic and angry tones. Ere long the two men had drawn their swords and were just entering upon a combat, when the youthful master appeared on the scene and placed himself between the two parties.

"What in the name of our Lady is happening?" he asked. "What are you doing, Hans?"

The two men dropped their weapons and turned towards the speaker.

"He was nearly preventing one of your best friends from appearing at the Rookery to-night," said the stranger addressing the Yonker.

The latter looked at his servant and again at the stranger with a certain degree of astonishment expressed on his face.

The stranger proceeded—

"Hans might have spared his energies for a foe worthier of his skill and power than I am."

Master and servant interchanged a rapid glance.

"You seem to know my servant, friend?" said the Yonker, coolly.

"And you too, Yonker," said the stranger, bowing slightly. "Peter Blink did not give me his detailed description in vain. I think I am not mistaken in believing that I address Yonker Karel Galama; I would know him were he to travel a hundred times under the disguise of a Spanish officer."

This latter part of his speech was said so softly that the whisper was not heard by the host or his wife, who stood at some distance looking with wonder at the scene. The youth, who had been addressed by the name of Galama, stood for some moments irresolute as if he found it difficult to determine in what light to regard this new comer. He scanned him closely from head to foot, a test which the latter stood with perfect composure. At last, seeming somewhat assured by his investigation, Galama said :

"You spoke of Blink just now. Explain yourself. Do you know him ? "

"Perhaps this scrap will explain better than I can do," said the stranger, putting his hand in his vest, and pulling out a little roll of paper tied round with a bit of silk. The Yonker opened the paper and read in old Gothic characters the following, while Hans looked over his shoulder :—

"The bearer is to my knowledge a good assistant. He can use the steel-yard very well and is quick at cyphers. You can trust him. His name is Gerard Bock. God speed you. Peter Blink."

"Your name I perceive is ? " said Galama, looking up from the paper after he had perused it.

"Gerard Block," said the stranger, bowing politely.

"Gerard what ? " said Hans, and made a movement as if to press upon the stranger from which he was restrained by his master.

"Gerard Block," answered the stranger when the Yonker also repeated the question. "Does it not say so in the letter ? "

"It does not," answered Galama, "the name mentioned here is Bock."

"That must be a mistake," said the stranger. "I think I was baptized Gerard Block in St. Nicholas' Church, Amsterdam. At least, so my mother says."

"I don't think you should have been either baptized

or born," grumbled Hans, giving his helmet a push to one side.

"I am not astonished at Peter Blink's making a mistake," said Galama, "for he never was very much of a writer."

"Ah, but Yonker, an L takes a long time in making," said Hans, "and if it were a mistake why did *he* not see it before. Surely he has read the letter." And he pointed to the stranger.

The latter bit his lips, and, as if he had not heard Hans words, he said—"It seems strange to me, because Peter has known me for such a long time and is generally very careful. I am glad, however, that I have further proofs in my possession which will convince you of my friendly intentions."

He again put his hand into his doublet and pulled out a blue silk ribband, which hung round his neck, at the end of which was attached a little brass medal. On one side of the medal was stamped the image of Philip the sovereign of the provinces, on the other, a beggar's wallet with the inscription around it. *"Fidelles au roy jusqu' à la besace"* ("Faithful to the King even to beggary").

The young nobleman looked at the medal and smiled as he said in a tone in which every trace of distrust seemed to have vanished :

"That alone, Master Block, would make us friends. I am curious however to know how you found me out and why you are here. But the hour is getting late. Go inside and finish your beer, Hans, and then let us be off. I suppose you are going our way, if so, we can become closer acquainted on our ride," he continued, turning to the stranger, with a courtesy and a manliness which showed that though young, his character had to a great extent been already formed by the experiences of his life.

"Humph!" muttered Hans, as he took his way slowly inside where a can of beer awaited him, "I don't half like that fellow. Block? Bock? Block? They do sound a good deal like each other, and yet there's a difference enough for Peter to stumble over. And then he had a coat of mail on, that's queer. I don't remember ever seeing any of us with one on. It's too heavy and not strong enough. I'll keep an eye on him, that I will. The Yonker's no good for looking after. He ain't got my eye, by a long way, but he's always thinking, thinking, thinking."

He finished his beer, and returning to the yard found the two men already mounted. He jumped on his horse, and after some moments the clatter of the hoofs was dying away in the distance.

Chapter Third.

AN ODD TRICK.

"AND what was the cause of this deadly quarrel?" said Karel Galama to the stranger when they had for some moments been riding in silence.

"Upon my word I do not know," answered Gerard Block. "In these unhappy days the cause seems to be often forgotten, so the result be but pleasing."

"Have you been picking a quarrel again for your own amusement," said Galama, turning sternly to Hans, his servant, who was riding on his right. "How many times have I told you that your noisy behaviour will do us more harm than good."

"Well, what is a fellow to do, Yonker?" answered Hans, doggedly, "when he is singing a Beggar's ditty and some lean, ill-looking,—I beg your pardon, when some stranger stands by and watches you. I could not run him through with my sword at once, so the only thing I could do was to pick a quarrel and do it. And I do not know, but what it would have been best," he added, softly.

"Silence," said his master frowning. "You must not sing your ditties anywhere, least of all where strangers can hear you, do you understand?" Then turning to the stranger, he said, "I am grieved that your introduction to me should have been in so unpleasant a manner——"

"Nay, Yonker," interrupted Block, "do not excuse. I cannot but admire the conduct of your servant, though it endangered my person. If I had been in the same position I dare say I would have acted like him. I confess it was somewhat careless of him to sing or even to hum that song, for had I not been as determined a patriot as I am, I might easily have become suspicious. As it was however he kept to his word, and but for your help might have done away with me for ever."

"You are very humble, Master Block, as to your own abilities in the art of defence," said the Yonker, smiling. "You look as if you had seen something of this world, and could call this neither your first nor your tenth quarrel. Have you belonged to us long?"

"I have been a friend of the Prince ever since I can remember," said Block, "and I wore his badge at the time that Count Brederode was at Amsterdam. I think I had the pleasure of seeing one of your family with him, at least a nobleman of the name of Galama was his constant companion."

"I know," answered Galama, in a gloomy tone, "both my uncles were beheaded yesterday or the day before, unless some miracle has happened, for I heard that Alva commanded that they and six other nobles should be hanged."

The stranger looked at the youth with some astonishment. "And are you nevertheless going to Brussels yourself?" he asked "for I presume that your way lies thither."

"Where duty calls us, we can have no choice," answered Galama. "But you seem to be pretty well known in the environs of this city."

"I should think so," answered Block. "I was born in Brussels, and I left it only a few days before the Duke entered it."

"Hallo, that's wrong, Master," said Hans, looking across his master's horse to the stranger, "you said just now that you were in Amsterdam when Count Brederode was there, and now you say you were in Brussels just before Alva came there. There is not more than a week between the two events."

Block bit his lips. He evidently disliked Hans' familiarity; but he saw that he must give some explanation. So he said in a haughty tone.

"There were nearly four months between them, and Peter Blink advised me to return to Brussels and sell all I had, before Alva came. Which very good advice I followed, and thus saved a greater part of my slender fortune."

"How did you become acquainted with Peter?" asked Galama. "To judge by the manner in which you speak of him he must be an old and intimate friend of yours."

"We did get acquainted in rather a peculiar manner," said Block, after a moment's pause, "and I suppose the recollections of it will not vanish from our memories very soon. It was about the time that the Inquisition and Granvelle were in the zenith of their power, that somehow or other our family became an object of suspicion. We were living in Long Lane, where I, my mother and my sister occupied a house, and my skill in the art of embellishing with gold, silver, and ivory, procured us a very comfortable living."

"Was your father not alive then?" asked Galama.

"He died in the seige of the city of St. Quentin," continued Block; "but as I was already grown up and knew my trade, there was little difficulty caused by his death. But one day a priest brought me a crucifix, which he desired me to ornament with ivory and gold according to a peculiar pattern. I fulfilled his command, but he never returned, so that I was obliged to sell the cross for what I could get for it. A few days after the sale some unknown person asked me whether I had ever decorated a cross of such a design. I acknowledged that I had, upon which he told me that it was a most blasphemous design, being a sentence written in some language I did not understand. I told him it was made to order, but having lost the piece of paper I could not prove this. The person went away, but that same night I was seized in the road, and would have been carried away but for Peter's timely interference, who put my assailants to flight and enabled me to reach home. I packed all my money and clothes together, and left the city that same night."

"And did your mother carry on the business?" asked Hans, in an interested tone.

Block shot a glance of ire at the servant, and addressing himself to Galama, continued. "The next day my mother and my sister were seized, and if they have not since died, they are yet lingering in prison, suffering for a crime which they know not."

"Oh, I see," said Hans, again, with the most persevering suspiciousness. "I thought you said that you returned to Brussels just before Alva left it in order that you might sell your all. If your people were seized, and you took your things away with you, you cannot have had much left."

"My work-place and my valuable stock-in-trade I gave to a friend to take care of, and he pleased my customers so well, that he fared better than I did. I had always had a longing to go back to my native city, and when I did so, my friend most generously gave me half the value of the business."

"I suppose you were born in Brussels, weren't you?" asked Hans, somewhat more politely. But Block seemed to dislike his questions thoroughly. He frowned, and shooting another glance of anger at the servant he said to Galama :

"I do not know what may be his object, Yonker, perhaps it is spite, but your servant seems determined to persecute me with silly and unimportant questions."

"Not I, Master Block, not I," said Hans, spurring his horse, "only you know, you said you were christened at St. Nicholas' Church, Amsterdam, and so if you were born in Brussels you must have taken to travelling very early."

"Thou seemest to know amazingly little of the state of the country to think that would be impossible, nor, I believe, does the Yonker share in thy ignorance. I would advise thee to wait therefore till thou hast a trifle more experience. At any rate molest me no longer, or I shall feel compelled to continue my way alone as heretofore."

"Ha!" said Hans, not heeding Block's resentment, "there is another thing I wanted to say. I do not think Peter Blink was ever inside Brussels in his life."

"Come Hans," said the Yonker, sternly, "hold thy tongue and give vent to thy feelings at some other time and place. I feel for you, Master Block, for I too have lost a father through this cursed Inquisition. Accept my hand as a token that I have that sympathy for you which your misfortunes command."

Kind though the words were, the tone in which they were spoken was not very warm, and the hand which Block grasped was not offered with great enthusiasm. Though he would not confess it, it was plain that Galama had quite as much suspicion as his servant, but possessing more tact than the latter he had resolved upon his own line of conduct. He therefore bade his servant ride a little in advance, and began a conversation with Master Block in which he showed himself exceedingly versed in the art of evading answers, of asking questions, and of getting as much information as he could from his companion without imparting more than he chose. But his dexterity seemed almost thrown away upon Block, who was perfectly frank and good-natured, and showed not the least reluctance in telling all about himself, his connexions, and his deeds, in all of which he did not spare either the Duke or the Church.

They had thus been riding for some hours, and the conversation, which owing to their brisk pace was rather broken, had stopped for some time. The sun was gradually sinking in the west, and above their heads, through the green foliage, could be seen the rosy hue of the clouds. The multitude of birds, whose voices had enlivened the sombre silence of the forest with an endless variety of song, began to prepare themselves for rest. Suddenly Hans rode beside his master and whispered something to him.

"Oh yes," said Galama, awakening out of his reverie, "we must halt here. It will be dusk in an hour, and then we shall want our horses doubly. Will you halt too?"

Gerard nodded assentingly, and presently the three men pulled up before an inn which had all the appearance of prosperity, and differed greatly from the one at which they had stopped before. It was a large house standing in the middle of a spacious yard, in which were five or six troughs. Our travellers soon dismounted, gave their horses to a man, and entered a large room, the oaken floor of which was neatly strewed with white sand, while the plastered walls and the small but clean windows, as well as the luxury of a few chairs in addition to the benches round the table, gave the place the appearance of comfort. The stout and contented-looking landlord stood in the middle of the room, and gave Galama and Hans a smile of recognition, as they entered and sat down at a table under one of the windows. Wine was ordered, and in a few moments the three men were refreshing themselves with the cool and delicious beverage which was in those days far commoner and cheaper than it is now.

"And do you really intend going to Brussels to-night, Yonker?" asked Block.

"I do not know whether I shall go there to-night," answered Galama; "I shall go there some day this week, but it depends upon circumstances when. What is your plan, if I may ask?"

"Well, to say the truth, I came down here principally to help the Beggars with my knowledge of the city, and with the information which I have been able to pick up. I think of going to the town first, and then to the Rookery."

"Do you know the Rookery?" asked Galama, somewhat astonished.

Before Block could answer, the bark of a dog was heard at the back of the inn, and a woman's voice bidding it be silent. Immediately thereupon the landlord entered the room and approached the table.

"Beg you a thousand pardons," he said, giving at the same time a mysterious nod to Galama, "that dunce of a stable-boy of mine don't know what to do with the horses. Would you mind going to see, for I 'm afraid there's something wrong with one of them."

"Indeed!" said Block, jumping up and running to the door, " I would not have any harm befall my horse for a hundred ducats;" and he ran round to the stables, followed by Hans, who was grinning within himself.

No sooner had they left, than the host turned towards the back-door of the apartment and whispered, "I'll tell him."

The next moment a tall form, wrapped in a cloak and covered with a wide-leaved, loosely-shaped felt hat of a dark colour, entered, and going up to Galama grasped him by the hand very cordially saying—

"Welcome, thou intrepid messenger of our Prince. What news from him?"

The speaker had thrown back his mantle, and taking off his hat he revealed a head which was exceedingly well-formed, and as dignified in its expression as it was aristocratic. A high and lofty forehead, large and intelligent eyes, a pleasant mouth, a brown moustache and peaked beard were its principal features. He was very plainly dressed, and his tawny leather doublet, his wide-slashed underclothes, and his shoes with steel buckles would have made him known as an artisan or respectable burgher, had not the magnificent hilt of his sword, and a beautiful signet ring of pure gold on his finger revealed a higher rank. There was courage, determination, but above all, thoughtfulness expressed in the whole of his face and bearing, and by the side of Galama, in the very manner in which they walked towards each other, one could see the difference between the calm and experienced soldier, and the youthful and enthusiastic volunteer. He was William de Blois, Seigneur de Treslong, one of the foremost amongst the presenters of the "Request," and destined to become a great leader in the struggle.

"I know no more of him than you do, my lord," said Galama. "I have been hanging about Ghent for the last month trying to find some means to liberate the Counts, but two nights ago they were taken away. I suppose you know that they are in Brussels at this moment."

"Rather; and they have taken lodgings with a very good acquaintance of yours, Yonker. They are in the Broodhuys," answered Treslong.

"So I have been informed," said Galama; "but I

could hardly believe it. I have, however, come hither on the strength of the report. We each owe the Duke a new grudge now, my Lord."

Treslong's brother had been one of the nobles beheaded at the same time as the two Galamas.

"Ay, my poor brother," sighed Treslong. "I wonder when I shall follow him. And poor Adolphus of Nassau is dead, too."

"Not, hanged, surely?" said Galama, quickly, and with something of terror in his tone. "The Duke would never dare to do that."

"I daresay he would *dare*," said Treslong, "but he has not had the chance. Adolphus fell at Heiliger Lee fighting against Aremberg—that renegade. But whom have you with you, and what do you propose doing?"

"As to what I shall do, now that you, too, tell me that the Counts are in the Broodhuys, I shall go there to-night and see Agnes. It is quite possible that between us we may hit upon some scheme for the liberation at least of Egmont. I am willing to risk my life, my everything, in the attempt, were I to be flayed for it to-morrow. I need not ask you whether you will aid me, my Lord, but, think you, are your Beggars willing?"

"Karel," said Treslong, earnestly, "most of these men are vagabonds, I confess; but not one of them would hesitate a moment to begin the most perilous undertaking if there were a chance of freeing Count Egmont. But you who have shown yourself so valuable to the Prince, do not risk your life in going into the city to-night, where all but certain death awaits you."

"My Lord," answered Karel, rapidly, "it is by the

D

express wish of the Prince that I am engaged in this —"
he paused. A loud shouting outside made both look
out of the window. They saw Hans seated on a horse
which was rearing, and plunging, and kicking most wildly,
and eventually threw him on to the soft grass which grew
at the side of the house. The landlord and the inmates
of the house were standing by, laughing heartily at the
ludicrous sight. As the two men looked at him with a
smile, the face of Block appeared at the back-door.
He threw a hasty but intense look at Treslong, and immediately pulled back his head. The next moment he
came running into the yard laughing heartily, and holding
another horse by the bridle.

"I have dedicated my life to my country and to
glory," said Galama, turning away from the window.
"I hope that I may be engaged in the most dangerous, the most care-requiring expeditions, and I shall be
content to die the most miserable and inglorious of
deaths if I could thereby further our most holy cause
one finger's breadth. You see that I am determined to
count no dangers, and as to my getting into the city,
am I not a Spanish officer?—and moreover read this," and
he handed the other a paper from under his cuirass.
It was a despatch from the Governor of Ghent Castle to
the Duke, having no interest for our readers.

"How did you get your disguise? and this?" asked
Treslong, having read the despatch and handing it to
Galama.

"Hans procured these," said the Yonker, "though I am
afraid their possession has been gained by blood. It is a
very valuable thing to me and cleverly got, too. Will

you be at the Rookery to-night, for I shall go there as soon as I have seen Agnes ? Then we can take counsel what is to be done, for I do not suppose Alva will wait long for their execution."

"I hear it will be in three or four days' time," said Treslong, "so we have not much time to lose. I came down here in consequence of your message, and I shall return to the Rookery, where all the Beggars are to be to-morrow night. But who is that stranger ? "

"I do not know him very well. A certain Gerard Block, recommended to me by Peter Blink. He accidentally fell in with us on the road. He seems to know Brussels and the Rookery well, and he is a Beggar. He may be of some use to us. He thinks of going to Brussels first and then on to the Rookery."

"Oh, but he must not go to Brussels to-night," said Treslong. "Three of you are too many to enter a city at night. Tell him to stay here and I shall keep an eye on him. He's a good horseman whatever he is."

"I can't give him any command yet," said Galama, "as he has not put himself under our control. Besides, there is little harm in Hans going with you to the Rookery, and he with me to Brussels. I must have some one as servant, you know, being a Spanish officer. We can't be certain yet of his faithfulness, and therefore I took care to see you alone ; but I have told him nothing, so he can do no harm. Here he is coming. Away with you. Till to-morrow night then."

Treslong flung his cloak over his shoulder, put on

the felt hat, and had just slipped out of the back-door, when Gerard Block followed by Hans entered the front.

"I have given your servant a lesson in riding, Yonker," said Block, smiling.

"I never saw such a brute in my life," said Hans, rubbing his shoulder with a scowl. "But I managed him at last."

"Since you are going to Brussels, Master Block," said Galama, "we had better go together, and after having done our business, meet somewhere in the city, say at the corner of the Nassau Palace. Then we can go to the Rookery, and give our respective experiences. I just thought it would be rather suspicious for three men on horseback to enter the gates after sunset, but now you can pass for my servant."

"Which I will be honoured to call myself, Yonker," said Block.

"Then Hans, you must remain here till we are gone, and go to the Rookery alone. If you should be there ere we return, which will not be before to-morrow night, tell the guards that we are coming. And take care you do not become uproarious again;" and the horses being brought round at that moment he stepped outside.

"Here, good Hans," said Block, mounting his horse and holding out a ducat to Hans, "drink my health and never ride a spirited horse again."

Hardly had he said these words, when his horse began rearing and plunging in the same manner as it had done with Hans, who stood at his master's horse grinning from ear to ear.

Block, however, was quicker than Hans had been, and jumping out of the saddle, he began adjusting the straps. A moment afterwards he remounted, and rode off with Galama in the direction of Brussels.

And Hans, who looked after them, shook his head and said, " Block ? Block ? I don't like him at all."

Chapter Fourth.

TWO CONVERSATIONS.

WE shall anticipate the swiftness of the two horsemen, and enter the city of Brussels by the Coudenberg Gate. The beauty of the evening seems to have failed in calling forth from the citizens any expression of enjoyment, and the poetic feeling which it is wont to inspir even in the dullest souls, has left their troubled spirits quite untouched. The city formerly so gay about this time, is almost silent. The troops of girls or young men, who with noisy merriment used to patrol the streets, the knots of burghers who then stood talking to each other in the doors of their houses, and discussed with pleasure or pain their past, present and future affairs, they are no more. Troops of soldiers fill the beerhouses, or make the streets echo with their Spanish, German or Walloon songs. Here or there a group of men are talking in hushed tones, with grief or anxiety expressed upon their faces ; or some proud priest, who views with satisfaction the submission into which the haughty city has at last been frightened, paces about like a conqueror.

What a difference to Brussels thirty years before ! It was then, too, the seat of the government, the place where the nobles congregated, where the wealthiest, the most beautiful and the most learned of the nation met. A day scarcely passed that some great feast was not given, and that upon the squares and outside the town the free and thriving burghers were not shooting with the cross-bow or playing at quoits. But perhaps the life then was too careless, too gay, and needed the heavy hand of God to make the people consider.

As we enter the gates and follow the road, a sudden turning brings us in front of the Nassau Palace. It is a noble building, the property of the Nassau family for ages, but having now been forsaken by the Prince of Orange on his flight to Germany, it is confiscated by the Duke, and all its costly furniture has been sold or taken away. It was formerly the rendezvous of the principal and most influential nobles. All that was talented or distinguished by bravery and wisdom had free access, and in those rooms many schemes had been discussed, many plans projected, and many wise measures taken, in order somewhat to counterbalance the influence of the Cardinal, and his evil companions.

Turning to the right, we find ourselves in a square, called the Sablon, where on one side the famous Culemburg Palace rears itself. It is at present being destroyed by the orders of Alva, who, furious about the defeat of his troops, intends to annihilate around him all traces of the yet living spirit of national independence. It was there that two years ago the nobles congregated, at the request of its owner, Count Brederode, the handsome but reckless descendant of the old Counts of Holland, and it was from the doors of that mansion that they started their memorable procession to the Duchess. It was in one of its rooms too, that a few days afterwards the celebrated banquet took place, at which the order of the Beggars was instituted. Its massive blocks of stone, its handsome halls are now being demolished. Ere long a pillar of triumph shall mark the place where it stood.

A broad and spacious street leads from thence to the Castle, the seat of the Duke's government, and the place where he resides. *There* is life, *there* is gaiety. Bustle and business are going on on the square in front of the castle. Soldiers are running hither and thither, officers with an air of native Spanish dignity and *hauteur*, or of French liveliness, are pacing up and down or chatting gaily in groups. They do not care for the sufferings of the inhabitants, they have their pay, or what is equivalent to it, credit, and they justly reason that the less leniency they show the longer will be their stay.

"And so, Pierre," says one officer, who belongs to a group of captains, "you think we shall have to march in a few days. How do you always get hold of your information?"

"Don't you know, garçon," answers another, "he confesses to the priest, and in return he gets all the gossip and news the holy man has got hold of."

"Bah!" says a third, "I hope Pierre is not so silly as to go confessing."

"Well," says a fourth, somewhat earnestly, "it is unmistakably an easy way to get rid of sins."

"Especially if you give the priests half of your spoils," said the second speaker.

"Pooh! I don't believe in them at all," said the third,

"since I read that little book of Erasmus on them. He calls them the dogs that ought to eat the crumbs, but have climbed on to the table and stolen the dishes."

"Now I cannot understand this," said the one who had been addressed as Pierre, "we are sent down here, and we are paid in order to uphold the Roman Catholic religion, and the Pope, and all that sort of thing, and I am blessed if every one of you is not a worse Catholic and a greater heathen than these poor people, take whom you like."

"Oh, that's nothing," said an old German veteran who had seen many a battle, "I used to belong to a Saxon regiment; and some twenty years ago now, we were ordered by the Emperor Charles to march into Guelderland and help the priests in punishing those who would not bow down before the host. But the lark was, that half of us were Lutherans ourselves, and helped the people instead of the priests."

There was a general laughter at this, when a heavy coach was drawn up to the door of the castle and a lady descended. She was magnificently though sombrely dressed, and her beautiful and noble face was deadly pale.

"Who is that, Schwabel?" asked one officer of the veteran who had saluted the lady as she passed quickly into the house.

"The Countess of Egmont," answered he, gloomily. "Heigho," he continued, "I served under him at St. Quentin, and traitor or not traitor, I would rather have him free again than keep a single priest or inquisitor about us. May God help her, I say."

The captains were silent and looked up at the window where they knew Alva was. They also knew that the Countess's visit would be in vain.

Such were the men which the Roman Catholic church employed as a means to bring back its erring sheep. Most of them had forsaken it themselves, and were of no religion at all. Some even had secretly adopted the reformed one which they were employed to put down; it may be imagined however that their hearts had little to do with that religion, as they could continue serving such a master as Philip and for such a purpose.

But let us turn away. We have a better visit to make. Following the road we come at last to a great square —"The Square" of Brussels. On one side stands the town-hall, a fine old building; on the other, between the spires of the church of St. Nicholas and the meat-house stands the Broodhuys. It has a highly and costly ornamented façade, with all manner of quaint figures in stone and five rows of windows embellished with rich garlands. It is an old building and was formerly used as bread-market, but having been altered and almost rebuilt, it was now used by different corporations or guilds for their assemblies, and often too did the estates and nobles hold their meetings in its spacious halls. Two of its rooms are at present used as prisons for the two counts. Two broad stairs, one on each side of the door, give access to the great hall, which, as well as the stairs and their vicinity, is full of soldiers. We shall, however, enter by the lower door which leads to the ground-floor of the house, the apartments of which are occupied by the warder and his servants. Following the corridor we find it crossed about the middle by another at right angles, which leads by a stair to the hall. Proceeding along the first corridor, we find a door in front of us and one on each side, giving access respectively to a little lane at the back, the private kitchen and the sleeping apartment of the daughter of the warder, Agnes Vlossert.

The latter was but a little room, and wanted many of those ornaments which betrayed the devout Roman Catholic, and though it had not even the little crucifix, without which no room in those days was reckoned complete, it was yet tastefully and neatly arranged, and the gentle touches of a woman's hand were easily distinguished. The spotless curtains around the bed and on the windows, the little bits of ornament and finery on the chimney, and the beautiful flowers on a little table before the window, are all tastefully arranged. Strange to say, on such a beautiful evening, the window is shut, and the rosy light of the departing sun as it is reflected by the clouds, has to find its way into the little room through some fifty small panes of glass set in lead.

And yet, the two girls who are sitting in the room do not seem to be desirous of having the window open. They are engaged in conversation. In those days conversation between lay people upon any subject was dangerous, and all precautions were taken against being overheard. There was but little difference of age between them, and a certain family likeness in the otherwise very dissimilar faces, betray their relation to each other. One of them is sitting upright and supporting with one arm the figure of the other. Her features are

noble, without being hard.   Her eyes shine with feeling
and intelligence, and the look which ever and anon she
throws upon the other girl, is so full of affection and
tenderness that they fully redeem a certain expression
of sternness which their conversation seems to have
called up.

The other girl, who is apparently an invalid, leans upon
her friend as much out of physical weakness as natural
timidity.   She, too, is beautiful, but it is a different
beauty.   She is the sister of Karel Galama, but the
determination, the haughtiness, the enthusiasm which
are expressed on her brother's face are not to be found
on hers.   There are the same fair locks and blue eyes,
denoting a Frisian descent, but the whole cast of
face is far more indicative of gentleness, of timidity, and
even fear.   Her cheeks are pale, and the little flush
upon them shows that health is either slowly returning
or slowly vanishing.

Both of them were orphans, but Agnes Vlossert had
lost a treasure, which to a girl can never be replaced.
Some four years ago her mother died, and thus forced
early to act and think for herself, she has already
had many a hard trial.   But it had been for her good.
Her father, the warder, who had the management of
the whole house, for which purpose a set of domestics were
under his control, had naturally but little time to look
after her, and she thanked God many a time afterwards
that just then she had made the acquaintance of an
apostle of Calvin, a certain Wouter, or Walter Barends,
who was preaching in the neighbourhood.   She listened
with intense interest to the words of grace which he

preached, and accepted the glorious truths which he held out to her, with delight.

Her mother being dead, however, she begged her aunt, the Baroness Galama, who was living at Brill, to allow Maria, her cousin, to pay her a visit, and as the times were yet comparatively peaceful, and no apprehension of Alva's coming agitated the minds of the people, her request was granted ; the more because Karel, her brother, had been sent to the neighbouring University of Louvain to complete his studies, and brother and sister would thus be near each other. It was not long ere Agnes, whose heart and soul were full of her new faith, induced Maria to accompany her to the house where Walter Barends preached, and she too began to doubt the truthfulness of that faith in which she had been educated. They were also frequently visited by Karel, and by his two uncles, the brothers Galama, whose company however, little contributed towards confirming them in their new opinions, since the three gentlemen, though advocating the good cause of liberty heart and soul, had not as yet found that true liberty wherewith Christ makes His disciples free.

While Maria's mind was yet unsettled, Alva suddenly appeared in the country. The two uncles and many other noblemen were imprisoned or executed ; many of those who had congregated and worshipped with her and Agnes were seized by the Inquisition, which had now recovered its old bloodthirstiness, and were burned or hanged often before their eyes. To crown all, her brother's name was mentioned as one of the most determined Beggars, and the warder hinted that he would like to see Maria return to Brill. She, too, wished to return, but the events had made too deep an impression upon the simple girl, who had never been outside the little seaport of Brill. She fell into a fever, from which she had only a fortnight since recovered. It is she who is leaning against Agnes, and listening to her words with earnestness.

A little book is lying open on Agnes's knee. It is a New Testament, which was then recently translated into the Dutch language by Liesseldt.

"Yes, it is true," said Maria in a pensive tone, " I cannot deny it. But still——"

"No ' buts,' dear, where the Word of God speaks," said Agnes, laying her hand upon the open book. "You see it is clearly stated that the blood of our Lord Jesus *alone* cleanses us of all our sins."

Maria was silent. She took the book and looked again at the text which her cousin had read to her.

"No priest can take away our sins," said Agnes, animatedly. " Jesus alone can do it."

"Ah, but mind," said Maria, "our good Lord has ordained the priests to administer the forgiveness of our sins to us in His stead."

"No, dear, you are mistaken. I have searched the Word of God from the first to the last page, but I have nowhere found such a statement."

"But hasn't our good Lord given the keys of heaven to Peter ? And isn't the Pope Peter's successor ? And hasn't he called and appointed the priests, and haven't they consequently the power to lock us in or out, and ——?"

"No, dear, that's altogether erroneous," said Agnes,

turning up the passage of Scripture referring to Peter. "You see that it is not merely to him, but in fact to all His disciples, that Jesus gives the authority of proclaiming remission of sins in His blood. And as to the power of opening and shutting the gates of heaven, listen to what the Lord says in the Revelation of John :—" I am He that liveth, and was dead; and behold, I am alive for evermore; and I have the keys of hell and death, and I have the key of David. I am he that openeth and no man shutteth, and shutteth and no man openeth."

There was a pause. The words evidently made a deep impression upon Maria.

" The priests are but sinful men like us," Agnes continued. "They have no power to take away their own sins, much less those of any one else. No one, but Jesus, can do it, dear. To Him we must go, and not to the priest. Believe on Him ; give up your heart to Him and you are saved, your sins *are* remitted unto you."

"Oh, but Agnes, do you know what you are saying ?" said Maria. "It is so fearful !"

" Fearful ?" Agnes exclaimed, her eyes beaming with enthusiasm. "Fearful," she repeated, folding her hands on her lap, and staring Maria in the face, with an expression of utter astonishment. "How can you say such a thing, darling ? Can there be anything more rejoicing than to have free access to Jesus himself, than to receive from His own word the assurance of the perfect forgiveness of sins ? What is true peace, if it isn't that ? That, is salvation and unspeakable blessedness."

"Oh, certainly," Maria answered, a little taken aback by her cousin's ardour; "but I did not mean that. I meant that the consequences of adopting the new religion are so fearful. If the priests had heard all you have been saying just now, I am certain that you would be a child of death. I shudder at the thought."

And while saying these words she covered her face with both hands, while a shiver of horror thrilled through her frame.

"Yes, these are sad and heavy times," said Agnes, "and may the Lord give us wisdom to walk prudently. But it would be more fearful still if we denied Jesus before men. He would be sure to deny us before His Father and His Angels. We might escape the temporal death, but the everlasting one would surely become our lot."

"But we need not deny Jesus, need we?" said Maria, "the priests do not require us to deny that Jesus is mighty to forgive our sins."

"True; but they require us to kiss the crucifix and to worship the Virgin Mary and the saints, and to kneel down before a wafer, and to believe that there is a power of salvation in all these things. And to believe this is to deny Christ."

"Yes, you are right," sighed Maria. "It is distinctly said that there is but One Mediator between God and man even Jesus Christ."

At that moment a rustling was heard at the door. It was only one of the servants who passed by, but a shock passed through Maria's frame.

"Holy Virgin! she whispered, "can anybody have heard us?"

"Do not be alarmed" said Agnes with a sad smile. "They won't be so very quick upon us."

"Ah, but it is horrible," ejaculated the poor girl; "just think of the Inquisition, and the rack, and the screws, and all those horrible things."

"Maria, Maria," said Agnes, reprovingly, taking her cousin's hand in hers, "how weak is your faith. Is Jesus not mighty to protect you, and did He shrink back from the cross, by which He has saved us?"

Maria's eyes filled with tears.

"Oh, do pray for me," she said, "I wish I had a faith like yours." "I am just thinking of the two Counts," she said, after a pause, "who are lingering at present above our heads, hourly expecting their death. Is it not sad to think of these noble sufferers?"

"And especially hard for the Count Egmont," said Agnes. "For Count Horn is a Protestant, and he may look upon his death as a sort of martyrdom. But Count Egmont is a devout Catholic. He has ever obeyed and venerated the priests, he has even persecuted us adherers to the reformed religion, and in spite of all he has done he is to be executed."

There was a moment's silence. The laughter of the soldiers and the measured tread of the sentry, who was posted at the back-door, were heard in the room.

"I hate these soldiers," said Maria, "they are such profane and godless men, they care for nothing. I do think they deserve death as much if not more than the Counts."

"I wish I knew some way of getting them free," mused Agnes, "I would try it. I know Count Egmont will have learned by this time that he must not put his trust in princes. But Maria, my dear, you must go to bed

E

again, you are not strong yet, you know, and we must soon make you ready to go to Brill.

"I am not very eager to return to Brill," said Maria, 'for you know I shall be very dull there, and have no companion now that Karel is away."

"You will have the Baroness," said Agnes, archly, "you had no other company before. For surely Karel was not much of a companion, was he ?"

"Oh, Agnes, how can you say that ? " said Maria in a gently chiding tone! " have I not seen you yearning in silence for the last five months, since Karel has been here no more ? And whenever there is a story about the Beggars, you ask with such interest after his name, even more than I do. I would have thought you the very last person to say this."

Agnes kissed her cousin tenderly and said nothing, for the simple reason that there was nothing whatever to say. After a little remonstrance she prevailed upon Maria to lie down on the bed, and having waited till her cousin fell into a slumber, she softly crept out of the room, and crossing the passage, entered the little private kitchen where Gritta, the servant, was busy scrubbing some brass utensils, and humming a tune.

After having exchanged a kind word with her she passed through the door at the other end of it into the sitting-room of the family, and presently her busy little feet were turning the wheel of her spinning-machine.

Chapter Fifth.

A SELF-CONTENTED MAN.

ADRIAN VLOSSERT, the warder of the Broodhuys, was a man of no uncommon type. With a fair amount of personal bravery when in danger, he possessed an equal amount of cupidity and superstition, while his conduct in all cases was marked by a total absence of principle. To please those who were in power, and especially in power over him, and to fawn on the great was his chief occupation ; to be in disgrace, even for a noble cause, was with him utter ruin, and pitifully did he look upon those, who rather chose to give up all they had than denounce what they had once adopted as truth.

He did not, however, consider himself in this light, but regarded the respect, or rather indulgence, with which he was treated as a just reward for his merits. It is true, some thirty years ago his merits were different from what they were now, but he neither loved to speak nor to think about that time. *Then*, vehement protestations were made in his native city, Ghent, against the arbitrary acts of Charles V., and believing that little danger was attached to it, he allowed himself to be prevailed upon by some stout burghers to clamour as loudly as the rest. He had even gone so far as to attend meetings of the heretics outside the town, and protested to all his friends that liberty of religion was the thing to be desired.

But when he saw the glittering armour of the Emperor's suite in the spacious streets of the old town ; when he saw some of his friends swinging on the gallows, and others kneeling in forced submission at the Emperor's feet, clad in a single shirt and with a halter round their neck, while his own purse testified to some part of the punishment inflicted upon the rebellious city, he confessed that Charles's logic was the most powerful, and his line of conduct was changed accordingly. He entered the army, and after some years rose to the dignity of captain, showing himself all the while a jealous supporter of the reigning family. No matter how ruinous or how arbitrary their edicts and their placards he applauded and defended ; but when they became too unpopular and had to be repealed, he forsook them and praised their successors. When, some twenty years ago, he obtained his present post his loyalty knew no bounds, and he even dared to assert that Philip, the new king was as handsome, a man and as able a potentate as his father. The Duke of Savoy, Cardinal Granvelle Orange, Egmont and other nobles were in their turn taken up and dropped successively, the late favourites being each time buried under a load of abuse.

He had become a zealous Roman Catholic too, and the Inquisition and the Jesuits found in him as pious and ardent supporter as he was a devoted invoker of all the saints in the catalogue. Being at the same time convivial and good-humoured he was rather liked as a companion, especially amongst soldiers, in whose company he dismissed some of the pious and loyal glitter with which he shone. Had the Netherlands known no other citizens, they would long since have been crushed under the yoke of slavery. A little more talent might have made him another Noircarmes or a Virgilius. As he was now, he was comparatively harmless ; but in the absence of those higher qualities, what remained there for those who knew him, but to despise ?

Perhaps the only one with whom this was not the case was Agnes. She still honoured and loved him as her father, but could she also obey him in everything, and acquaint him with all that took place in her heart ? Not only was it impossible for her to make him her confidant —and who should be this more than a father, especially to an only and orphaned daughter ?—but to her inexpressible grief she could not but look upon him as an enemy in relation to everything which she loved and revered. She loved Jesus ; he used that holy name, if he used it, as an oath. Alas ! it is a sad thing for a believing and loving child to have such a father ; and yet what else but the possibility of such painful trials has the Lord prophesied, when He said " Think not that I have come to send peace on earth ; I came not to send peace, but a sword, and to set a man at variance against his father."

The warder is just leaving the room, where he has been playing cards with the officers of the watch appointed to guard the illustrious prisoners, and whose money, won at the game, has put him in a high goodhumour. He is expensively and somewhat gaudily dressed ; a light-blue silk doublet, laced and embroidered, a wide hose of violet velvet reaching to the knee, coloured stockings, a broad linen collar, a felt hat, the plume of which is fastened with a magnificent diamond hook, a like ornament for his broad belt, and silver buckles for his shoes, and you have him *in toto*. Traversing the hall he descended the broad stair which led to the ground-floor, and jingling his money he stroked his beard with a contented smile and entered the apartment which he and Agnes used as a family room.

It was not a large room, but for those days handsomely furnished, though at the present day, the furniture would certainly be called clumsy. At the high window with its small panes set in lead, and its heavy and somewhat sombre velvet curtains, sat Agnes on a high backed chair, and though ever and anon she touched the spinning-wheel before her with her little foot, it was easily seen that her thoughts were far away from her work. It was too dark to work, as the long shadows of the house which formed the other side of the lane, soon deprived them of the light of the sun.

"Well, my daughter, thou lookest pale ; dost ail anything ? " said her father as he went up to her and playfully pinched her marble cheek.

"And have I no reason to look pale, father dear ? " said she, rising and kissing him affectionately.

"Ay, what, Agnes ? " he said, slily, " has that rascally Captain Pedro spoken to thee about anything ? Well, I am glad to see thee taking it to heart. He is a likely man I trow, though somewhat soldier-like."

"No, father. My reason is the same as that which makes almost every woman in Brabant and in the Netherlands look pale——"

"What can that be ? " said her father, as he threw himself in an arm-chair, "they surely haven't all got Captain Pedros to speak to them, have they ?"

"They have either him or some other of these foreign and mercenary oppressors about them," said Agnes with a touch of disdain in her sweet low voice. "You know as well as I do, father, that they are chiefly sent here to burden the poor people and rob the most virtuous——."

"Jesus ! Maria ! child ! Stop thy dangerous tongue or, by St. Ann, we shall both be marched off to prison to-night. Remember that you are easily heard through these thin windows, and such language has brought many a better one than thee to the scaffold."

"As it will again in a few days," said Agnes, little heeding his injunctions. "I am only saying what is true, father, and what can be proved by thousands of witnesses. Do you not feel for the two Counts that are sitting upstairs, and are you still willing to serve a man who rewards his best servants in this manner."

"By our thrice blessed Lady," said Vlossert, impatiently, "don't speak so loud whatever you do, and hold your tongue if you can't say anything else. Don't you know that you are in open rebellion against the King and his excellency the Duke. As a true and faithful soldier I ought to inform against you now, but I warn you in time, that you may repent of your rebellious spirit and thank me for my leniency."

"Rebellious spirit ?" repeated Agnes. "Is it a rebellious spirit to pity the man that is being murdered in the street ? But I know you say this because you are afraid, of being overheard, because a free burgher of the city of

Brussels cannot live in his own house, without being afraid that some treacherous Jesuit may be listening at the key-hole or the window. But you need not fear, father," she continued, stroking his hair, "you are too zealous a partisan of theirs to be suspected. And, moreover, the bloodhound's attention is now directed to nobler martyrs than Adrian Vlossert."

"Martyrs? what martyrs are you talking of child?" said he. "Keep to your spinning-wheel and take care of that guest of ours, that sister of the greatest Beggar and vagabond under the sun, whom I should like to see hanged to-day. The fellow and his connexion with us will bring us into trouble yet."

"Karel is no vagabond, father," said Agnes, indignantly, and with flushed cheeks. "He is a noble defender of our liberties, and neither he nor his uncles have deserved hanging any more than the Prince himself."

"Ay, I should like *him* to keep Count Egmont company. He brings nothing but disturbances about, and whenever there is news of him the people go half mad."

"I remember the time when you thought differently about both of them, father," said Agnes pouring out some wine and handing it him. "I remember the time when the news of the Battle of St Quentin came, you said that you considered Count Egmont the greatest general of his age, and that if he and the Prince could be governors of the provinces, it would be a splendid thing for us."

"Yes, Agnes," said Vlossert, hastily, "there has been such a time, I acknowledge, but even the King was pleased with them then. But affairs have very much altered since then. Were they not both the first men to act against the Cardinal? Did they not draw up a letter to the King in which they said that the Cardinal was a despot, and that consequently he ought to go? Did Count Egmont not threaten to bring an army into the provinces, and did he not congregate with traitors, and talk treasonable matters? Why, I remember one day when he was banqueting here in the upper room with the masters of the fleecer's guild, that he drank a toast to the speedy removal of all fools and fools'-caps from this country, and the speedy restoration of all our old liberties. Whom did he mean but the Cardinal? Besides, what business have we to ask whether the Count is guilty or not, when the Duke and his councils have condemned him after due examination?"

" But have they a right to condemn him? That's what I want to know," said Agnes, who was not thus to be convinced. " Of course, they won't execute him and say that he is innocent; but the charges against him cannot be proved, at least not sufficiently to justify their death. And I very well remember the evening of which you speak, father, when the Count proposed that toast, you told us afterwards that you cheered———"

"Hush! Agnes, Hush! Our Lady preserve us! Be silent child, give me pen and ink and paper. I came down to write a note. Now say no more."

" You cheered and applauded as loudly as the rest," continued Agnes, with obstinacy, " and you said you liked his speech very much."

" No; nonsense!" said Vlossert, anxiously. " Did I? You must be mistaken, I never applauded against the

Cardinal. It would have been very foolish, for he is a
mighty man. St. Ann preserve us! I hope it did not
come out on the Count's trial, or I am a lost man."

"Trial!" said Agnes scornfully "what trial has he
had? What trial can a man have when he is all the
time shut up in prison and is not allowed to defend him-
himself in person or get legal advice? He has not been
outside a prison for nine months since he was kidnapped
by the Duke. And if he is really guilty why is he not
judged by the other knights of the Golden Fleece, for you
know very well that such a knight can only be judged by
his peers. But against all rule and right they have both
been tried and condemned, and will be executed in an
unlawful and disgraceful maner. Woe, woe to this unhappy country, when men even of such importance can be
brought to the scaffold for no greater crime than that they
loved their own countrymen better than a false and
deceitful Cardinal, whose very name must sound detest-
able in every one's ear."

Vlossert listened to his daughter with admiration, for
her enthusiasm and indignation had heightened her
colour and made her look doubly beautiful. He secretly acknowledged that her words were true, but he
thought it prudent to protest against her denounce-
ment of Granvelle.

"Hush, my daughter," he said, "you must remember that the Cardinal is a pious and holy man, and
that your confessor will not give you absolution for
so great a sin as to speak against him."

"I thank God I can do without it," said Agnes,
from the bottom of her heart.

Vlossert started.   He knew that his daughter was very liberal and patriotic in her views though she was careful enough to hide them.   He had often been afraid, too, that she would turn a heretic, for she went to mass but seldom, and she treated Father Florisz, her confessor, with little better than contempt.   These words seemed to confirm his worst suspicions.   He started up, and seizing her by the arm, said in a trembling voice :—

"What do you mean by these words, girl ? speak ! Do you require no absolution ?   Holy Virgin ! has your head been turned by these damnable heretics ?"

Agnes covered her face with her hands, and dropped into a chair.   Knowing her father's character, she had not deemed it advisable to tell him of her conversion as yet.   Now however, in the heat of her argument she had parted with her secret, and as she sat there she prayed God from her inmost heart that He might strengthen her.   Her father, however, mistook her attitude for fear, and glad that he found her so soon repentant of her own rashness, he thought the occasion good for a little sermon.

"The Holy Virgin," he said, gravely, crossing himself, "is looking down upon you just now with sorrow and compassion—and so am I for that matter—because of your great wickedness in thus speaking of her holy servants. I shall go forthwith and send father Florisz here, who will speak to you about this great sin of yours, and show you how to obtain absolution of it."

He turned round to leave the apartment, but his daughter seized his mantle.

"Do not send Father Florisz to me," she said, speaking as if with difficulty, yet calmly, "for he would do me no good whatever. I have not said a single word against the Mother of our Redemer. But I have spoken against the folly of having your sins forgiven by any but Jesus Christ."

"Agnes, I cannot hear you say such things," said her father ; "for the sake of everything that is dear to you. for the sake of your eternal salvation, I beseech, I implore you, say that you do not mean these words, and that you spoke them thoughtlessly."

But Agnes was firm now. She was prepared for her father's opposition.

"My dear father," she said, sadly, "it is just for the sake of my eternal salvation that I do say these things, and I would that you said them too. It will be such a blessing to you, I am certain, when you begin to see that there is no salvation in priests and gaudy dresses and crosses, and incense, and all that rubbish."

"Jesus! what shall I do?" said the alarmed soldier wringing his hands in despair at the fate of his beloved child. "Agnes! think to what fearful dangers you are exposing yourself! If my Lord the Inquisitor heard one word of what you said just now—O God! I shudder to think what would become of you."

"My Lord the Inquisitor, can do no more with me than God shall allow," said Agnes, boldly, "and if I should have to choose, I'd rather have temporary pain here, than everlasting pain hereafter. But why are you so alarmed, my dear father? I love you as much as formerly, nay more, since I feel a greater love for allmen."

"Ay Agnes, my child," said Vlossert, standing before her and speaking with a voice trembling with emotion, "I have been a good father to you. You have never been in want of anything that I could procure you. I have allowed you to learn everything that suits your position in life, and I expect that you shall obey me as behoves a dutiful child. I command you to repeal these words and never breathe them again. You must, you shall!"

Agnes shook her head. Tears were flowing from her eyes, and in a voice almost inaudible she said.

"I cannot, father. I have never disobeyed you yet. But in this I must follow God's command more than yours. But do not be angry with me——"

"Ha, that is surely a very perfect religion that teaches children to disobey their parents, and bring disgrace and ruin upon the house! You, who profess to serve God, you will tell me that you can disobey me and excuse yourself as you do! You who denounce the priests and holy fathers, you will set up a moral of your own! This then is your religion that you have been preaching, for some time. I shall leave you to yourself to-night, but to-morrow morning I shall bring Father Florisz to you, and cursed be you till your dying day, if you do not confess all to him and do penance for your heresies."

And swinging round he left the poor girl sobbing and bending down in her chair. The anger of her father had touched her more than she had expected, and though she knew that she was in the right, she could not refrain from giving vent to her grief in a flood of tears.

Suddenly, a strong arm drew round her waist, her

hands were seized tenderly, and a voice said lowly and compassionately :—

"Do I find my Agnes in such grief? What causes these tears?"

She looked up, a smile brightened her face, and jumping up she fell on the breast of Karel Galama.

Chapter Sixth.

A DARK INTERVIEW.

To explain the somewhat sudden and mysterious appearance of our old acquaintance, Yonker Karel, let us for a few moments step through the door, which he has left open, into the kitchen. It has already been noticed that a corridor or passage ran through the ground-floor from the market to the little lane dividing it into two equal parts. Each of these halves was again divided by a cross passage, thus forming four square blocks of rooms to the North, East, South and West. Those to the North and East had their windows looking out upon the little lane, and consisted respectively of the private kitchen and the family room on the North side, and three bedrooms on the East, while the two blocks on the S. and W., looking out upon the square were set apart for the domestics belonging to the Broodhuys.

It will thus be seen that the room, where the above scene took place, could be entered by two doors, one opening into the cross passage almost at the foot of the stairs which led to the hall, and the other opening into the kitchen. At the time at which the interview just described took place, this kitchen was occupied by Gritta, the neat, buxom and active little servant who was engaged in spinning the flax of her mistress.

"I think it a great bother," said she to herself, "to have the house that full with them foreign soldiers and their noises. I wish these Dukes and Counts wouldn't keep a-quarrelling amongst themselves, and disturbing the rest of a poor body, as does them no harm."

"Ah, Gritta, you be a vine liddle woman," said a German soldier who had been pacing up and down, on guard before the back door, resting his halberd on the stones of the passage, and looking at Gritta through the kitchen door.

"Get out," said she, with a toss of her head, "I don't like speaking to any of them butchering boys as crawls about here. My mother was a respectable woman, and she always said that I was born at the striking of twelve, which to be sure means that I am respectable too."

"Eh! that is a curious thing now," said the soldier, "and I was done that way myself exactly, at the striking of the twelve, so I must be respectable too."

"Were you though?" said the girl looking up with interest, "and did you put your foot in your mouth immediately, because she told me if I had done that I would have become very rich?"

"Well, I can't speak to that myself," answered the man of the sword; "but my mother did tell me I put my left foot down my throat and they couldn't get it out for some time. But I don't remember that myself, at least I couldn't do it now."

"Dear me! dear me!" said the girl, astonished, "you are the first one whom I have met that has had it, and I have asked ever so many. And have you become rich, then?"

"Haven't I, Gritta, just look at this," said the soldier, pulling some pieces of gold from his pocket and chinking them in his hand, to the apparent delight of the simple-minded girl. "And the best of these pieces is that they never grow less, and the more you use them the bigger they get, what think you of that?"

"That's like our good lady of St. Gudule," said Gritta, coming a little nearer the door, "for Father Florisz told me himself that they had a new lady put up, and he poured some costly oil on her head one evening at vesper, and the next morning her hair had grown right down to her feet, and now he says it grows twice a week, and I've got some of it," she added with an air of importance.

"And won't you let me have a look at it, Gritta?" said the soldier, coming nearer the kitchen door. At first Gritta was inexorable. At last, however, she gave way to the entreaties of her admirer, and proceeded to look for the little box where the precious relic was stowed away. But as it had grown too dark for her, she proceeded to light a little brass lamp with a taper which she lit at the smouldering fire on the hearth. Suddenly, however, while she was standing lamp in hand before the table which stood under the window, she heard a very soft knock at the glass. She looked up, gave a scream and dropped the lamp.

The halberdier jumped into the kitchen, weapon in hand, expecting to pin some foe with it to the ground, but was requested by Gritta not to make a fool of himself. She had only burned her fingers with the taper, and he thought it was Black Herman who had

F

played her a trick. So presently lighting another taper she lit the lamp, and soon after found the little lock of hair of St. Gudule.

It seemed, however, as if the relic in question did not please the enamoured warrior so greatly as another specimen of hair which was within his reach; at any rate he protested that he considered Gritta's own hair by far the better of the two and craved permission to cut off just a little lock.

"Go away," said the girl, giving him a sound box on the ear, as he endeavoured to seize her hair. "I have vowed to our good lady that I shall allow no one to cut a bit of my hair except on one condition."

"Tell me the condition," he said, "and I swear by all the saints in heaven I shall do it, were it ever so bad."

"Oh, it is not the least use telling you," said she, shaking her head, "for you daren't do it, I know. You would get arrested if you were found out, and I couldn't bear that, I'm sure." And she turned her head away.

The poor fellow being thus put upon his point of honour, swore and protested high and low, that he would die for her.

"Well then," said Gritta, "you must take this taper and light it, and take this can, and go to the wine cellar below here, and go to the big vat you'll see in the farthest off corner, and beat on it three times with your fist and cry, 'Come! come! come!' and you must count slowly from one to a hundred, and when nothing comes you must draw a can of wine and come back to me. There now."

The bold warrior stood for a moment in hesitation.

"What if the officer comes?" he said, "I'll catch it, by St. Ada!"

"There now, I knew you daren't. Get out and don't molest a poor girl or I'll scream. Here! Help!"

"Hush! give, me the can and the taper," said the fellow putting his halberd to the post of the door with a desperate effort. Gritta gave him the two articles, and preceded him to the door of the wine cellar.

"The large barrel in the farthest-off corner," she whispered as he went downstairs, cautiously holding the burning taper before him. He soon reached the bottom of the stairs and turned into the cellar. No sooner, however, had he disappeared, than Gritta locked the door of the cellar, put the key in her pocket and ran to the back-door. She looked outside, but not a soul was visible in the little lane, not a figure was distinguishable in the dusk. And yet, when Gritta had peered for a moment and sounded a 'Pst!' a figure which stood in an opposite doorway, and was wrapped up in a large dark cloak, crossed the lane and made one leap into the kitchen, where the servant followed him and closed the door. The mantle fell off and revealed Galama.

For a few moments it seemed as if terror and astonishment at his sudden movement into the kitchen had deprived the superstitious servant-girl of her power of speech. She stared at him with her hands clasped and her heart beating violently.

She had seen his face through the window and immediately resolved to get the soldier away, but she had not expected him to come into the house.

"Oh, Yonker Karel," she said at last, rapidly, "fly, fly quickly. Don't you know that the house is full of soldiers, and they'll murder you when they find you here. Fly! O holy Mother of God, help us! don't stop here another minute."

The young Frisian looked at her for a moment with an air of abstraction.

"Is Agnes here?" he asked in a whisper. "Where is she, and where is my sister? She must be here, too. Don't disturb yourself Gritta, there's no fear."

"Yes, there *is*," she said seizing his hand, and pointing to the door." "Did you not see me speak to a soldier when you looked through the window. I managed to get him away, but he will be back presently, and then when he finds you here it will be all up with you. I thought something awful would happen to-day, for the cat scalded itself with the hot water, and that's a sure sign. I think I hear him coming up the stairs, Yonker. Oh! you're a lost man."

But in the same degree as Gritta's terror augmented, Galama's presence of mind seemed to become greater. He passed his hand over his forehead and seemed to think for a moment. Then he said quickly and softly :

"Silence, Gritta, and answer me. Go and lock that door. Where is Agnes? I *must* see her. There is no fear of any harm befalling me. Don't you see I am a Spanish officer now, and that fellow would be too frightened to look too closely at me. But, quick now, is Agnes in here?"

And he made a movement to the door which communicated with the sitting-room. But Gritta sprang up and seized his mantle ;—

"Not there, not there, for God's sake!" she cried in a hoarse whisper. "The warder is in there with his daughter, and they have been quarrelling for the last half-hour. He never speaks about you but he flies into a rage, and if you were to go in now, you would never get away again. But here, go into this cupboard, and I'll tell my mistress that you are here, or come—I'll bring you to your sister's room, quick Yonker, there's no time to be lost. What are you——?"

The Beggar turned round and pressed his finger to his lips. Instead of going into the cupboard, he had softly opened the door of the room about an inch or two, and with his ear to the opening thus made he could hear every word of conversation between Vlossert and his daughter. It was at that moment that the warder, as reported in the above chapter, had commanded his daughter to forswear her new religion and had met with her sad but firm refusal.

Just at that moment soft raps were heard at the cellar door in the passage. The terrified servant sank on her knees and seized her rosary.

"Oh, our lady of St. Gudule, God Almighty, here is the soldier wanting to get out. Oh Yonker, I have known you from a boy, and I'll see you killed before my eyes. Oh!——" The thumps became somewhat louder, and a voice was heard indistinctly.

"Go and let the poor fellow out of his prison," whispered Galama; "but don't let him come into this room, do you hear," and he slipped softly into the room and went up to the figure of the weeping girl.

For the first few moments the two lovers gave themselves entirely up to the enchantment of the unexpected meeting, but then simultaneously, a recollection of the danger of their position made them start, and Agnes, looking at Galama with an expression of unutterable tenderness, said in an anxious tone :—

"Karel! do you know what you are doing? Do you know that my father may be back here any moment, and that if he finds you here he will have you locked up ?"

"Do you wish to hunt me away so soon as this, Agnes ?" he said, encircling her with his arms. "We have not seen each other for nearly a year, since the Duke arrived in the provinces. Surely you won't send me away yet. I heard your father say that he would leave you alone for to-night. Can you not shut that door, so that we may have some warning of his coming ?—then we can open the window and I can escape that way if it should come to the worst. You see, we Beggars are getting accustomed to these kinds of interviews, and I think I have entered a house as often by the window as by the door. Can't you do that, my own Agnes ? for I have a great deal to say to you and I *must* say it now."

The thought of the imminent risk of her lover being discovered, had caused Agnes for a moment to lose her accustomed presence of mind, and trembling, nervously, she rested passively within the outlaw's strong embrace. But when she heard his advice as to the precautions that might be taken, she aroused herself out of her stupor, and pressing her hands before her face which was still wet with tears, she controlled herself with one strong effort. Then walking with a firm step to the door she locked it, put in the bolt, with which every door in those days was provided, and stepped to the window, but in the act of endeavouring to open it she paused and said—

"I don't know whether it is advisable, Karel, for if we open the window some of the spies that are always crawling about might hear your voice. I think we should just unfasten it and draw the curtain before it, so that———." She paused and stepped back with a quick gesture, pressing her hand to her beating heart.

Galama had just filled a bumper from a can of wine, which was standing on the table, and was emptying its contents when he saw Agnes's movement. He put down the cup and ran to the place where she stood.

"What is it?" he asked, in an alarmed tone. "Are you ill?"

"Nothing" she said, smiling faintly. "Only, while I was trying to unfasten the window, I thought I saw the face of a man staring into it. But I must be mistaken, for it is so dark that I should not be able to distinguish it, if it were a man."

"Well, it would be nothing if there were a spy," said Galama, "he can't see me, but for prudence' sake draw the curtain, and shut this door too," and he pointed to the kitchen-door through which he had himself come.

"And now, my darling," he said, as he led her to the seat where he had found her, and took a seat himself on a stool at her feet, "let us talk for a few moments about the important matters for which I have partly come here."

He paused, and unfastening the band of his heavy and pressing helmet, he put it beside him on the ground. Then leaning his head against the chair he looked up into Agnes's face, though it was hardly visible in the faint twilight which still lingered in the room.   But he could see that a great change had come over that face in the short space of time that he had been in her presence.   At the moment when he first found her, the poor motherless girl had well-nigh received a curse from the only relation she had about her, and the only person, except her aunt Galama in Brill, whom she had not seen for years, to whom she could look up with reverence. She felt how lonely she had become, now that the only one who should have been her support, threatened to become her enemy.   But there Galama enters as if sent by God, to occupy that place at her side which her father had so cruelly left.   No, she was not alone in this world! his appearance brought the roses back to her cheeks, and his words reminded her forcibly of the great and sacred questions in which she was engaged.   It brought most clearly to her mind that it was no choice with her as to liking or not liking, but a question of deep, of holy principle. She forced back her tears and though she knew not what were the reasons of Karel's visit, she was determined to hear him and help him if she could.

"I do not know, Agnes," he said, after a moment's silence, in a low voice, "whether your opinions have undergone a change since I saw you last.   I do not mean whether you love me less than formerly, for I know you don't, but whether, like your father, you look upon me as an outlaw, a rebel, an enemy of the country. I remember your former indignation at the oppressions of Granvelle, and at the arbitrary and disgraceful manner in which he infringed every one of our ancient and sacred liberties and privileges. I remember, too, that you spoke with enthusiasm about the heroic conduct of the Prince of Orange, God bless him! But I fear lest the continual influence of the slaves amongst whom you live, the company and the talk of those degraded men who reckon their country, their great and glorious country, and their sacred rights of less importance than their own miserable bodies, that will be rotten in the course of a few years, I fear lest their example and arguments have weakened the grounds of noble patriotism upon which your enthusiasm was built. Tell me whether my fears are just. If they are, farewell! The holy Virgin be with you, for *I* shall love but leave you for ever." He paused and seemed to wait anxiously for her answer.

"It is quite true, Karel," she said somewhat hurriedly, "that when we last met, I spoke to you with indignation about the oppressions which the poor people at present have to suffer, but I think you were and are mistaken as to the grounds which made me feel so indignant. I know the only, at least the chief, reason, why *you* have seized arms against Alva, is the violent and unbearable manner in which all the liberties of this country have been trampled upon and the life of every inhabitant imperilled. I fully approve of this reason. But above this I have another, a more sacred one, and I would to God you had it too. You know that three years ago I used to attend the lessons of Master Wouter Barends, the godly disciple of Calvin, and through him I saw the folly and sinfulness of worshipping any one but God. The chief reason for my indignation, is the manner in which the priests try to withhold from the people the Gospel of salvation. It is not they I hate, but their wicked system. I pray that mine be a holy anger and not vengeance. I trust that God shall make me day by day stronger to walk in the Spirit of Christ. For I confess that it is sometimes very hard to pray for our enemies, when we see them hang our relations before our very doors. But oh, Karel, if we remember what Jesus did for us and how He prayed for his oppressors, even at the very moment when they crucified Him, we *must* try."

Tears of emotion smothered her voice. Galama was silent. Certainly, this was a different reason from his, though it did not exclude it. He seized her hand, and pressed it to his lips.

"You are better than I am," he said. "God knows that the recollection of those things which you have said to me before, has been with me always, and has kept me from doing many a thing which I would otherwise have done. And yet your words have somewhat disappointed me. I thought that your religious ideas would not have prevented you from helping me, helping us, helping the nation in a matter so grave. Oh, Egmont! Egmont! shall you then have to die like the meanest culprit, when you might help us in destroying the monster that threatens all of us with perdition? O God! is there no help? Is there nothing, nothing that I can think of?"

In his agitation he had risen and stood before Agnes, with his hands lifted up to heaven and his voice broken with agony.

"Egmont? What do you mean?" whispered Agnes, half-rising and pressing Galama down again to his former position. "Sit down and tell me."

" I forgot," said he, smiling faintly, " that other people think not as I do. And that, while there is the least chance of rescuing that man, they can think of aught but that. Is there a chance, a shadow of one ?"

" Of rescuing the two Counts ?" asked Agnes, as if she could not as yet realize the idea. " There is not."

" For neither ? Think ! There *must* be. Where are they ?"

" They were only brought in here this morning. Count Horn is in one of the front rooms on the second-floor. For him I am certain there is not a shadow. Count Egmont is in the room of the bowman's guild, and with him, too, it is impossible."

But the tone in which she uttered the last words was hesitating.

" It *is* possible," said Galama catching at that, " all the Beggars are ready to try."

" All the Beggars would be of no use," answered Agnes. " But hear me, and you will be convinced that it is impossible. There is a soldier in his room armed to the teeth. Then there are two before his door, two at the top of the stair, and the next staircase is also well-guarded. The only way by which you can enter the room is by the one door that is guarded, or by the chimney, to get at which you would have to go to the garret and pass all the soldiers, which you could not do without an order from the captain of the guard or my father."

" But does not Father Florisz go up and down the stairs without being stopped by the soldiers ?" asked Galama, after a moment's silence.

"He does," answered Agnes, "but he won't be here to-night or to-morrow————"

"Yes, he will, Agnes! Did not your father say that he would send him to you to-morrow morning?"

"True," said Agnes, sadly, as the recollection of the scene came back to her. "And may God strengthen me to sustain his visit. But he would not help us for all the world."

"But he must without knowing it," whispered Karel, speaking rapidly; "my plan is made. Remember the grave nature of my plan, and do not shrink back from its dangers. To-morrow morning you must pretend to be unwell and when Florisz comes, you must tell him that you had rather see him in the evening. When he comes in the evening put him in Maria's room, who as I hear from Gritta is not quite recovered. In the meantime I shall come in a similar dress; he is a Dominican, is he not? You take me up to the garret, and if God and my dagger do not help me further, I am willing to die even if my attempt should fail. There is a chance of escaping on to the next house, the fish-market, at any rate."

For a moment Agnes sat speechless and horror-struck as the full audacity of this plan revealed itself to her. She was unable at first to understand the mind that could conceive such a plan, but when she saw the reality before her, she started back from the idea of lending her hand to accomplish what seemed to her nothing short of her lover's capture and death. She tried all her powers of persuasion to alter his mind; every danger, and there were many, every obstacle, every likelihood of discovery, every chance of being overcome at the last moment she put before him in the most vivid colours which her love for him, summoned to her aid. She implored, she wept, she threatened to reveal all, but it was in vain. She might have known beforehand that the most powerful of persuasions are shipwrecked upon the obstinacy of the Frisian character, especially when it is heightened by patriotic enthusiasm.

It was a touching sight to see her, when, at last exhausted, her whole body shaking with sobs, she lay almost breathless in her chair, and her tearful eyes searched for the all but invisible, erect and warlike form of the young Beggar.

"For the last time, Karel, and answer me not rashly, choose another of your companions and I shall risk every thing; but do not come yourself, for your life is more precious to me even than my own, and I would not for anything put you in such a danger. Let any other Beggar come and I am ready for him."

"Is this then your patriotism, Agnes?" said he in a somewhat stern voice; "do you prefer me to your country to the whole nation? Fie! promise me this, for I must go, that whoever shall come, you will help. I shall let my companions choose, and if they choose me, promise me that you will treat me as the rest. In a cause so sacred as ours, no man is different from another. Will you promise?"

"I will," said Agnes in a low voice; and she gave a sob.

"God! I know Thee but little, but Thou wilt hear my prayer. Keep this beloved child of Thine under Thy care, and guard her against our enemies!" Kneeling

before her and with her head resting upon his cold
breastplate he breathed this prayer to the God whom he
saw as yet but dimly by the light of her piety. One
long and passionate embrace and he rose.

Cautiously opening the window and looking out he
saw no one. One light jump placed him outside on the
street. He quietly shut the window behind him, wrapped
his mantle around his body, and crept away through the
darkness, which, as a symbol of the shadow of death
that hung over the inhabitants of the provinces,
enveloped the city in its impenetrable folds, and cast its
gloom alike upon the magnificent palace of the noble,
and the humble dwelling of the artisan.

Chapter Seven.

"AD PATIBULUM."

Turning to the left as he alighted from the window, Yonker Galama stepped onwards with long strides and keeping as near to the houses as he possibly could. It was now completely dark; threatening clouds swept with incessant rapidity before the moon. It seemed almost as if with the daylight all traces of life had disappeared from the city. The brawling of the wealthy nobles who were wont to congregate in its halls, or the gay voices of burghers as they went to or from a place of entertainment were no longer heard in the street. The shop-windows formerly representing a lively appearance were closed, and but for a faint glimmering of light which shone through an occasional shutter, one might have thought that the inhabitants of one of the first cities in the world spent their nights indoors in complete darkness.

When Galama had passed the building which flanked the Broodhuys and which was used as a meat-market, he turned a little to the left, and found himself presently in La Chausée, the principal street which ran from the *Coudenberg Gate*, and the Palace, to the market-place. It would now-a-days have caused great astonishment, if such a notorious rebel as Galama were to walk through the streets of the metropolis even at night ; but my readers must remember that the streets in those days were not lighted at all, and that every one who desired to see how and where he was walking found it necessary to carry his own light, or in case he were a rich man to have it carried for him.

There was thus not much danger in Galama's walking along in the darkness ; but he kept his ears wide open, for it was possible at every turning of the street that he might meet with some foe who was thus provided with light and attendants, in which case he foresaw his danger would be very great.

Happily, however, he encountered no one. After having walked for some five or six minutes at a smart pace, he paused before the palace of the Nassau family, the spot where he was to meet Block, but where the latter did not seem to have yet arrived. Suddenly, voices were heard approaching him, and gleams of light fell upon the palace. It was clear that a party, and probably a numerous and armed one, was coming through the street which led almost from opposite the Nassau Palace to that where the Duke of Alva was then residing. Galama looked round for a place where he could escape the observation of the approaching party. A porch, which was somewhat deeper than the others, and had moreover a corner in it, seemed to offer a very good shelter. In a moment he jumped into the corner and covering himself with his mantle pressed closely against the wall.

It was not a moment too soon. A number of men turned round the corner and followed the road by which he had just come. The party consisted of about a dozen torchbearers, some five or six of whom were Spanish soldiers, while the gentlemen whom they surrounded seemed by their dress and the loudness of their tones to be men of rank and authority.

"Well, your worship," said one of the gentlemen, addressing a stoutish man, who, with one other companion, was not dressed in the military fashion. "I think that I can boast of having fairly gained my bet and that the *gladius* has conquered the *patibulum* in this case, at any rate."

The answer of the person thus addressed was lost in the distance ; but the Yonker had heard and seen enough to make him gnash his teeth. He had recognized at least the two principal men in the whole group. The one was Julian de Vargas, the famous president of the "blood-council," whose incredible cruelty and ferocity are even now, after nearly three centuries, a proverb in the Netherlands. The other one was the scarcely less famous Hessels, also a member of the same council, whose conduct however was mixed with just a little touch of the ludicrous. It is not out of place here, perhaps, to say a few words in explanation of what I mean.

Being convinced that through the regular and lawful courts, but few convictions, and still fewer confiscations would be obtained, the Duke of Alva instituted on his arrival in the provinces a council, or tribunal, of his own, which he called the "Council of Troubles," and which was to supersede all other institutions. . It was composed of

G

twelve members, of whom only two could vote as to the
ultimate fate of the accused, while the rest were present
to give the proceedings the appearance of lawfulness,
however little they might possess it in reality. For it
must be known that the council was purely an invention
of the Duke himself, unauthorized by any act, charter, or
decree whatever, and merely maintained through the force
of the soldiers which he had brought with him.   So great
was the ferocity of this council, mainly owing to the
activity of its president, De Vargas, that within three
months of its institution nearly two thousand persons of
all ranks had suffered death by its decrees.   We have
mentioned that only two members could really vote, the
one was De Vargas, the other Del Rio, also a Spaniard ;
but amongst the members who composed this board,
and whose nominal voice was sometimes given, was
the above named Hessels.   This man used to pass his
time at the council-board, comfortably seated and
dozing while the cases under consideration were being
heard, and when a soft shake from one of his neighbours
warned him that his opinion was wanted he lisped a
sweet "Ad patibulum" (To the gallows) and forthwith
returned to his former occupation—that of snoring.

It was to this, the more blood-thirsty De Vargas
alluded, for with the above words he meant that the
fate of the two Counts had not been conformable
with Hessel's sentence, but with his.

It was the appearance of these two men which
made the Yonker's blood boil in his veins.   He
grasped the hilt of his sword with a fierce and violent
gesture, and felt as if the greatest pleasure ima-

ginable to him would have been nothing compared to the luxury of plunging the weapon into the miscreant's heart. He had stepped out of his corner and looked at the retreating party as the red glimmer of their lights could be seen fading away in the distance. From what he had heard he concluded that the subject of their remark was the fate of the unfortunate Counts which had now been definitely settled, and shaking his fist at the retreating hangmen, he cried in a bitter voice :—

"Oh that my country should ever be so deeply disgraced by one of her own sons !"

"Hallo ! what have we here ?" said a voice in Spanish behind him. He turned round. A soldier, probably belonging to the party which had just passed, came running along, torch in hand, followed at a little distance by two others with a second torch. He had arrived within two or three paces of Galama and seemed uncertain what to do. The Frisian's attitude and face contrasted strongly with his dress ; but his being alone and that without either torch-bearer or attendant seemed to settle the question in his mind to the detriment of Galama. He approached the Yonker, at the same time calling out to his companions to come on. Action with Karel was a thing which required but little consideration. He had gone through a great many dangers already, young though he was, and he was seldom at a loss what to do. He quietly awaited the soldier. Suddenly, when he had come near enough, he made himself with a quick movement, master of the flaming torch. Striking the fellow with the burning end in the middle of the face, and turning round to fly before the two others, as he saw his aggressor fall under the heavy and un-expected blow, was the work of a moment. In another, the two other soldiers were in full pursuit, but they had reckoned without their host.   After having run a little distance, in which Galama allowed his pursuers to come close to him, he suddenly turned round, dashed between them, and flew as fast as he could in the opposite direc-tion, towards the *Coudenberg Gate.*

He was aware that he was in great danger, but he did not lose his presence of mind.   He knew that there was but one way which he could go, and that was to the right, through the little passage which ran along the Palace of Nassau, and which led into a labyrinth of little streets and lanes between the *Chaussée* and the High Street. If he kept on to the *Chaussée* he knew that he would come to the gate where the soldiers would find it easy to stop and arrest him. The left turning would bring him into the vicinity of the Palace, which, being always surrounded by soldiers, would be more dangerous still. So, trusting to chance, he turned to the right, and flew along with his pursuers panting and swearing behind him. But in his great speed he became less careful. He had not ran far when, making a false step, he stumbled and came down heavily upon the earth. Scrambling upon one knee, and drawing his sword, he turned round to face his antagonists, who were coming along at a distance of several yards from each other. His first blow was aimed at the torch which the foremost of them carried in his left hand, while with his right he drew his sword. At the same instant that the naked blade shone in the light of the torch a blow from Galama dashed the light to the ground, and presently the two swords were heard upon each other. The combat upon such unequal terms, however, would not have lasted long, had not an unexpected help extricated Karel from his highly dangerous position. At the moment that the second soldier arrived at the spot and was ready to help his comrade, a dark figure which seemed to have followed them, leaped like a tiger upon his back. The fellow uttered one short howl or rather snort, and fell lifeless at the feet of his comrade. A moment afterwards the other one felt his legs knocked from under him, and measured his length on the ground at the feet of the astonished Galama.

The dark figure ran to his side and seized him by the arm.

"Come along, Yonker, and let us get to the Rookery, for this game is getting dangerous," whispered a voice which he recognised to be that of Gerard Block, his new acquaintance.

"Not until I have thanked the preserver of my life," said Galama, seizing the other's hand. "May God reward you for the service which you have done me and my cause, noble Gerard, and now, whither?"

"Come along, I have got the watchword as I promised, and the sooner we get outside, the better, for there will be a pretty kettle of fish when any of these fellows come to again. I have had better success than I dared to hope, and I have got some information that will serve us excellently. But let us get outside, for walls have ears, say I."

While saying, or rather whispering these words, he

had seized Karel by the arm, and not long after both appeared in sight of the gate.

It seemed as if Gerard Block had been quite as successful in obtaining information as he had anticipated. When they arrived before the heavy and clumsy iron gate, they found it closed, and a soldier with a matchlock on his shoulder walking before it, while some dozen others could be seen playing at dice in the adjacent guard-house. The soldier on guard looked with a somewhat suspicious eye upon our two friends as they bore down upon him and called out the sub-officer who was inside. As soon, however, as they saw the outfit of a Spanish officer, they became more respectful, and when Gerard Block passed the watchword, the door flew open and the two Beggars stood outside the town. Galama drew a deep breath when the imminent danger had passed, but he was fully aware of their perilous position. For a moment he stood still and considered how best to proceed, as he was certain that soldiers would be sent out to pursue them. Rain had begun to fall, and came down with ever-increasing violence.

"We have not much time to lose," said Block to him as he remained motionless within a stone's throw of the gate, " let us first fly to the inn, and then to the Rookery."

" That would be a bad plan, indeed," answered Galama, "we are sure to be pursued, and the first places they will search will be the forest and the inn, whither consequently, we must *not* go. Follow me."

He turned to the left and ran along quickly and noiselessly, followed by Block. It was not long before they reached the bank of the Grelle, one of the numerous, little branches into which the river Senne divides near the city. The two fugitives walked along the bank for some moments, until they reached a fordable spot, where they crossed, and arrived on a sort of island formed by the Grelle and another branch of the river.

" There is a small farmer on this island," said Galama, " who is a partisan of ours, and who will give us shelter for the night. But methinks I hear some one approaching. Let us lie down in the corn till he passes."

It was a false alarm, however, and the two men proceeded for some distance in silence. At last, the bark of a dog was heard, and Galama once more bade his companion hide in the corn while he went to the house to reconnoitre. After having been absent for a short time he returned, and led Block to the house, where the old farmer and his wife, two honest and generous people, received them as drenched fugitives with every kind of welcome.

" I haven't got long to live, nor much to lose, your honour," he said to Galama, as he prepared for each of them a bed and a good supper, " but please God I'll give it all to Yonker Willem and his friends."

" Yonker Willem," was the familiar name which the people gave to the Prince of Orange ; in later times when the people really began to see what he had done, suffered and sacrificed for their sakes, that title was altered into " Father Willem " by which he is known to the grateful Hollanders to this day.

Happily for the two Beggars no one dreamed of coming to the lonely and insignificant, though very much exposed farm, and that night and the following day they were perfectly safe, and burning with desire to discuss and execute the plans which they had made.

Chapter Eighth.

THE BEGGARS' HAUNT.

WE must now return to the inn, where Blois de Treslong and Hans were left behind. The host, who was a secret favourer of the Beggars, and a friend of the Prince, was well-known to all of them, and through him they often received very valuable information. In return for this the Beggars never molested—nay, secretly protected him, whereas they often proved a heavy scourge to those inn-keepers, who, whether from fear of the lawless band, whether from dread of discovery, showed no inclination to follow the example of mine host.

As soon as the two horsemen had disappeared Hans returned to the stables, where he began to alter the trappings of his horse, and to look after his pistols, while he muttered to himself:

"What a vicious brute that was. I used to think myself a tolerably good rider, but I 'm dashed if anyone could ride *him* at all. That fellow Block could not manage him either, so that makes it all right. I wonder where my Lord de Treslong is. He hasn't surely gone back already—confound these pistols, they are of no nse whatever—hope he won't return to the Rookery without me, because I don't know but what I forget the exact way."

"Hans! Hans!" Treslong's voice here whispered. Hans looked round, but could discover no one, until after having heard another call he perceived an opening in the ceiling through which by means of a ladder, the hay-loft could be reached. Through this opening Treslong's face appeared.

"Come up as soon as you can. We must not be seen, and cannot very well leave until after dark. You had better take the trappings off your horse."

Hans obeyed these orders and was soon up beside the chief, who had made himself exceedingly comfortable in the hay, and invited Hans to sit down beside him and take part of the wine with which he was regaling himself. Just at that moment bells were heard tinkling in the distance.

"Do you hear these?" said Treslong, "these bells have warned me not to go till it is dark. They belong to the transport vans, and it is quite possible that they are attended by a number of spies who might follow us to our haunt. But what have you been about that you have such a fine horse for yourself, eh?"

"Ah! it is a fine one too, my Lord, and no mistake," said Hans, greatly pleased; "it is a very vicious brute, I can assure you, and very few men *would* be able to ride it."

"So I thought," said Treslong, gravely, "when I saw your performance on it in the yard."

"That was Block's horse; not mine," said Hans innocently "it is an old brute, but unhappily the saddle got loose, you know, and I slipped off. But it could not be compared to mine, you know."

"Oh, indeed," answered Treslong, "I thought it was a vicious brute, and in fact you know I expected that nobody could ride him at all."

There was a twinkling in his eyes as he looked at Hans, who, finding that his confession to himself had been overheard, looked rather sheepish. Treslong laughed, but said good-naturedly :—

"Never mind, Hans ; your fall was by no means to be attributed to bad horsemanship. From the movements of the horse I concluded that, wanting to play you a trick, Block, or whatever his name be, put a beech-nut under the saddle, the irritation of which no horse can bear. So when it was brought back here I quietly told the ostler to repeat the process, and you saw yourself that he experienced the same result as you did. So much for his tricks."

At this moment a bustle was heard in front of the house, and presently the yard at the back of the stables was filled with unsaddled horses tied together, and led by five or six dragoons.

"What a pity," whispered Treslong, "that I did not know of this. Had we been at Dirk's Castle to-night we might have attacked these fellows on their way. They are sure to have a good sum of money about them, and we would have killed the horses, for they are destined for the coming expedition to Friesland."

Dirk's Castle was another and more frequented haunt of the Beggars, and lay not far from the present Waterloo.

"I do not suppose there will be anything doing to-night?" asked Hans. "Have you assembled all the Beggars at the Rookery, my Lord ? "

" Nearly all will be there by to-morrow," answered he, " but I do not like the place much for anything but a store-room. It is too near Brussels, and I do not know but that it is being already suspected. We must be very cautious. How have you and Yonker Galama fared of late ? Have your perils been great ? "

" The only blood I have seen for two months, my Lord," said Hans, as calmly as if he were discussing his dinner, "was this morning. The trooper was quiet enough, but the captain would not give in, so what else could I do ? " It appeared from his tale to Treslong that they had followed a Spanish captain and his servant out of Ghent to a little inn, and there they had picked a quarrel with them, tied and gagged the servant; while the captain, who, as Hans said would not give in, was killed or mortally wounded in the encounter. They had then appropriated the outfits, and thus disguised, proceeded on their way. Thus, even the most noble-minded men found themselves often constrained to spill the blood of their fellow-creatures, and, much against their will, to employ means from which they inwardly revolted. Yonker Galama had seen the necessity of capturing the two men, but it was Hans who having completed his task with the troopers, and exasperated at the captain's resistance, dealt with him in a manner, which his coarser nature could not regard with such aversion.

While they were thus speaking, the door of the stable below was heard to open, and voices sounded through the floor of the loft. Treslong motioned Hans to be silent, and crept to the opening through which the latter had reached his present quarters, and which he had taken the precaution to close : after having drawn up the ladder,

Treslong opened the trap-door for about an inch and looked through. Notwithstanding the dusk he could perceive the host in conversation with three men, who were enveloped in large cloaks, but whose helmets made them known as Spanish dragoons.

"You see, mine host," said one who appeared to be the most important, "we cannot reach Brussels to-night in good time, for it is more than seven miles yet, and we have travelled a good distance already. Besides, it is raining and dark on the road. You must make room for our waggons in this stable, and those of our men who are not on guard must sleep in your hay-loft. Be not afraid, they shall do you no harm."

"Well, Sir Captain," answered the host, "I will serve you with all I have. Let your waggons be removed hither, and your men remain on guard. As to the others, they may sleep in my hay-loft, but they won't find any hay there to sleep in. I have not been able to find more hay than would suffice for the meal of two or three steeds. The grass has not been yet cut in the fields."

"Let them remain in the front-room then, and give us a separate room and plenty of wine, and cards," was the officer's rejoinder, as he left the stable. Treslong turned to Hans, and looked at him, smilingly.

"We are nicely caught," he whispered, "the house is surrounded by Spanish dragoons and we can't get out. What's to to be done?"

This question, however, was answered by the host himself, who came up to them by another door leading out of his own bedroom or kitchen. He assured them that, thanks to his lie about the hay, no one would

be likely to come up, and that they were at once safe
and sheltered, for the rain was coming down in torrents,
and several waggons, which, as the soldiers said, contained
powder and money, were being rolled into the stable.
Nor were Treslong and Hans sorry for being thus
forced to remain in the hay, for had they gone that
night to the Rookery, they would have had to walk
five miles in pouring rain, and there would, after all,
have been no certainty of getting shelter. They resolved
to watch in turns, and when the next morning broke
upon them the Spaniards had already left, unaware
that their deadliest enemies had been so near them.

As the road, however, was full of troops of soldiers,
all going to the metropolis, Treslong deemed it advisable
to wait until it was again dusk. When at last it
came, they emerged from their place of shelter, and followed for some time the road Galama had taken the previous night. Then striking off to the right, they entered by a
little path into the very midst of the dark and sombre
wood, and proceeded cautiously and in absolute silence
to the haunt of the Beggars.

It may not be out of place here to say a few words
about the origin of this confederaey, which has played so
considerable a part in the history of the foundation of
the Dutch Republic. We have seen how, much against
his will, yet unable to resist the force of public opinion,
Philip was obliged to recall Cardinal Granvelle. Those
nobles, however, who had hoped that with him the Inquisition would leave the country, found themselves direly
mistaken. It is true, it somewhat relaxed its violence,
but it was there, and as long as it remained, the nobles

and the people felt uneasy and indignant. They resolved
to draw up a petition, or *Request,* in which the Regent was
humbly solicited to remove the so obnoxious Inquisition, and restore to the most loyal subjects of the King
their ancient liberty and happiness.

On the third day of April, 1566, three hundred noblemen, headed by Count Louis, of Nassau, and by Count
Brederode, the brave, reckless, dissipated, yet kind-
hearted and generous descendant of the old Counts of
Holland, walked in procession to the Castle of Brussels,
where the Duchess of Parma, surrounded by her counsel-
lors, received them. The Request was read, and the
nobles withdrew to give the Duchess an opportunity to
consult her advisers. It was then that Berlaymont, her
confidant, perceiving that the warlike and haughty appearance of the nobles had made a deep impression upon
the Duchess, said in a tone of disdain, " Of what, madam,
should you be afraid ? These are but a troop of
Beggars." This expression was heard by Brederode and
a few others, and it sunk deeply into their hearts. In
the evening of the 6th following, an evasive answer having in the meantime been received from the Regent, the
nobles assembled in the magnificent Culemburg Palace,
the mansion of Brederode, and partook of a splendid
supper. Heated with wine, and yet indignant at the
taunt, the eloquent and witty host rose up, when the cloth
had been removed, and told the assembled guests
by what name they had been called. As his speech
reached its climax, his cupbearer handed him a wooden
mendicant's bowl. Filling it with wine to the brim, he
raised it in the air, and then, under the exclamation,

"Vivent les Gueux !" (Long live the Beggars!) he emptied it, and handed it to his neighbour.

He was answered by shouts and roars of applause. Each guest emptied the bowl in his turn, and repeated the cry. It was adopted as the war-cry, and the taunt was taken as the name of the new confederacy. And thus, though born as it were out of the fumes of wine, and nourished in its infancy by the inconsiderate and often foolish enthusiasm of its founders, the confederacy soon developed itself into maturity, and within a few years it presented to Alva, both on land and on sea, the form of a giant, who, like the genii in the Arabian tales, was all the more terrible because he was so seldom visible, and often dealt his fearful blows where they were least expected.

As we have already said in our first chapter, when Alva came into the land, part of these nobles fled, and another part formed guerilla bands, retaining their old name of Beggars. That many of their followers adopted this name to be better able to ply their trade, which was no other than that of common highwaymen, was a matter of course, considering the state of the country. Still, notwithstanding this, they performed real service to the cause of liberty by intercepting letters and supplies, and keeping the Prince informed of all that happened.

Many were the efforts made by Alva and by his helpers to put down these bands, and to a certain extent they succeeded. But their great end, namely, to lay their hands on the Prince's secret correspondence, they were totally unable to attain. Letters, it is true, were sometimes seized, but they were so disguised and the names so arbitrary that nothing could be made out of them. The Duke, the Jesuits, the Inquisition, were at a loss. They knew that the thing was done almost under their nose, yet they were unable to lay their hands upon the culprits. Such was the vigilance, the caution, of these otherwise reckless, debauched and defiant forerunners of the Dutch Republic, whose haunt we shall now enter at the side of our two friends, Treslong and Hans.

Though it was still early it had grown quite dark in the forest. The sky was clouded, and it would have been impossible for anyone not well acquainted with the locality to find his way through a mass of underwood, which, to all appearances, had never been disturbed by the hand of man. The two men, however, seemed to know their path perfectly. Treslong leading and Hans following, they proceeded cautiously but swiftly. At one place they had to brush away the branches that almost obstructed their passage, at another spot they had to wade up to their ancles through a pool or marshy place, and here and there it seemed as if they could only proceed by cutting their way with the sword, when some unexpected turning which both of them seemed to know almost by instinct brought them on the path once more.

Suddenly, as they were thus proceeding, the harsh shriek of a barn-owl re-echoed through the wood, and the rustling of the leaves was heard as the frightened animal flew up from its shelter. No sooner had Treslong heard this sound, however, than putting his hand to his mouth he gave vent to two clear and prolonged notes, such as the nightingale utters, and paused to listen. A moment afterwards a dark form appeared from behind a stout tree about two or three yards in front of them.

"Who is with you?" whispered the figure, advancing to Treslong.

"An acquaintance of yours, Jonathan, Black Hans."

"Bravo!" said the figure, in accents of pleasure, seizing Hans' hand and shaking it cordially. "How art thou, Hans? I haven't seen thee for a while!"

"The owl is splendid to-night," said Hans, as he gave a cordial welcome to the guard who had been addressed as Jonathan. "Where is he?"

"The northern one is up in yonder tree. It is Thomas to-night."

Treslong and Hans now passed on. After having proceeded about a hundred yards, the sombre and indistinct form of what appeared to be a ruin, rose amongst the underwood, at a spot where the larger trees had all been cleared away or had never existed. It was the Rookery. Some three hundred years ago, it had been the castle of a plundering baron who had made the forest the scene of his violence, and drawn many a victim either by fraud or by force within the immensely thick walls of his castle. Only two of these were now left, and even they were broken and rugged at the top. There was a large area covered with masses of stone and mortar, and overgrown with ivy and brushwood, which plainly indicated that formerly the castle had stood there. The north and east walls, which were several feet in thickness, and a tower, apparently of but half its original height, were now the only remnants of the dwelling of the rich and mighty; but ruined though it was and decayed, its splendid halls

H

had never been so greatly honoured by the presence of its haughty, defiant, and wealthy owners as it was now, when its vaults sheltered men who were one day to raise their country to a greater glory than ever, and who surpassed in all but wealth their famous predecessors.

Stealing cautiously along the above-mentioned area, Treslong directed his steps to the middle of the north wall, and at a spot which was completely covered with ivy he halted and whistled softly. Suddenly a gleam of light appeared through the ivy, and a voice whispered "Watchword!"

The answer was given, and a summons to pass followed. The light disappeared, and pushing away the ivy, the two men entered an aperture in the wall, which gave access to a long and narrow passage, at least threescore yards in length. At the entrance, they found the man who had carried the light, which at closer sight appeared to be only a burning match, and who gave them as hearty a welcome as his colleague Jonathan had done.

"Have you laid a new train of powder?" asked Treslong of the sentry.

"Ay, ay, my Lord, and I'll undertake to send a whole regiment of Spaniards back to Spain with it, in no time, if they try to walk about here. Is there anyone else coming?"

"Yes, two more, Yonker Galama, and another."

Treslong passed on, and arriving at the end of the passage, he stooped down and felt about for a moment. Suddenly, the ground before them seemed to open, and a volume of light and sounds of laughter and merriment rose through the chasm. Treslong then descended a ladder, and Hans, following his example, took care to close and bolt the immensely thick trap-door, which had given them entrance.

The apartment which they had entered was an oblong quadrangle, with a vaulted roof. It had been one of the prison-vaults of the old castle. Massive iron rings could still be seen in the walls. It was partly situated under the tower, and a mine or train of gunpowder had been laid by the Beggars in such a manner that the roof of the vault could be blown up, and receive as a crowning piece of destruction, the tottering walls of the tower. Another and smaller vault, the entrance to which had been hung with a velvet curtain, had a door which opened into a long passage, and provided a safe exit in case of surprise.

The first vault was about fifteen yards long, and ten broad. A large wooden board, supported by two huge stones, served as table in the middle. Two lamps, which looked as if they belonged to some church, were hung up at each end. At the side of the table, nearest the ladder, five men, between forty and sixty years of age, and of a grave and dignified appearance, were engaged in a discussion which was interrupted by the appearance of our two friends. At the other end, a totally different group was seen. There the floor was covered with straw, and on it, reclining in sixteen different positions, lay sixteen men of all ages and appearances. A more picturesque group it would not be possible to conceive. Here lay a thin, delicate-looking youth, with the blouse of the rough farmer around him; there a jovial and purple-nosed soldier was dressed in the monk's cowl, and drinking wine out of a silver censer, which had apparently been carried away from some altar. In one corner, a broad-shouldered fellow was cleaning and polishing a cuirass, and vigorously applying his chalk and water out of a baptismal font; in another, a figure lay unconscious in sleep, though his flushed cheeks, his irregular breathing, and the bandages around his head showed that this sleep was produced by a wound-fever; by his side as if in direct contradiction to the moral which he taught, another Beggar was sharpening his sword.

The table was covered with weapons of every descrip-tion, and various dishes of silver or other metal, which constituted part of the plunder of churches, abbeys, and convents, lay amongst them. The light, as it shone upon this motley group, and upon the curtain before the en-trance of the second vault, displayed indeed a very curious and picturesque scene.

Most of them were passing their time in joking with each other, and in playing at dice.

It was natural that each of the two men who entered the place should join that party with which his rank and disposition most agreed. Thus, after having respectfully saluted the five men nearest the ladder, Hans walked to the other side of the table, where he was cordially and somewhat uproariously received by his more jovial and numerous associates, with whom he seemed a great favour-ite, and who speedily assigned him a place in their midst.

"Has any one brought any new intelligence from Brussels, since I have been away?" asked Treslong of an elderly man of a dignified and somewhat sad appearance, whose name was Verveen.

"Not that I am aware of," answered he; "but I suppose there is very little doubt now about the execution taking place to-morrow, or the day after. But I thought you were going to bring Yonker Galama with you; where is he?"

"He has gone on to Brussels and will be back here within a short time. He has procured the costume of a Spanish officer, and has little to fear. He will be able to give us the best information, for he is going to the Broodhuys, where, as I suppose you are aware, he knows the warder and his daughter."

"I don't suppose he will show himself to the warder," said the first speaker; "but has the Yonker no news from the Prince? I heard that he was going to reinforce Count Louis, in Friesland, for if it be true that Alva is going thither himself, the Count will have a hard battle to fight. He is not a match for the Duke, in my opinion. He is too young and impatient."

"That is just what spoils every one of our undertakings, and I am afraid will spoil our whole cause," said another, opposite him, impatiently. He had a martial appearance, but his face indicated that he possessed none of the independence and originality of Treslong, and that, excellent though he might be as a servant, he was but ill fitted for the post of commander. He was a scion of the ancient family of van Hagendorp, and had been one of the presenters of the Request. "I know," he continued "that nine out of the ten inhabitants throughout the Provinces would at once declare openly for the Prince, if we could but get an able general in whose abilities we could put our trust. But now, who is to blame them if they do not respond to the call, when, as we have seen in the case of that traitor Villars, the whole band is cut to pieces by an enemy of half its number?"

"Nobody says they are to blame, my dear van Hagendorp," said Treslong, "but————." He was interrupted by a burst of laughter from the other end of the table. Turning his eyes in that direction, he saw Hans sitting on a wine barrel, clothed in a beautifully embroidered mass-chasuble, while he pretended to read or chant out of a book in his hand. The Beggars around him seemed highly delighted, and laughed, and chuckled at the ridiculous figure before them.

Treslong gave three smart raps upon the table with the hilt of his dagger, and said, in the silence which was thereby occasioned, "I hope the confederates will not forget that our cause is a sacred one, that we are within three miles of Brussels, and that it is most unadvisable to make an unnecessary noise. We should recollect that our business here is not pleasure," and seeing that his words produced their desired effect, he continued his interrupted answer to van Hagendorp.

"I do not blame the people for not rising, but what I blame the people for is, that they do not contribute their money more profusely. You know very well that the Prince was very much disappointed in finding that he had received barely half the amount which was absolutely required for levying an army. And how can you expect a good general to consent to take the command of an army when he knows that within a month the troops will become mutinous for want of pay. Why, if the people dread being imprisoned, or executed, because

their wealth makes them an object of desire for the
Duke, why don't they give it to work out their own
safety? Count Louis might be marching on towards
Brussels now, if his troops were not in mutiny."

"Do you think that we may expect help from France?"
said Verveen who was more of a politician, and had occupied the post of secretary to one of the influential
nobles. "The King has made peace with the Huguenots,
and seems favourably disposed towards us. De Coligny
has great military talent, and might persuade him to
help us if he knew that we would acknowlege him as
Lord of the Provinces."

"And would you?" asked a fourth, whose dress was
a mixture between the civil and the military, and whose
face, when he spoke, shone with enthusiasm and life. In
him the priest and the warrior were united. He had
preached to great assemblies, and had been the means in
God's hands of bringing the truth home to many, but having no opportunity at present he was content to take up
the sword and defend those liberties which he proclaimed.
"Would you accept his help upon that condition? I
would as lief have Philip. If it were purely civil liberty
we were fighting for, it would still be doubtful, for France
is not the country, nor are the de Medici the family to
allow us to manage our own affairs. But one of our
great reasons, nay, the greatest, is liberty of religion, and
that, you must acknowledge, they would not grant."

"And has not the King granted it to the Huguenots?"
asked Verveen.

"For how long?" said the other. "For a month, for
a year, perhaps. Believe me, Master Verveen, as long as

a king or a sovereign has a power above him which he must obey, such as that of the Pope, he cannot perpetually allow liberty of any kind.   And besides, in a country where the acts of a sovereign are so entirely arbitrary, who knows but the next king might annul all our mutual agreements, supposing we had made any. No, if we have to get foreign aid, let us not seek it there. Let it come from the free, from the Protestant England and its Queen."

"I tell you," the voice of Hans was here heard, "I am a different fellow from what you think.   When I was at Dillenburg last, the Prince says to me, 'Well, Hans, what would you advise?' Says I, 'Well, your Highness, I would send one army, under your Highness's brother, into Friesland, and another under some first-rate fellow, into Brabant. Alva can't fight 'em both, and p'raps won't fight either.' 'But,' says I, 'don't take Villars, 'cause he's no good.'   'Oh, yes,' says he, 'Villars is all right.' 'Very well,' says I, 'we'll see.'   And who was right, eh?   I can assure you now————"

He paused, for as he sat with his back to Treslong, he had entirely forgotten him, but now by the ironical smiles, the winks and the silence of his listeners, he perceived that he was the centre of all observation. He looked round, and at that moment all in the cave but himself, burst out into a laugh, which, considering that he was the object of it, he bore with great calmness and magnanimity.

"What a conceited fool that fellow is," whispered Verveen with scorn, as soon as the laugh had been silenced, or at least subdued.

"I wish I had some more of these fools, Master Verneen," said Treslong. He is given to bragging, it is true but it is quite harmless, and I know of no more faithful, intelligent, or honest member of our confederacy."

"And it is possible," said the preacher, "that upon such ground, the seed of God may yet bear good fruit; for I am perfectly assured that with many of the fellows round about him, it would be choked by the thorns in a day."

"To resume our conversation," said Verveen, to whom this allusion seemed to be distasteful, "you recommend Queen Elizabeth as a help, and you were pleased to call her Protestant and free. But may be, you know not that Protestant though she be, she has refused to help the Huguenots in France, and yet I am sure she would rather wage a war against France than against Spain. She is, perhaps, not so relentless and hateful as her sister, but she has but little affection for our brethren, the Puritans."

"And yet, Master Verveen," said Treslong, "if I understand rightly my friend Marnix de St. Aldegonde, her principal adviser, Sir William Cecil, with whom Marnix seems to be intimate, is not, by any means, so adverse to these Puritans as she is, and I am assured that if we do put ourselves under her protection, we shall eventually be delivered from this yoke, and enjoy a thousand times greater liberty than we do now. You must not forget that Queen Elizabeth is in a very difficult position at this moment, and that she has shown nothing but kindness and benevolence to those of our countrymen who have been able to escape to her dominions. She may not be a Puritan, but she is most decidedly not a Catholic."

Here their conversation was again interrupted by the

other Beggars, who, perhaps somewhat heated with wine, had formed a circle round two of their companions, who were proceeding to attack each other with their swords, by way of pastime. The opinions as to their comparative merit seemed to be divided, for there was a great deal of encouragement on both sides, though but little noise was made. Treslong, however, who foresaw that it might easily become a cause of quarrel, had just made up his mind to put a stop to it, when the shrill cry of the owl penetrated into the vault.

The effect was electric. Every one seemed to know his particular duty. The lamps were taken down, and kept in such a manner that they might be extinguished in a moment. Every one rose and listened, with his hand on his sword or pistol, and not a sound was made. The opening to the other vault had been cleared, and showed a ready exit in case retreat were necessary. Suddenly two knocks were heard above head, and immediately the lamps were restored to their former position.

A moment afterwards, the trap-door was opened, and Treslong who had gone up, re-appeared, followed by our two acquaintances, Yonker Galama and Gerard Block.

Chapter Ninth.

AN ELECTION.

FOR a moment after their entrance, there reigned a dead silence, and the whole band now being assembled, its members drew, as by instinct, closer together, and ranged themselves round the table. Those of them who had before passed their time in jest and carousal were now attentive and respectful, for they knew that the time for action was at hand. The roving life which they led, the frequent changes and dangers, the little, though strict discipline, and the desperate undertakings in which they engaged at a moment's notice, had forced them to accustom themselves to all situations, and to sleep, eat, joke, or fight, at any time, without being influenced by the rapidity with which these actions succeeded each other.

Treslong, Galama, Block, and the five other chiefs had taken their stand at the head of the table. The rest took their places around, and all eyes were turned upon Galama, from whom the great news was expected, which was to decide what was to be done. And as he stood there, with his fair locks hanging around his pale features, his eyes shining with hope and enthusiasm, and his lips parted with a smile, as he saw all eyes turned upon him, he looked the personification of undaunted courage and noble patriotism.

"I have first to introduce to your notice, gentlemen, a new member of our confederacy," said Galama in a clear voice, after he had greeted his particular friends cordially, and conversed with them for some moments. "He has been sent to us by our friend Peter Blink, who, as we all know, is very active in promoting our interests in the province of Holland, and who has sent him to me with a written introduction, in which he assures us that Gerard Block, for such is his name, will be of great service to us, as he has known Brussels from his childhood. I need not ask you, Master Block, whether you have taken the oath of allegiance to his Majesty the king of Spain as the Count of these provinces, to the Prince of Orange as his lawful and sole representative, and to our confederacy as their faithful and loyal support."

Block, thus addressed, bowed his head in token of assent. Many of the Beggars, however, looked at him with unwilling, if not suspicious eyes. Galama saw this, and hastened to remove their suspicions.

"If any doubt of his fidelity to our cause had still lingered in my mind," he continued, "it would have disappeared by this time. For I must tell you that within the few hours that I have known him, he has already endangered his own life to save mine. Indeed, I have little doubt that but for his timely and courageous help, I would be swinging on the gallows in Brussels within a few days."

The Beggars looked kindlier at Block, and Galama proceeded, "I must now call your attention to the heavy blow which threatens all of us at this moment. The manner in which the most sacred and tender ties which can bind human beings together, have been severed by the bloody servants of the Duke and his predecessors, who, under the pretext of protecting the most holy Church, have destroyed our homes and robbed our properties, need not be here enlarged upon. I do not believe there is one amongst you who is not smarting under some heavy and cruel blow, who has not lost some beloved relation, or friend, and seen him die like the meanest and deadliest of malefactors."

He paused, and his face assumed for a moment a tender expression, as he thought of her who had impressed him so deeply with the nobility with which she looked upon these wrongs. Then he proceeded—

"But it is not vengeance that we are now contemplating. It is a service to our cause, an act for promoting our sacred liberty, which we are now called upon to execute. All of you will remember in how base and treacherous a manner the Duke of Alva possessed himself, nine months ago, of the persons of the two Counts, Egmont and Horn. When the rumour spread through the length and breadth of the land, that they had been imprisoned, it was not believed. But when day by day the report was confirmed, and when even the king was said to have given his consent, even the most unbelieving began to fear that it was true. Shall I remind you of the immense services which they, and especially the Count Egmont, have rendered the king? Shall I speak of the brilliant and valiant exploits by which, at the outset of his reign, his arms redeemed their somewhat tarnished glory? Has not the whole world repeated with admiration the name of Lamoral, and do not our neighbours, the French, at this moment, remember with shame the names of St. Quentin and Gravelines? And how think you are his services to be rewarded? This morning, his public and private enemy, the Duke, resolved to have him and his friend and fellow-prisoner, Count Horn, beheaded pub-licly, on the market-place in front of the Broodhuys, and that to-morrow morning——"

He paused, and looked round the assembled Beggars. The piece of news, which had spread like lightning through the town, and had, in fact, been known some time before, though up till that day its confirmation was not official, seemed to be known to most of the confede-rates, and a deepening of the gloom upon their brow, as they looked at each other, at Galama, or on the floor, was the only response which they gave.

"Almost the whole time during which the two Counts were confined in Ghent," continued Galama, "I was secretly engaged in endeavouring to liberate them, b all my efforts failed completely. At last, I was informed that they were to be removed to Brussels for execu-tion. I sent you word, for it is possible that we may effect here what proved impossible at Ghent. I need not tell you of what immense value the Count of Egmont would be to our cause, and what great assistance he would be to our glorious chief, the Prince of Orange. His military talents, which match those of Alva himself, the adoration in which he is held by the people, and especi-ally by the soldiers, would make him the greatest sup-port of the Prince and his brothers. I have been inside

Brussels, last night, in company with Master Block, and both of us have learnt a great many particulars, which make our case at once more easy and more difficult. Let our friend Block first relate us what he has heard. I shall afterwards give you my story."

All eyes were now turned upon Block, who said in a very calm manner,

"The information which I have been able to obtain, though not very extensive, is important and reliable, having been given to me by my own cousin, who occupies the post of one of the Duke's chamberlains, and who is secretly on our side. Through him I know that a rising in the city in order to effect the liberation of the Counts will be a total impossibility, even if we were a hundred times our present number. Two thousand men are to be drawn up on the square, and two companies will patrol the streets during the execution, so that even if the burghers did assist us, we could effect nothing in that way. But the unfortunate burghers are so stricken down, so discouraged and altogether so afraid, that I do not think we would get ten people to listen to us. Alva has sent for the Bishop of Ypres, who is with him now, I suppose, and who has orders to go to Count Egmont at 12 o'clock to-night, and acquaint him with his approaching end. He is closely guarded, and unless some means or other is found to liberate him, the greatest general of his age, and the man who could help our cause more than almost any other, will be a corpse within four-and-twenty hours."

The last words were spoken in a low and tremulous tone, and the impression which they created was very

deep.   It was to be seen that every one present felt the
leaden hand of the impending calamity press heavily
upon him. Treslong, who saw this impression too, frowned,
and resolved to alter it if possible.   Quickly taking up
the word, he said cheerfully—

"We are surely not going to despond because our
enemies at present are stronger than we are, and because
we have no army to oppose theirs. We know that one of
their armies has just been defeated, in Friesland, by an
enemy about half its number ; who knows but what we
may defeat them somehow with less than that. We can try
at any rate, and I for one have made up my mind to it,
though I die in the attempt. When Yonker Galama arrived,
I thought I saw his face lit up with a smile of hope. We
have not heard his story yet.   Perhaps the burghers are
not so downcast after all, and perhaps, if they knew that
we were present they might be induced to risk a rescue.
What is your news, Yonker ?"

Having been already informed by Galama what the
result of his going to Brussels was, his words had the desired effect.   The men awaited with the greatest interest
what Galama was to communicate.

"You are right, my Lord," said Karel, "and you, too,
Master Block.   I fear, indeed, that the poor burghers of
Brussels have suffered too much to run the risk of being
beaten by the Spanish soldiers.   But still there are some
amongst them who know not what fear is.   Last night I
visited the Broodhuys, the place where the two Counts are
confined, and it seems that there is some hope of one of
us being able to liberate Count Egmont, for Count Horn,
I am afraid, is beyond our reach.   But the attempt is

fraught with peril, and must moreover be made with great caution, in order to involve no one but ourselves in any danger. One of us must go, dressed as a friar of the Dominicans, to the Broodhuys, where he will be conducted through a host of sentries to the garret. Thence he must descend the large chimney into Count Egmont's room, and in some noiseless way disable the sentry. The Count then will change clothes with his liberator, and in this disguise leave the prison, while the other makes his best way from the garret to the adjoining fish-market. One of us, meanwhile, must scale the wall of the town, surprise the sentry, let the others in, and, at the moment that the Count approaches, attack the guards and open the gate, which is not difficult. Those of us who have horses will accompany the Count on his flight to France, with the others it is *sauve qui peut.* This is my plan, and the only one which has yet the slightest chance of success. It is a desperate undertaking, and I hardly suppose any of you will become a volunteer. Consider the dangers well. He who goes to the Broodhuys must put but little value on his life, for the escape once discovered will involve his almost certain death, and that of—— "

His voice faltered, but he quickly recovered himself. There was a dead silence amongst the Beggars. At last Treslong said—

" Who volunteers for the post of surprising the sentry on the wall ? "

" I do."

It was Block. He stood erect and looked round the circle.

I

"I would not be so bold, my Lord," he said, "but that I have known Brussels from my very childhood, and have climbed almost every inch of the wall before the town was in a state of siege. Well do I know the place near the gates, where I used to wade the moat and creep through a sewer to the other side. It is still there and I'll stake my life on its being accomplished to-night."

It seemed, however, as if both Treslong and the other confederates were still hesitating how to receive so daring an offer from one who had only that night come amongst them, and was personally known to no one. Block perceived this.

"I do not doubt," he said, "that there are many amongst you who look with some sort of suspicion upon my offer. But let me briefly give you the reasons that prompt me. We have only three hours and a half in which to do everything, as after that the Bishop of Ypres is to be with the prisoner. Nobody would be of the slightest use for the post to which I have volunteered except one perfectly acquainted with the walls and everything belonging to them. One attempt failing, we need not try a second, for the sentries, after having been put on their guard, are not to be duped. So all depends upon one stroke. If anyone thinks he can do better than I can, I am willing to let him go. But my hands burn to pay back a little of the debt, the fearful debt, which I owe them."

He spoke rapidly, and as it seemed with deep feeling. He had gained his object, and saw with satisfaction that many of them gave a nod of assent after he had spoken. Treslong seemed to think for a moment and then looked up.

"Yes," he said, "it is better as it is. I had thoughts of taking the post myself, but, after all, I believe I am better fitted for the friar. I have not forgotten all my Latin, and I am weary of this life of idleness. So who can get me a cowl?"

But here he met with a violent opposition. None of the Beggars would consent to his taking that post. Some remarked that he must stay behind to lead them to the walls—others that he must remain to keep order, as no other could take his place. Some made laughing comments upon his unclerical appearance, and protested that he would never pass the gates. Treslong seemed to hesitate.

"What say *you*, Yonker?" he said, turning to Galama.

A heavy struggle had in the meantime been going on in Galama's breast. He burned to offer himself for the post, and yet his promise to Agnes closed his mouth. He stood with compressed lips and flushed cheeks. When the chief addressed him he fetched a deep breath, but said not a word.

There was a moment's silence amongst the confederates, during which some seemed uncertain how to interpret the Frisian's conduct. At last Block spoke in a low and somewhat humble tone.

"Pardon me, my Lord de Treslong, but in my opinion the objections which have been raised against your going are not without ground. Your face is known to almost every inhabitant of Brussels, for the gallant companion of the brave Brederode will not soon be forgotten by any Dutchman. And why should you go? The noble Yonker at my side, is, I am sure, burning with desire to fill the post of honour.   He knows the Broodhuys, he can speak Latin, and he is at least more of a friar in his appearance than you, my Lord, and that he is not want-ing in courage and presence of mind, the little affair of last night has shown to me."

The proposal thus given by Block was received by all the confederates with the loudest tokens of satisfaction which they dared give.   There were only two exceptions —Treslong and Hans.   Hans was silent and looked with a sombre scowl at Gerard Block.   Treslong, on the other hand, openly expressed his disapproval, but the Beggars, with whom Galama's qualities seemed to be well known, negatived all his objections, and the Yonker himself agreed to the proposal with the utmost pleasure. He seized Block's hand cordially, and then turning to Treslong he said—

"Come, my Lord, let us waste no more words.   I go, and please God I shall send you the Count within an hour or two.   I shall make my best way out, and if I can't I'll die with pleasure, so the Count be freed.   Get me a friar's cowl, Hans, and help me to take off these things, for it is growing late, and every moment is pre-cious.   Only this I must yet say.   The Count shall halt at the corner of little Cross Street.   There some of you must await him.   He shall whistle twice and pass the word 'Liberty.'   The rest you must arrange yourselves. Where is Hans?"

He was told that Hans had gone into the other vault, to find suitable outfit, and in order to lose no time he lifted up the curtain and joined him.

Hans was standing amongst a disorderly heap of

clothes of every imaginable kind with which the floor of the second vault was covered. A good stock of arms was suspended on the walls, and two or three barrels in a corner contained the two most necessary things for the Beggars—wine and powder. The moment he saw his master he put down the lamp which he held in his hand, and unbuckled Galama's cuirass, as this would be but ill-suited for the underclothing of a confessor. He then bent down as if looking for some articles of dress, but in reality he was closely examining the cuirass and the embroidered band to which Galama's sword had been attached. Though the examination lasted but for a moment, it seemed to satisfy Hans, for he put the two articles aside, and stood erect as if in momentary thought.

His master watched him with some interest, for Hans was as much his friend as his servant, and there were times when his advice was as valuable, and his views as clear, as those of the most intelligent; and many an ingenious suggestion of his had been attended with the best result. He now stood looking at his master with an expression upon his face as if he knew he must say something hard, and as if that something was at the same time difficult to say. All traces of frolic and careless gaiety were vanished, and his dark eyes were shining with a steady and thoughtful fire.

" Well, Hans," asked Karel, " what are you thinking of ? "

" Hm, Yonker, I was thinking of the Count," answered Hans, slowly, " and as how *he* 'll feel to-morrow about this time."

" Is that all ? " said Galama, " give me the friar's cowl.

He will feel extremely comfortable, when he is on the other side of the frontier."

"May-be he won't feel at all," said the servant, bending down once more and tossing the dresses about.

"How so?" asked the master, "you seem to be particularly unhopeful about this affair."

"Well, Yonker, you know it *is* dangerous. Firstly, you know, they know your face by this time at the gate, and they'll think it jolly queer that an officer comes dressed as ——"

"I know the watchword. Make haste, will you?"

"Then there's Mistress Agnes ——," continued Hans, as if speaking to himself.

"Agnes is perfectly aware of what is going to happen," interrupted Karel, impatiently.

"—— and I do not suppose she will be as cool and as considerate as she ought to be, and may be she'll cry again, and then the whole thing will come out and we'll lose ——."

"We'll lose all our time if we stand talking here," said Galama, growing more and more impatient," give me the cowl, or make haste if you have not got it yet. It must be going on for nine by this time, and I must be there at ten."

"Now Yonker," said Hans, with some hesitation in his voice. "I really—I don't think, you know—you shouldn't—you mustn't——"

"What do you mean?" cried Galama, stamping with his foot. "Are you going to keep me here all night, or what? Give me that cowl instantly, or let me find it myself. I dare say I can dispense with your services."

The Yonker saw perfectly what Hans was aiming at, and it is possible that a voice within him whispered that the faithful fellow was quite right. That, at any rate, would be sufficient to explain why, obstinate Frisian as he was, he resolved to follow his own plan. But if Galama could be obstinate, Hans could be firm.

"Dash it all, Yonker," he said determinedly, as he threw away a monk's cowl, and looked his master fairly in the face, "don't you see that you can't go. What is the good of being obstinate, when the fate of Count Egmont, of mistress Agnes, and of your sister depend upon it. I'm not going to say that you are not cool enough at other times, but I'll stake my life you won't be this time, when you have to be there by the side of mistress Agnes and your sister."

"That remains to be seen," said Karel, haughtily stretching forth his hand. "I thank you for your consideration, and I will allow that your reflections upon my courage spring purely and only from noble motives. But since I have been chosen for this post, I shall not shrink from it, and difficult though it be, the difficulty is appreciated both by Agnes and myself, and I feel naught but honour at the trust which the confederates put in me. Give me the cowl?"

"Och," said Hans, almost in the tones of a father, "the confederates would not have put that trust in you if they knew what I know. They don't know you, and they don't know mistress Agnes, and they don't know that she has been weeping the colour out of that scarf too. Come, Yonker, you can't deny that either she or your sister, or both have been crying over you, and I know they could do a good deal of it a year ago. A woman is a woman I say, and dashed if she'll ever turn anything else ; if she cried to-night already, what will she do when she has to go through danger with you. One will be so afraid for t'other that you'll both be caught without fail."

But it was no use. With an expression of insulted dignity upon his face, Galama tore the dress out of his servant's hands, and notwithstanding his remonstrances, he proceeded to put it on. Hans shook his head, and turning round he walked to the entrance of the first vault and lifted the curtains. The place had become quite altered. The table had been put on one side, the blocks of stone deposited in a corner. Gerard Block had already set out on his enterprise. and all the Beggars were busily preparing themselves for the undertaking. As Hans put his head through the opening between the two vaults, he perceived, almost touching him, Treslong, Verveen, and the preacher in earnest conversation together, and he immediately tapped the chief on the arm. Treslong turned round and seemed rather astonished to find Hans.

"Hoping you'll excuse me, my lord," said he, respectfully, "but the Yonker is rather obstinate, and I think you are the only one who can make him listen to reason. You must not let him go to the Broodhuys, for he is sure to make a mess of it. I can't make anything of him."

Treslong smiled and looked at the other two men, while he said, "You see my fears are well grounded. Just let us go to him," and the three men went into the vault where Galama was still busy, followed by the astonished and delighted Hans.

"I have been thinking, Yonker Galama," said Treslong calmly, and with a tone of authority, "that you are, after all, not the best fitted of us for this enterprise. I think you told me that your sister was staying at the Broodhuys, and that you are well acquainted with the warder and his daughter, all of which are so many reasons why you should not go. Remember, it is not glory you go for, but Egmont."

Karel Galama, who stood totally equipped in a friar's cloak and a rosary on his girdle, frowned when he heard these words, his cheeks turned pale, and on his lips there played a smile of haughty defiance. The idea of going to Brussels again, and braving the danger by the side of Agnes, of defending her whom he loved so deeply, and of dying for her and for Count Egmont, was so pleasing, so romantic, so seductive for him, that he was ready to resist even Treslong's authority. But glancing at the chief's calm and commanding features, he reflected that Treslong had had far more experience, and possessed, at any rate, the power to retain him, and as he remembered what Agnes had said to him he resolved to give in. Thus, after a moment's silence, he said in a low voice,—

"I place myself at your lordship's command."

Treslong extended his hand and shook Galama's cordially. He understood fully what had passed in the youth's mind, and resolved as he was to be obeyed, he appreciated the spirit in which his words had been received.

"The next question is, who shall go in your stead?" asked Verveen.

"I might as well, since I have been at that work before,"

said Hans, stepping from a corner of the vault whither he had withdrawn. He was dressed the same way as his master, but being stouter and fuller in the face, he presented so exactly the appearance of a monk, that even Galama smiled, and when with a low voice he repeated "*Ave Maria, ora pro nobis*," the dissimulation was complete.

"He's our man" said Verveen, "he knows the Broodhuys as well, and the ladies less intimately, than you do, Yonker," and he playfully poked him in the side.

After some discussion Treslong consented, and Hans was fully informed what he was to do. Some barrels and clothes having been removed silently and quickly, Treslong pressed on an iron knob, and a door, wide enough to allow one man to pass, opened in the wall, and gave access to a passage of the same dimensions. Hans entered it with the burning lamp in one hand and a dagger in the other, and disappeared.

For a few moments the men looked in silence at the open door, through which the cold night air entered the vault. The glimmer of the light became fainter and fainter. At last it vanished, and the shriek of an owl was heard, disturbing the stillness of the night. Treslong stepped forward, and closing the door he hid it again with the dresses and the casks. Then turning round to Galama, who had remained in his thoughtful position, with his hands crossed over his breast, he said, pointing to the door:—

"God watch over that fellow, and bring him back in safety. For noisy and bragging though he be, no truer or more faithful servant ever trod this earth."

And Galama bowed his head, and softly said "Amen."

The four men now returned to the first cave, where a great change had taken place amongst the confederates. The fantastic dress of some, the defective or shabby equipment of others, were put aside. Each sought out what he wanted, and supplied it as best he could. Iron helmets were exchanged for the famous felt hat, the girdle was charged with pistols and dagger, every superfluous article of dress was laid aside, and deposited in the store-room. It was not long before most of them were ready, and stood in a group under the lamp in the middle of the vault. Treslong, whose dress had ever been simple, had watched the whole proceeding attentively, giving a direction here, an advice there, and shortly explained to the somewhat astonished Beggars why they saw Galama amongst them instead of Hans. When everything was ready he stepped into their midst.

"Comrades," he said, in a low but distinct voice, "this is probably the last night that we shall be together in this neighbourhood. We are on the eve of a great day, and a few words as to our future line of conduct may not be amiss. It is possible that our schemes for the liberation of Count Egmont may succeed. If so, most of you will follow me in his defence on his flight across the frontiers. But it is as possible that it may fail. In that case you must take your own counsel. I shall endeavour to make my way to the army of Count Louis. I have heard that Alva has issued orders to move towards Friesland as soon as the execution is over. There will be plenty of fighting, therefore, and every man will be welcome in our army. Those, however, who think they will do better by remaining here can do so, though I would not advise it. This place is being suspected by the Spaniards, and some day you may be caught in it. At any rate should our attempt fail to-night, and we be obliged to fly into the forest, let no one fly hither, nor appear in its neighbourhood, until to-morrow evening. In case we are unsuccessful, my command over you is at an end, and I place it in the hands of Yonker Galama. Let me thank you here heartily for the manner in which all of you have supported me. Remember always the great cause in which you are engaged. Think that the eyes of the whole world are upon you, and disgrace not by any mean or ignoble act the name of our confederacy, or of its illustrious chief, the Prince of Orange. Let us drink at parting a bumper to his health and our success, and then we must move.

The bumpers were soon filled. The cry "Vivent les Gueux !" was repeated softly, the Prince was blessed, Treslong was cheered, and Alva's name repeated with a curse.

"We must go separately," continued Treslong ; "we shall meet at the outskirt of the wood, at the corner of the road to Ixelles, about a hundred yards from the gate. Yonker van Hagendorp lead the van."

Van Hagendorp mounted the ladder, and his footsteps were heard in the passage. A few moments afterwards, the owl's shriek was heard, and a second man left. In a short time the vault was cleared. Treslong and Galama were the last to leave. They were saluted by the man with the burning match, who had kept a continuous watch the whole night.

"You have kept excellent watch, Frank. Take this and keep it as a remembrance of me, and give this to the two owls," said Treslong, giving the sentry some golden ducats. "Not one of us is to be here till to-morrow night, at least, so you can take some rest. In case the place be attacked in our absence, the warning cry is that of the wild cat. All the rest remains as it is. Goodbye. We shall see you no longer."

"Are you going to leave us, my lord ?" said the man, sinking down on one knee, and kissing his chief's hand with reverence. "I am afraid that our place of shelter will not remain long unknown. In that case, if both you and the Yonker go away, the band will be as a body without a head."

"I shall return here, at any rate," said Yonker Galama ; "I am resolved not to go to Count Louis. I shall first wait here to see whether Hans may, perhaps, come back. If, however, I find that there is no chance of that, I shall make arrangements here, and resume my old business, that [of letter-carrier between the Prince and Master Paulus Buys. It was at his desire partly, that I went hither, and I have done him too many services not to be missed. So good-bye, only for the present, I hope."

And parting the ivy before the entrance, the two men stepped into the area.

The night was very dark. Black masses of clouds hid the stars from view, and scarcely anything could be distinguished even at the distance of a foot. The weather was excellently suited to the occasion. Silently the two men followed the path which led towards the city, and heard with a smile how the sentry in the air saluted them at their departure with a series of owl-shrieks, which were as natural as they were shrill.

.

After having thus walked silently and cautiously for rather more than half-an-hour, they halted. They found themselves at the outskirts of the forest, and at about a thousand yards from the walls of the city. The distance between the city and the spot where they at present stood was covered with low underwood, with only an occasional group of trees, the larger trees having been cut down for building purposes. It was the most dangerous spot of all, for a person could be easily seen rising above the low bushes, while but little shelter was afforded by the few straggling trees. All precautions, however, were taken. Bending low, they moved on slowly and softly, until presently they arrived at the last group of trees, where the road to Ixelles is crossed by that going to the little village of St. Giles, and by the other numerous cross-roads which intersect the forest. A group of men were assembled under the trees, and could be indistinctly seen amongst the slender stems.

"Are we all here?" asked Treslong. He was answered by a soft "Yes."

The names were called out, and the owners responded in turn.

"Lie down in the bushes, and you, Jonathan, go and reconnoitre. Gerard must be opposite this spot, if he is anywhere. Give three low and short whistles, which he shall answer in the same manner ; wade through the moat, and he will throw down a rope. Tie this rope-ladder to it, and come back here."

The command was given sharply and softly, and a moment afterwards, Jonathan, the same who had formerly addressed Treslong and Hans, stole like a cat through the darkness and disappeared.

"Attention," whispered Treslong. The confederates moved closer to him. "We shall have to go up the ladder one by one. I shall go first, then Yonker Galama, then Yonker van Hagendorp," and he proceeded to arrange the order. "On the wall we shall have to lie within a stone's-throw of the guard-house, until the Count comes. Should we be discovered or betrayed, however, we must keep together, and either force our way through the gate, or back over the wall. At any rate, do nothing until you hear my command. And now, silence."

No one passing the spot would have been aware of the presence of any living being, such a death-like silence did there reign. At last, the voice of Jonathan was heard again. He had approached without even their knowledge, sharply though they had listened.

"The way is clear. The ladder is hanging, and there is but half a foot of water in the moat. Block says that the guard is almost entirely drunk."

In a moment the men had softly risen and advanced, sword in hand, led by Jonathan, Treslong, and Galama. Sombre and ominous did the walls of Brussels rise before them. The city, which is shaped somewhat in the form of a pear, was surrounded by a wall of about ten to fifteen feet, and a moat or ditch of about twice that dimension in width. It receives its water from the river Senne, which flows through the city, and when in a state of siege it is filled, and has a depth of at least six feet. At that time, however, the water in the river being low, and no danger of an attack upon the city being apprehended, the moat was allowed to remain comparatively dry, and had at some places no more than half a foot of water.   One by one, the men glided into the moat, and a row of dark shadows formed as it were a bridge to the wall, which rose straight up out of the mud.   Treslong seized the ladder and gave it a pull.   It remained fixed.

"When I am above, I shall give a jerk," he said, turning round.   Then seizing his sword between his teeth, he began to ascend.

In a few moments, Yonker Galama felt a jerk, and he likewise ascended.   He soon reached the top, and was helped upon the rampart by Treslong, who lay on his stomach.

"Where is Block?" he whispered to Treslong, who was bending down to help up another man.

"Here I am, who asks?" said Block's voice.

"It is I, Galama."

"Galama?   Yonker, you here?   Who is at the Broodhuys?"

"Hans."

Block pronounced a curse.   It was short, but passionate, as if the speaker had been taken entirely by surprise.

"What's the matter, Gerard?" asked Treslong, helping up another man, who, like his predecessors sat down on the grass.

"Nothing," answered Block, "only I thought the Yonker would have done far better at the Broodhuys. But no matter, it can't be helped now, and so, silence." And another man appeared above the wall.   It was not long, ere all were up and seated upon the grass.

"Follow me, and tread softly," whispered Block.

Everyone rose, and proceeded in silence. They were as yet on the top of the wall. Behind the wall was a road, from four to five feet lower than the wall itself, and running right round it on the inside, constructed so as to enable the garrison to open fire upon the enemy without being itself exposed. This road is commonly called a curtained, or covered way, while the wall, upon which as yet the confederates were treading, is called a rampart.

"We must get down on to the covered way," whispered Block. "Walk in single file." They walked on silently, and were soon upon the covered way.

Suddenly a shot flashed upon them, and a bullet whistled through the air.

"We are discovered," said Block, half audibly, halting, and turning to Treslong and Galama, who were foremost. "Let us fly to the gates and force our way through."

"Stop!" commanded Treslong. "That shot was fired intentionally, though too soon. We are discovered, there's no doubt of that, and you——"

A cry of men in front of them made them start.

"To the gate!" shouted Block, leading the way, but four more shots flashed, and he fell down with a yell. It was answered by the soldiers on the wall, who came rushing on in a body, and shouted.

Treslong did not lose his presence of mind. He turned round to the men who stood behind him.

"Back! up the rampart, and jump into the moat. *Sauve qui peut!*"

"Block! let us rescue Block," cried Karel, but no one heard him, and he found himself carried away with the rest.

K

In a moment, the whole band flew up the ramparts, followed by the soldiers. Most of them made the dangerous leap without hesitation, and arrived safely in the mud. Two, who hesitated, were brained by the soldiers, on the spot. To plunge through the mud, and fly into the forest was the work of a moment. Balls whistled past them. The gate opened, and some fifty men set after them in full pursuit, but as they were scattered in every direction, not one was caught.

After a good quarter of an hour's run, Treslong and Galama, who had kept together, halted in a part of the wood far away from the Rookery. They lay down amongst the bushes and waited. It was then that the full consequence of what had happened came upon them. The Count was hopelessly lost, even if he had managed to make his escape from the Broodhuys. To pass the aroused guard was now out of the question.

"Who can have betrayed us?" said Treslong. "I am very much afraid that it is your new acquaintance Block. If he had not fallen himself, I should be certain of it. I wonder how many of us have been killed."

"I do not suspect Block," said Galama. "He is the truest of us all, I think. You must acknowledge that it was a bold game, and that it is a marvel we were not all killed."

"Ay," said Treslong, gloomily, "this Brussels has been no good to me. I shall leave it to-morrow. Let us go to Ixelles, and leave the two Counts to their fate; and may God have mercy upon them."

They rose and went towards Ixelles, where Treslong's

horse was stabled. And as they turned their back upon the city, Galama threw a last look towards it, and said in a voice almost choked with tears, " Farewell, headless Counts."*

---

* See Note " Headless Counts."

Chapter Tenth.

CAUGHT!

In the same room of the Broodhuys, where we have already witnessed the scene between Galama and Agnes, the latter sat alone, pale, sad, and thoughtful. A beautifully ornamented lamp shed its light through the room, and in the breast of Agnes, as in the room, there seemed to be a combination of sentiments, as opposite and as conflicting as light and darkness. A deep sigh escaped her breast at intervals; sometimes her lips moved as if in prayer, while her clear and liquid eyes turned towards heaven with a beseeching look. The spinning-wheel before her, which often enlivened the silence of the room with its cheerful hum, was mute, and for all the work it did, the little machine, with its beautiful carvings and ornaments of ivory and gold, might have been made to please the eye alone.

While thus she sate, the door which led to the kitchen was softly opened. Agnes started, and turning round her head with a quick movement, threw an anxious and somewhat bewildered glance at the door. But her look softened, and her face assumed an expression of kindness when she saw the eyes of her maid regarding her with a mingled look of pity and beseeching.

" What is it, Gritta ? " she asked, in a kind voice.

Gritta, thus encouraged, came in, and running up to her mistress, kneeled down beside her, and seized her hand. It was icy cold.

" Ah, mistress," said the sympathising girl, covering the thin fingers with kisses, and endeavouring to warm them between hers, " it is not right of you to be thus sitting and musing alone. You look so pale and weary. The colour which I so much loved to see in your cheeks is entirely gone, and I have hardly seen you smile this last year and more. It grieves me to see you suffer so ; for though you never complain, Mistress Maria, who has been far worse, as the doctor says, looks ever so much better than you do."

" Gritta," said Agnes, looking kindly at the girl, " the illness from which I am suffering cannot be cured by a doctor. But do I then really look so alarmingly ill ? This light perhaps makes me look paler than I am."

" No," said Gritta, shaking her head, decidedly, " I have watched your face in the daytime, and I have seen it paler than it is now. And you are trembling all over. I am sure you must be ill, and it's all from reading them books. Father Florisz always tells me that I must throw them into the fire whenever I see them, for that I am sure to get an evil spirit within me if I read any of them. Oh, mistress, it may be the evil spirit that's shaking you now, for all you know. Let me go and fetch Father Florisz. He'll cast it out."

Agnes leaned her head upon her hand and endeavoured to control her emotions with one powerful effort. She was thinking how best to get the girl to help her in executing the plan without making her acquainted with it.

After Karel had left her she had remained within that dark room for some hours, battling with her feelings, and trying to look calmly at what she had to do. For though Agnes was morally courageous and could not bear the idea of cowardice, yet after all, she was but a weak girl, and for the execution of great deeds she was almost as badly fitted as Maria. The next morning, however, she was in a much more favourable mood, and to her own surprise acted the invalid so well both before her father, and before Father Florisz, that the one was very near renouncing his favourite saint for allowing his daughter to become ill, while the latter himself proposed to return at some more appropriate time, which Agnes fixed for that night.

And then she made her second move. She told her father that it was no use speaking with Father Florisz down below, where their words were interrupted by the sounds of the soldiers, and that, were they to go to the little room on the top floor, their interview might be attended with far better results. Vlossert listened to her request for a pass with astonishment, for the little room was but seldom used, and never within his recollection had it been used by her. And it is possible that at other times he would have refused her request; but he was partially possessed with the spirit of wine, and eager to join the party of officers with whom he was engaged in playing at dice. Moreover, the quarrel with his daughter was fresh in his recollection, and as he looked at her, standing there with downcast eyes, and revealing an emotion which he ascribed to every cause but the true one, his heart softened towards her. He gave her a loving kiss, blessed her as a pious and obedient daughter, snatched up a pen and scribbled the order. Then, as if a whole load was taken off his mind, he gave her another kiss, and left the room whistling a tune and jingling his money in his pocket.

And Agnes remained behind vainly stirring to calm herself for the coming event. She had told her father that she sought to go up to the little room in order to be free from the noise of the soldiers who occupied the ground, first, and second floors, and whose rude laughter was but a sorry accompaniment to a Pater-noster. But now that she began to think about the details of the matter, she felt that difficulties beset her path at every step. With her father's look bent upon her she had felt herself tremble, and how would she be able to pass between and listen to the rude criticisms of unknown soldiers ? And with Karel by her side, whose haughty temper she well knew, and by whom she feared the insults of the soldiers would not be taken in so meek a spirit as a holy father was supposed to possess, she almost despaired of ever reaching the little closet. She earnestly hoped that some other confederate would be chosen, for, she owned to herself, that with him at her side her courage might forsake her.

But how was he to get inside the house with the sentry at the door and nothing arranged ? Suddenly, when Gritta offered to go and fetch Father Florisz, a thought struck her.

"No, Gritta," she said, soothingly, "Father Florisz promised to be here to-night, and ought to be here by this time. Watch at the door for him, and when he comes let him go to my cousin Maria. I have asked another holy father to come to me. When *he* arrives let him come in here, and do not let Father Florisz see him. You had better watch at the door for him too. Now leave me, and let me know when Father Florisz is here."

Gritta threw a look of pity at her mistress, and left the room. The large clock of the neighbouring church of St. Nicholas struck the hour of ten, and the tones trembled long and solemnly over the silent city. They seemed to be answered by sounds of another, though not less solemn kind, for blows as if carpenters were at work in the neighbourhood fell upon Agnes' ear. She started, and put her hand before her eyes, for she understood but too well what these sounds meant. They were those of the men who were erecting the scaffold on the square, the spot where, within twelve hours, the bloody deed was to be done.

"If he does not come speedily we shall be too late," said Agnes, stepping towards the window and pulling aside the curtain. "The Bishop of Ypres is to be here at eleven, and it is ten now. Where is Karel?"

She turned her head. Through the kitchen door, which was partly open, she could see all that happened in the kitchen and at the back door. A man dressed as a priest was speaking to the sentry and to Gritta. For a moment he turned his head slightly, and then followed Gritta into the opposite room where Maria was. Agnes had recognised him as Father Florisz. A crowd of thoughts came upon her at this moment. Was it right of her to leave her weak, her faltering cousin in the hands of a priest? The conversation of that evening recurred to her, and she thought how the undecided and gentle mind of Maria was still hesitating between the religion in which she had been born and bred, and the one, all the arguments and reasonings in support of which even clearer heads than hers had at times been unable to comprehend. Should she be the cause of her cousin's falling off? Was it not her duty to leave everything and guard her against that?

She made a move towards the door and pressed her hand on her beating heart. Suddenly a voice behind her said softly—

"*Benedictus qui venit in nomine Domini.*"

She looked round. A pair of black eyes stared at her from under a monk's cowl, but whether the person himself was outside the window or within the room she could not see, and her alarm at the moment prevented her from coming closer. She soon, however, recovered herself when the same voice said—

"Can I enter, my daughter, or is there any danger?"

"Enter," said Agnes, in an agitated voice, "but for God's sake take care," and she ran towards the kitchen door and locked it.

"Take care!" said Hans, jumping into the room and closing the window; "care and wine are the only two things that I sometimes have too much of. But how, Mistress Agnes, you stand before me trembling as a leaf? Do you not remember your faithful servant, Black Hans?" and he threw back his cap.

"Hans!" said Agnes, striving to appear as calm as possible; "O God be praised that it is not Karel. How are you my faithful friend, Hans?" and she gave him her hand.

Hans respectfully took the little hand, and looking round the room pressed a soft kiss upon it.

"Eh!" he said, holding it in his own big brown hand, "how it trembles! I think I was quite right in keeping the Yonker from coming here. Lovers, Mistress Agnes, are excellent in their way, as I found out just now, for I am sure I would not have known how to get in, if that lout of a German had not been so sweet upon Gritta. I stood here for about a quarter of an hour, and I could not get a chance. Lovers, I say, are excellent in their way, but when they come to face danger, side by side, they are no good."

His words, unmeaning though they were, effected their purpose. He stood there, so cool, so unconcerned, as if he had all his life been a monk, and as if he were, at this moment engaged as such, without a shadow of danger around him. Agnes looked at him, and unconsciously his manner calmed her.

"Do you not think that I look very much like a pious and reverend father?" he continued. "I have been told before that I would do very well for a bishop. But let me beg you to sit down for a moment, and tell me distinctly how we are to go."

He led Agnes to a chair, and stood before her.

"We have but little time left," she said, much more calmly than before. "In less than an hour the bishop will be here, and then our plan will be impracticable."

"An hour," said Hans, somewhat startled. "Block told me he was not to be here till twelve, and it is just past ten."

"He is coming at eleven," said Agnes. "I have a pass

for the staircases up to the garret. We must first ascend the middle stair. Then turning to the right, we must pass through two rooms occupied by the Guild of Trumpeters. Then there is another stair up to the second floor, and so on to the closet."

"And have we to go through the kitchen?" said Hans, looking at the other door.

"No, we shall go by this door, as soon as you are ready."

"Lead on, madam. Now for the Count, God help us."

Agnes had risen. She was almost perfectly calm, and the easy manner of Hans inspired her with hopes of success which formerly she had not felt. She opened the door which led to the cross-passage and listened. The uncouth sounds of soldiers' laughter, mixed with the noise of the preparations outside on the square, met her ear, and stimulated her to decisive and cool action. She advanced and beckoned Hans to follow. With every step she took her courage grew, and she walked up the staircase which led to the first and principal floor, as firmly as if she had been the lady of the house, followed by a train of attendants.

The large vestibule of the Broodhuys, with its marble pavement, its magnificent statue of the Virgin, and its hangings of costly and beautiful tapestry, was guarded by some dozen soldiers, who were pacing up and down, or sitting on a form. Two halberdiers stood upon the first step of the stair, like statues, scarcely moving a limb. A tall man, dressed as an officer, leaned against the balustrade.

To him Agnes applied, showing her pass and pointing

to Hans.   The officer threw a quick glance at the disguised Beggar, and turning round, ordered the soldiers
to let them pass.   Silently the soldiers moved aside, and
the two ascended, their hearts beating with joyful expectations.   There was a landing, however, in the middle,
and here some five or six soldiers were grouped, neither
so silent nor so tranquil as their lower brethren.

"Hallo," whispered one, as he stepped in the way,
seemingly by mishap.   "Who is this?   A beautiful girl
and a stout priest.   Is this another prisoner, father?"

"Son," said the monk, in a sepulchral voice, "*Praedi-
care captivis remissionem veni.*"

The soldier stepped back, discomfited by the look of
the holy man, and the terrible sound of his words, though
he had not the least idea of their meaning.   But another of
his comrades, who was at once bolder, and less awe-
struck by the appearance of the monk, stood on the
stairs.

"You cannot pass here, madam," he said, "and I
wonder how you could take such a black-looking cur for
your companion.   You might have found many a better
one than him, to be sure."   And he stroked his own
beard with apparent satisfaction.

"Stand aside," said Agnes, with a look and a tone of
command.   "The officer of the guard below has let me
pass, and thou shalt not detain us. ·I am the daughter
of the warder."

The insolent soldier looked towards his officer, and
observing his motion to let them pass on, he stepped
aside with a scowl, and allowed them to proceed.   They
soon arrived on the first floor, where two other sentries

were on guard. There, however, no difficulty presented itself ; the pass was shown and the couple allowed to proceed. It was almost dark on that floor. A small lamp united its feeble efforts with those of the larger ones on the upper and lower storeys, and managed to throw just a dim light over the scene.

"Go on, Mistress Agnes," whispered Hans. "We are drawing nearer to our object ; keep step with the hammers, if you cán. Time is precious."

At the same time, a series of blows delivered by a hammer, sounded over the square and through the house. A slight shudder crept over Agnes, for she knew they came from the scaffold.

"A light," she said, pausing. "I have forgotten to take a light with me."

"Move on," whispered Hans, "I have got one good enough when we get up there. Can you find your way in the dark ? Else we must go back."

"Oh, yes," said Agnes, "I was born in this house, and know every inch of it."

She walked on, and entered the little room before them, which they had to pass before they could reach the staircase that led to the next floor. Their steps sounded sombre on the wooden floor, and Agnes was glad when, by the little light which shone through the door behind them, they reached the opposite door. She grasped the handle, when to her astonishment the door would not open.

"What !" said she. "This door shut ! locked ! It cannot be ; I have never known it to be so in my life ! and the other one too ! Hans, did you shut it after you ? Try this door, or open the other one."

She spoke in short gasps, twisting and turning the handle all the while, and hurting her little fingers in the effort. It had become quite dark in the room, and though they had not heard it, they surmised that the other door must have been shut too. Agnes was silent, and Hans could hear her breathe heavily beside him.

"Be calm," he said, groping about, "and we shall soon get out of this. Where is the handle? Ah, here it is— no," he said, after an attempt to open the door. "I'll try again;" he gave another pull at the door. The handle came off in his hand, but the door remained unmoved.

He paused a moment, and retracing his steps, soon found the door by which they had entered, and which proved to be shut also. Softly grasping the handle, he twisted it round, but with no other result.

"What!" said Hans, vainly applying all his strength, "it must have been shut from without! Is there no other outlet to this room?"

"None whatever," sounded the trembling voice of Agnes, in the dark.

"Caught! by my Beggar's pouch!" cried Hans, and he stamped impatiently with his foot on the floor.

Chapter Eleventh.

A LITTLE TIGER.

FOR some moments both stood without speaking, and listened involuntarily to the sounds without—the hammering, the tones of the mess-room, and the regular tread of the sentry. Agnes was bewildered. She thought of nothing, she stood like a lifeless image, and her breath came and went almost imperceptibly. Hans, on the contrary, was not long without becoming fully aware of the dangerous position in which they found themselves. He stood for a moment collecting his thoughts, and then feeling in his pocket he produced the implements for making light, which he had been so cautious to take with him.

"Let us at any rate see what kind of prison we are in," he said; and striking a light he lit a little wax candle and looked round the room.

It was a small room, or rather ante-chamber. It was in fact part of the corridor or passage, but for the convenience of the Guild of Trumpeters, which occupied the large room adjoining, it had been converted into a little room. Four naked walls, a door at each end, a few wooden seats, and a small wooden table in one corner were all the room presented. No chimney, no window, not a mouse-hole which Hans could discover to serve for an escape. There was not a room in the whole house which would have served better for a prison than this.

When Hans had finished the survey of the room, he allowed the light to fall upon the face of his companion. He started at the death-like whiteness of her cheeks and lips, and putting down the light upon the little table, he led the trembling girl to a chair. All her courage, all her firmness, all her strength, seemed to have fled, when she discovered that their attempt was crowned with failure. She sank down on the seat in a position of utter despondency. Hans regarded her silently for some moments, and an expression of pity came over his face.

"Poor girl," he muttered, "we ought not to have begun the thing. We might have known that her courage would last only as long as it met with no resistance."

Agnes heard his words, and turning her eyes towards him she said slowly and with a faltering voice—

"I am not such as you see me through cowardice. Had I to do this over again I would willingly do it a hundred times, so the Count Egmont and you were set free. But I tremble, because———"

She paused, and Hans could see by the faint flicker of the candle that she struggled to keep back her tears.

"I tremble," she said, at last, "because of the consequences which my deed may have for others. I have deceived my father———."

"Deceived!" said Hans with a sneer. "Can you deceive

the arch-deceiver? Can you deceive Alva? And is not
your father an instrument in Alva's hand. Did not
Rahab the harlot deceive the men of Jericho? Why, I
have deceived ever so many times myself, and I don't
think anything of an innocent dodge."

And as if this were a sufficient example for her to
imitate, Hans began pacing up and down the little room
with complacency. There was something striking in his
cool manner. He did not appear to realise his full
position, or if he did, he looked as if he had been
prepared for it all along. His only care now seemed to
be to set the fears of Agnes at rest.

"You need not be afraid, Mistress Agnes," he said after
a moment's pause, "Count Egmont won't be worse off
than before. They can't do more than kill him, and that,
I suppose, they will do soon enough. And as to myself,
why, I am used to this kind of thing. I have been in
almost all the prisons in the Netherlands, but I never saw
the one yet that could hold *me*. And this little, bare-
walled bit of a pigstye is worse than any I ever saw.
And after all, if they do have me, I suppose that must
come sooner or later, and I'd rather die for a good cause
than be caught in a plundering expedition and be shot
as a robber. But they won't do you any harm. I'd like
to see the man that would hurt a hair on so sweet a
head. I'll stand by you, Mistress Agnes, and when you
want me, just give the word, and this dagger will do its
work yet, though it should be for the last time." And
Hans drew aside part of his dress and showed underneath
a coat of mail and a girdle with a dangerous-looking
dagger in it.

L

But Agnes shook her head, and looking at Hans with an expression of humility and sweetness on her face, she said—

"No, Hans. You must not use violence on my part, or even on your own. I cannot bear to hear you speak of killing your fellow-creatures as if they were mere brutes. You must remember that they are men as well as you."

"They are rather troublesome at times, though," grumbled Hans.

"But the reason why I am afraid," continued Agnes, "is not because of any personal danger befalling me. I think that I can bear torture and death willingly for our holy cause; at least the spirit is willing, though the flesh is weak, and I may be brought to do or say things of which I would repent my whole life long. That is the reason of my fear, and may God give me strength to persevere to the end!"

She paused for a moment, and the flush which now covered her cheeks showed that her mind was fully alive to the perils before her. Hans looked at her with a puzzled air. He did not seem to understand what she really meant, at least he muttered within himself—

"What does she mean? She's willing to bear torture, and her flesh is weak, and she would repent of it her whole life-long? I don't understand her."

And probably Agnes saw the puzzled look in his face, for she went on—"We—at least I—shall fall into the hands of the Inquisition; I have long had a presentiment of this, and I have heard and seen too much of its working not to know what it can and what it will do. And oh, what a dreadful thing it would be if, through dread of their punishments and tortures, I should deny my Saviour ! What would Maria, what would many of those say, who are still hesitating between two opinions, and with whom one bad example will have more effect than ten good ones?   O Jesus! give me strength to suffer for Thee, and to confess Thee boldly before Thine enemies, that I may not only profess to follow Thy cross but be willing to take it upon me whenever Thy honour and glory demand it.   For whosoever shall deny Thee before men, him Thou wilt also deny before Thy Father who is in heaven."

She had sunk upon her knees by the table and buried her face in her hands.   Hans, no longer puzzled, looked at her with admiration and sorrow in his countenance.

"Ah," he sighed, shaking his head and wiping away a tear, "she has other reasons for belonging to us and our cause than I have—and I don't know that they are not better—ay, a good deal better," he added, with a sort of groan, as he turned with a fierce movement towards the door, at which at that moment a noise was heard.

It was that door which communicated with the larger room, and which they had first found locked.   Hans heard voices outside and the key in the act of being turned.   With one jump he placed himself firmly before it, and cried out to Agnes, who was still absorbed, and had remained in her prayerful position.

"Mistress Agnes, they are coming! Don't let them find you in that position. Sit down and be as calm as possible ; we'll get off yet."

Agnes looked up, as if she did not know where she

was. In a moment, however, she recovered herself and sat down upon the settee. Her face was perfectly calm, and there was even a look of cheerfulness upon it as she whispered, "Let them come."

"Come in, sirs!" said Hans, waiting for an opportunity when the pressure upon the door was for a moment suspended. He had pulled the cap of the cowl over his head, and with his arms folded across his chest and his head sunk down, he stood in the middle of the room in as venerable a position as the most pious of holy fathers could have assumed.

The door opened and a flood of light entered the apartment.

"Here we shall find the wolf and the lamb together," said a voice, which both recognised. It was that of the officer who had allowed them to pass at the bottom of the stairs. He entered by the side of another man, while some dozen soldiers followed on their steps and stood inside the doorway. The stranger was a short man, of very slender make and somewhat decayed figure. At any rate, his round shoulders and bent back gave him the appearance of being older than he really was. To judge by his face, which was regular and by no means unpleasant to look at, he must have been between forty and fifty years of age. It was browned by the sun, and worn by hard work; the peaked beard and moustache, together with his whole dress, gave him the appearance of a Spaniard. He was addressed by the officer with that respect and deference which is bestowed upon one higher in rank.

On entering the room, he eyed first Hans and then

Agnes, with a cool and scrutinising glance. Then turning to the officer, he said, in pure Dutch, a slight smile part‐ing his thin lips,—

"And are these the two liberators of the Count Egmont ?"

"They are, sir Inquisitor. Soldiers, seize this man and bind him !"

"Hold !" cried Hans, in a warning voice, and stretch‐ing forth his hand to the soldiers, "Touch not the anointed of the Lord !" and then turning to the officer he said, drawing himself up—

"I would know, sir captain, by what authority you presume to lay violent hands upon one of our holy order who has already been obstructed in performing his sacred office ? Is our order become so powerless, think you, that it is unable to make you an example of the punishment which it inflicts upon the profane and untoward children of the Church ?"

The soldiers had fallen back on seeing Hans's move‐ment, and even the officer seemed somewhat startled at the haughty tone of the man before him. The Inquisitor touched him slightly on the hand, and stepping forward, he asked in a reverential tone—

"What, holy father, is the cause of your complaint ?"

"I know not whether thou art a son of our most holy Church, or whether thou art one of the Philistines," said Hans, who had not heard the name of the stranger ; "but if thou hast one grain of the reverence which is due to my garb and to the sanctity of my calling—and to judge by thy dress, I presume thou comest from that great country where heresy has not made such fearful strides as to cause men to forget that we are the key-bearers of heaven;—if thou hast the welfare of our mother Church at heart, command these sons of Belial to let us pass, and suffer me and my daughter to proceed on our errand."

"It is strange, father, that you and this maiden should have been detained if your business was not of a suspicious kind. How came you within this chamber, at this hour of the night, and into this house?" said the stranger in a tone as if his mind were swayed to and fro by doubts.

"The natural man understandeth not the things which are *Spiriti Dei*," said Hans, gravely, not observing the smile which his blunder called forth upon the lips of his interrogator. "I was being conducted by my pupil to our little cell at the top floor, where we intended to spend some hours in holy meditation and pious reverence, and had for that end obtained her father's permission, when, passing through this room, both doors were locked, behind and in front of us, and we were thus detained in this little closet. Pray convince thyself that our errand was undertaken with the knowledge of the warder, our son," and he handed him the piece of paper which he had taken from Agnes.

The stranger threw a quick glance at it, and turning towards Agnes, he said in a kindly, interrogating voice—

"And are you such a pious and zealous daughter of our holy Church, that you would forsake your night's rest to spend your hours in prayer?"

Agnes looked at the questioner with calm eyes, and said in a distinct voice, "I am not."

The Inquisitor looked at her, and then at Hans.

"My daughter, my daughter, what means this?" said Hans in a tone of admonition, while he made the most expressive signs with every movable part of his face, to induce Agnes to follow his example.

But Agnes seemed to have no such intention. She shook her head and said,—

"I am a daughter neither of you nor of the Church. There is only one whom I call father besides the warder of this house."

"Sir stranger," said Hans, quickly touching the Inquisitor upon the arm, "I pray thee, do no longer detain us. Some damnable heresies have entered this young girl's head, and it was for the purpose of converting her from these pernicious doctrines that I intended to speak to her this evening. Suffer us to pass, and I will pledge my Beg—— my soul, that she shall become as dutiful and pious a child of the Church as I myself."

"Enough of this farce, Yonker Galama," said the stranger, turning himself sternly towards Hans, and looking him full in the face, "do no longer profane and desecrate the holy garb you wear. You and your intentions are too well known to us to need your explanation. Soldiers, pinion this pious father, but take care, lest he have some weapons about him as smooth and deceitful as he is himself. And let us gently lead this lamb away. We shall bring her to a place where she shall have plenty of opportunity to be converted, if such damnable heresies are really present in her."

Hans stood for a moment aghast, and a close observer would have noticed a change in his colour. His first movement was for his dagger, but seeing that such would be of little use, he folded his arms on his breast, and said—

"Take me. I am a man of peace, and not of strife. *Fiat voluntas tua.*"

The soldiers approached with their halberds pointed at Hans, as if he possessed as many hands and weapons as they. At the same time, the captain informed Agnes that she was his prisoner. The two were surrounded by the soldiers, and the troop was just putting itself in motion to quit the room, when a loud noise outside attracted their attention.

The voice of the warder, speaking hoarsely and excitedly, commanded the sentry, on guard before the door by which our two prisoners had entered the apartment, to unlock the door and let him enter. It seemed, at first, as if the sentry refused, but a moment afterwards the door flew open, and the warder, flushed with wine, and greatly excited by something or other, staggered into the room. But when he beheld the group before him, his daughter dressed in the gay colours of that period, with her hair streaming down her back, and the naked blades of the soldiers shining around her, the monk with his arms tied behind him, and above all, the little figure of the Inquisitor which he knew so well, he staggered and fell against the post of the door.

"What! Stop! sir Inquisitor!" he cried in a bewildered voice. "It is true, then, that you are leading my Agnes away. Agnes! Agnes! has it come to this? O Holy Mother of God!"

And in a burst of genuine grief he covered his eyes with his hands. He recovered himself in a moment, however, and turned to the Inquisitor who stood looking at him with an unmoved face, and said, in a tone at once respectful and reproaching,—

"There was a time when you would have rescued my daughter instead of taking her to prison. Is your gratitude so short-lived?"

"There was such a time, sir warder," answered the Inquisitor, "but that time is past."

Vlossert cowered before the cool eyes of the little man, but the sight of his daughter who stood in the midst of the soldiers, with her head half turned away from her father, seemed to revive all his courage once more, for he said,—

"Upon what charges is she being imprisoned, sir Inquisitor, and can you show me the warrant from any of the governing authorities ; for you know right well that when I entered upon the post of warder of this house, I had to swear that no one within its walls should be suffered to be imprisoned without proper warrant, and that oath has never been cancelled, nor the condition either, so far as I know."

"Nor so far as I know," said the Inquisitor, pulling a paper out of his bosom and handing it to the warder. "But you will find by this that I have due orders to imprison Agnes Vlossert, and Yonker Karel Galama, for being concerned with others in a conspiracy against His Excellency the Duke, for the liberation of one of the prisoners in this house and under your care, Count Lamoral Egmont." And the little man fixed his eyes upon the unhappy warder, within whose trembling hand the paper rested.

"Galama," he repeated, mechanically. "Galama! Would he dare to come here for such a purpose?"

For the moment he seemed stupified, and the look which he threw upon the assembled soldiers was bewildered. But suddenly he made a step towards them, his face lit up, and he cried out,—

"Why, there must be a mistake here, by our Patron saint, the Lady of St. Gudule! Galama? This great fat monk is not my nephew. He is only twenty-two years old, and this—what, is it Ha——"

"Ay, my son," said Hans, interrupting him just in time, "dost thou see how thy confessor is being insulted by these soldiers. Tell them to what holy orders I belong, and cause me to be liberated at once."

It would have been difficult for the most skilled pencil correctly to draw the face of the warder when he heard these words. At first, when he discovered it was Hans, who, as he could easily guess, was but a substitute for Galama, his heart misgave him, for he saw that the warrant was right. How Hans could be there in that capacity and for that purpose he could not understand. His words, however, gave, as Vlossert thought, a clue to the mystery. The look of abject misery left his face, and with ungovernable fury, shaking his fist at Hans, he said in a hoarse voice,—

"Thrice cursed be thou and thy master! May the most fearful punishments be thy lot here and hereafter, thou arch-rebel, thou viper. Is it not enough that I had to feed and shelter thy master's cursed sister, but must he send thee to impose thyself upon my pious daughter, and thus lure her into that destruction which is thine by right?"

This last accusation appeared to touch Agnes to the quick. It seemed as if she could not bear the thought of having deceived her father, for at his words she cast at him a look of pain, and covered her face with her hands. Her father seemed to understand that motion, for with a faltering voice he asked,—

"What, Agnes, has he not deceived thee? Has my daughter consented to conspire against her father with the king's enemies and his? Say that you thought he was Father Florisz; say that you had no evil intentions?"

While Agnes stood sobbing, with her face covered, not daring to look at her father, and he, in heart-broken tones, repeated his question, a murmur was heard on the stair, and an agitated female voice said, "Where is she? O let me see her! Agnes!"

The Inquisitor frowned, but ere he could shut the door of the little room Maria rushed in, her dishevelled hair streaming down her back, and her features deathly pale. For a moment when she beheld the group, the warder with his face distorted in agony, the Inquisitor whom she knew well, and her beloved Agnes surrounded by the soldiers, she paused, and pressed her hand to her forehead. Then, with a sharp cry of " Oh, Agnes, it has come at last!" she rushed into her cousin's arms, not heeding the soldiers, who were too surprised to resist her. And in the doorway stood the figure of another monk, who looked on the scene with a sarcastic smile.

Chapter Twelfth.

THE FLESH IS WEAK.

THE Inquisitor grew impatient. The whole scene had lasted but a few minutes, but accustomed as he was to do his work in secrecy and silence, even this time was too long for him. He was just going to give the order to remove the prisoners, when Maria turning round, fixed her streaming eyes upon him, and said in a voice of supplication, —

"Oh, sir, do not let her go. She is not guilty ; she has done nothing ; send these away," and she pointed to the soldiers. She did not notice Hans, who was standing behind her,—looking at the whole scene with the utmost *sang-froid.*

"Ay, Maria, my child," said the warder, grasping at a straw, "tell him that Agnes is a pious girl, and that she mistook this lying impostor for Father Florisz, for indeed they are much of a size."

"Are they?" said the voice of the monk in the doorway, who was no one else than Father Florisz himself. He was shorter, but quite as stout as Hans, and might have been taken for him had he not spoken, for his voice was high and full, that of Hans being low and almost growling.

THE FLESH IS WEAK.

" Your haughty and learned daughter, sir warder, cannot excuse herself by saying that she mistook some one
else for me, for it was by her directions that I was admitted into her own room. And yet I hear she has
trusted herself to another of my brethren, and is it he
whom I see there surrounded by soldiers ? What has
——"

" Ay, brother Florisz," said Hans in a sanctimonious
tone, "take note of my condition. *Benedictus qui venit*——"

" Silence !" said the Inquisitor sternly; and turning to
the officer he continued in a low voice, " Command your
men to separate the two girls and let us march."

" One moment, Father Hubert," said the confessor, stepping forward. " Would you separate the two girls ?   I
should advise haveing them taken away together, since
they are both guilty of the same iniquity;" and turning
to Vlossert, he continued, " Know ye not, sir warder,
that your daughter is deeply stained with heresy, and
that she has already greatly led astray the mind of her
cousin ?   Ask her whether she can deny having spoken
profanely of the Holy Church and its sacred servants, of
our blessed Virgin, and of all other matters; and if she
does, ask her how she can account for the presence of
this damnable heretical book, which I found in her room
this evening ? "

It was true.   Though Vlossert had not yet informed
him of his daughter's heresy, Florisz had for some time
doubted the piety both of Agnes and of Maria, and had
taken advantage of Maria's solitude to get at the truth.
He was clever, but so was Agnes, and she had always
taken good care to be at her cousin's side whenever the

priest appeared, which, as may be surmised, had not been often of late.   When he found Maria alone, therefore, he cautiously played his game, and by skilfully questioning her, very soon found out as much of the truth as sufficed for him.

Unhappily Agnes had left the little Bible, out of which they had been reading, upon the table before the window, not knowing that the room would soon be visited by one of its bitterest enemies.   Maria had partially covered it with one of her kerchiefs, but at an unlucky moment the confessor caught a glance of it, He snatched it up and looked with flaming eyes from the title-page to the girl who sat before him speechless with terror.   At last his gaze fell upon Agnes's name on the first page, and he smiled.

"What means this, my daughter?" he said, with a look which made the poor girl's heart beat faster.   She turned her eyes on the floor and was silent.   Indeed, what could she say?

"Know you not that this is a most heretical book, for the reading of which many a girl younger than you has been condemned to the flames?   But," he continued, as Maria remained silent, "I see the name of Agnes Vlossert in this book.   You must follow me to her; I cannot let this pass."

Maria rose mechanically and followed the priest out of the room, her heart throbbing violently and her limbs trembling with agitation.   But in the passage another surprise awaited her.   In answer to Father Florisz's question, the weeping and terrified Gritta told him that "Mistress Agnes and the warder were upstairs a-

quarrelling with some of them soldiers." No sooner did
Maria hear this than she set off to find Agnes, whose
help she now so urgently required. The sentry who had
been left on the stair dared not obstruct her passage, and
thus she appeared, followed by Father Florisz, in the
midst of that tragic scene. And long afterwards there
was a feeling of repentance within Agnes's breast that
she had allowed her little lamb to stray within the
clutches of that wolf.

It was an easily recognised book in those days, and as
the priest held it up to those in the room the effect was
immediate. The soldiers, who were Spaniards, and did
not understand one word of her conversation, stood
motionless, wondering what it all meant, and in that
disciplined order for which they were in those days
world-renowned. But when Agnes saw the book, her
manner changed. Her frame, which had formerly bent
with tenderness over her cousin, became erect and firm.
Her face beamed with a smile, and as she bent her head
down to Maria, who was hiding her face in her bosom,
she whispered,—

"Be firm, now Maria, be firm. Do not think of Father
Florisz, do not look at that little Inquisitor, but think
that Jesus is here, who is far mightier. He will help us."

"We're done for now," muttered Hans, adapting himself calmly to the new position.

The warder glanced at the book, and became, if possible a shade paler than before. He grasped for support
at the little table, and his breath came shortly and thickly.
Accustomed though he had been during the whole of his
life to bow to the priests, at this moment he felt something

like an inclination to resist, and if such had been possible with him he would assuredly have defended his almost adored daughter. The Inquisitor seemed to observe this spirit within him, for he said in a tone of fearful meaning :

"So ho, we have two fair martyrs here, and besides that a Beggar ! A good harvest," and he looked hard at the warder.

"I cannot believe it, Father Hubert," gasped Vlossert. "Father Florisz must have made a mistake. They cannot be heretics, not my daughter, and least of all, Maria. There must be some mistake."

Father Florisz frowned, but Hubert motioned with his hand, and directing his cold and cruel look towards Vlossert, he said, "We'll see."

Then addressing himself to Maria he said,—

"Be calm, my daughter, and weep not. There is no danger. But tell your uncle the warder here that you have never read that heretical book yonder, and that you and your cousin Agnes have not spoken profanely of the Church."

He paused, and there was a silence in the room. Maria had been separated from her cousin, and stood alone at a little distance, her face covered with her hands and tears tricking through her fingers. When the Inquisitor, who had spoken with a hollow and awful tone, ceased speaking, a shiver ran through her, and she sobbed almost inaudibly, "I do, I do."

"She does, she does !" cried Vlossert, joyously. "Ah, blessed be the holy virgin, I shall give sixteen pounds of wax candles——"

"One moment, Master Vlossert," said the Inquisitor, a malignant smile playing around his lips, "your joy may come a little premature, and would be all the better for suppression."

Then, turning to the trembling girl, he said—

"My daughter, I am glad that you deny having given your mind and soul to those most pernicious heresies of Luther, and as a true daughter of the Church, I would have you kiss the little crucifix which Father Florisz has on his girdle. He will at the same time absolve you from sin, I am certain."

Father Florisz came nearer and held out his crucifix. Maria sunk upon her knees and seized the little ebony image.

"Maria! Maria!" sounded the voice of Agnes, "Do not! You have rejected the truth before the servants of Antichrist! In the name of Jesus, consider. This will be looked upon as a sign that you are a Papist at heart. Don't Maria, don't! O God!"

Maria had bent her head under the hearing of these words. Every particle, every drop of blood had left her cheeks, and her hands trembled to such an extent that she could hardly hold the crucifix in them. For a moment it seemed as if Agnes's words would have the desired effect upon her. But, looking towards the Inquisitor, who had his eyes fixed upon her with an expression of cruelty, she closed hers, and pressing the crucifix to her lips, she muttered "Holy Virgin," and fainted. The terrors of the Inquisition, embodied in the Inquisitor before her, had so strong a hold upon the poor weak girl, as to vanquish the little faith she possessed.

M

"*In nomine Domini te absolvo,*" muttered the priest as he bent down to support the powerless girl.

"Thus does the Church absolve her children, after she has frightened them with her sword," said Agnes, with a touch of bitterness in her voice.

The Inquisitor turned sharply upon her.

"And you, my daughter," he said, "will you not kiss the cross, and show yourself a pious daughter of the only saving Church?"

"Never!" said Agnes, stepping back.

She spoke with a decision and energy that made the meaning unmistakeable. The Inquisitor seemed to have expected the answer, for turning to the warder, he said,—

"You see, sir warder, that my charge was well-founded."

Vlossert was silent. When he heard Agnes's word, his whole face became distorted with agony and fear. He began to see that his daughter was lost to him, and something of the possibility of being danger for himself too seemed to dawn upon him.

With trembling hands and lips he turned to the Inquisitor, who seemed to grow calmer as the other showed signs of fear.

"Pater Hubert! Old Friend! this is but the raving of an excited girl, upon whose mind circumstances have worked their injurious effects, I beseech, I pray you——."

"Father!" cried the voice of Agnes, half sad, half angry, "why will you misconstrue my words? I am not raving, I am not mad. I am as calm as I have ever been, and my mind is perfectly clear. I tell the Inquisitor here that I am no longer a member of the Church of Rome, but a member of the Church of Christ. Let him take me away, if such be his behest, and may the Lord Jesus have pity upon my poor unfortunate cousin."

"Yes, sir warder," said the Inquisitor, turning to Vlossert, and speaking to him in an undertone, "I have as yet abstained from threatening, but I can assure you that you are becoming suspected by the Inquisition. Your daughter and this girl have long been heretical, and think you we know not that you had a hand in the scheme to-night? For look you, Master Vlossert, whose handwriting is this?"—and the wily Jesuit showed Vlossert the pass. "Take care, Master Vlossert, take care; you are watched Let your daughter go, or by the Holy Virgin you shall go too."

The warder had no answer. The blow had been struck, and he lay prostrate before the giant form of the Inquisition.

" ake her away," he murmured, "and may the Holy Virgin protect her best servants, the holy brethren of Jesus."

The Inquisitor smiled disdainfully. He turned round and was about to give a command to the soldiers, when a noise was heard below. A carriage drove into the square, from the side of the Palace, and a horseman was heard to gallop from the opposite side.

Everyone was in expectation of what was to follow.

A servant came running up the stairs, and saluting the warder, said, audibly—

"The Lord Bishop of Ypres comes to see the prisoners."

Vlossert turned round to the Inquisitor.

"Let Gritta look after this girl," he said in a low tone,

pointing to Maria, and left the room without looking back upon his daughter.

At that moment another servant came up to the Inquisitor.

"Your worship is wanted below in great haste. A horseman waits for you in the hall, and gives you this," and he handed the Inquisitor a small gold ring.

Pater Hubert looked at the ring and frowned. For a moment he was absorbed in thought. Then turning round, he said to the officer :—

"Take the two prisoners into the next room, and guard them well till further orders. You"—turning to the messenger—"fetch the servant Gritta here to attend this girl, who I see is awaking out of her stupor."

Agnes gave a last sad look at the form of Maria, who was supported by Father Florisz, and then followed the soldiers to the next room. Wrapping his short mantle around him, the Inquisitor turned round and moved towards the door.

At that moment the Bishop of Ypres, preceded by Vlossert and the captain of the guard, ascended the stairs, carrying his message of death to the unfortunate Counts on the next floor.

Chapter Thirteenth.

MASTER AND SERVANT.

ARRIVED at the vestibule, the Inquisitor looked round, and perceived in the darkest part of it, a tall figure covered with a felt hat, and entirely concealed by the folds of a large hussar mantle, which hung from his shoulders to his feet. He seemed at once to know who the stranger was, for, after pondering a moment, he gave an almost imperceptible movement of the head, and descended the stairs leading to the lower apartments, on reaching which he entered the sitting-room already familiar to us, and threw himself into a chair. He was followed by the mantled stranger. Locking the door as soon as he gained the room, and having ascertained that the one opening into the kitchen was locked, for it had not been opened since Agnes shut it, the latter went to the window, fastened it securely, and drew the thick curtain before it.

Then, turning round, he again faced the Inquisitor, who had eyed these proceedings with indifference, and said,—

"I shall not give my enemies the advantage of my own weapons." At the same time he took off his felt hat, and his mantle dropping to the floor, disclosed our old acquaintance, Gerard Block, dressed as a common soldier and with his arm in a sling.

"Are you wounded?" asked the Inquisitor with some concern, noticing the sling.

"Slightly," answered Block.

There was a pause of some moments.

"You have failed, I presume?" again asked the Inquisitor.

"I have; but not altogether," answered the other.

"Are you sure that you are on the right track at last?"

"More than ever. I have said A this night to the best alphabet in the provinces," answered the spy.

"And how is it that you have failed?" asked Father Hubert.

"It was purely through the stupidity of one of the soldiers on the wall. The blockhead ought to be hung, drawn, and quartered for his carelessness," answered Block, with something of passion in his voice.

"You should not give way to your passion, Brother Sextus," said the Inquisitor, calmly. "The frequency with which you mingle with the outcasts of society, and the fact that you have to conduct yourself as one of them, should have no effect upon your piety whatever. Take a seat and relate to me briefly what has happened."

Brother Sextus, thus admonished, took a chair and sat down, silently smarting under the Inquisitor's dry tone of sarcasm and reproof.

"I hope you will pardon my anger," he began after a moment's pause, "but whenever the thought strikes me, that I might have brought you three of the most

notorious Beggars—Treslong, Galama, and Verveen—and
that they have escaped by the rashness of a common
soldier, I think even you, father, will acknowledge that
the idea is somewhat irksome."

"Thou shouldst forgive until seventy times seven,"
said the little man with an earnest voice. "But is that
arch-rebel Verveen in our neighbourhood too?"

"He was," answered Block, *alias* Sextus, "but I shall be
very much astonished if he has not by this time set out
for France in company with the other two. Let me briefly
relate to you what happened. When I saw you an hour
ago I told you that the arrangements had been made
just as I wished them, so that we might catch Galama,
without spilling a drop of blood, and the others either
dead or alive. Some alteration seems to have been
made since I left, for to my great astonishment the
second man who mounted the ladder was Galama, and I
had nearly betrayed myself in the momentary surprise.
It all depended now upon the suddenness with which
they were surrounded, whether we might still hope to
catch them alive ; for they are a desperate lot, and I
knew that if there were the smallest chance of success,
they would fight against any odds."

He paused and threw a longing glance at the can of
wine, which stood on the table. The Inquisitor, however,
bade him go on, and he continued,—

"You know it had been arranged that fifty arquebusiers should be hid on the wall, and fifty should take up
a position outside, to cut off their retreat. The moment
they fired a shot I was to jump aside, the arquebusiers
on the wall were to surround them, capture them, and

those who endeavoured to escape by the way they came would be equally well received. Suddenly, as they were all upon the wall, and the gate was about to be opened to allow the second fifty to go round, one of the soldiers fired a shot. I immediately perceived that it was a blunder, and wanting to make the best of it, I shouted out that we were betrayed and must at once fly to the gate; and I do believe the desperate fellows would have followed me, had not the first shot been followed by others, one of which struck my arm. It was a good thing that I wore a coat of mail, else I might have been much hurt; as it is, my arm is bruised, and I was staggered by the force of the bullet. It flashed through my mind that the only way to save myself was by falling down and pretending to be mortally wounded, which I did. The Beggars immediately turned round and fled to the wall, where of course their retreat had not yet been cut off, and consequently they escaped almost unhurt. That young fool of a Galama cried out that they should stop and rescue me. Ha! I wish they had. They would have found that rescue more than enough for them. But for that shot, we might now be in the possession of the key to the secret which puzzles us all, but——"

"But, in short, we have failed, Brother Sextus," said the little man drily, "and we have to get at the key yet. Have you any idea who that man upstairs is, and whether he knows anything worth troubling about? I first thought it was Galama, but he speaks very much like a priest, and is too old for the Yonker. He is a broad-shouldered fellow, with a black beard and a scar across his cheek."

" That's Galama's servant, Hans," answered Block, for thus we shall continue to call him. " He may know something, but it cannot be much. It is a good thing, though, that we have him here, for he is the only one that distrusts me."

" Why should he be the only one that distrusts you ? " asked Father Hubert.

" Because it was he whom I first saw yesterday morning as he was singing a Beggars' song."

" But why should not the master be as suspicious as the servant ? " asked the Inquisitor.

" You forget that I saved his life," said Block.

" Last night. But before that time, why should either of them have suspected you ? "

" Because ·I introduced myself at an unpleasant moment, and with nothing to recommend me but a very short letter."

"What were its contents?" asked the little man, fixing his cool and scrutinising glance upon Block, who turned down his eyes and hesitated. At last he repeated the words of the letter which we already know.

" I know the blunder you committed at the inn, Brother Sextus," said the little man after a moment's pause, "and I am not astonished that both servant and master should suspect you ; for that Peter Blink would have omitted an L in writing your name is, to say the least of it, unlikely. But you ought to have told me so at once, instead of hiding it from me. Remember, henceforth, wherever you are, the eye of our order is upon you, and that we can see what has been hid from the sun itself."

· A shade of astonishment, shame, and mortification

passed over Block's face when he heard that the Inquisitor knew what he had done, for he flattered himself that it was unknown to anyone but Galama, Hans, and himself.

"Why did you not seize Galama on the wall, before he could get away?" again asked the Inquisitor after a moment's pause.

"He or his comrades would have killed me and himself immediately, or they would have rescued him ere the soldiers could have come to my assistance."

"Is this Galama as great a heretic as his cousin, the daughter of the warder?"

"He is nothing at present but a Beggar. He seems to have dedicated himself to fame."

"*Qui non est mecum, contra me est, et qui non congregat mecum, spargit,*" said the Inquisitor, devoutly, "why did you not seize him when he was in this room?"

"I should not then have known the Rookery, which will serve us now as a trap to catch whoever comes near it."

"But you would have had Galama, who is worth the whole Rookery."

"I shall have him yet, Father Hubert, and better than ever."

"You seem to be very sanguine after your defeat," said the Inquisitor, a little angry at Block's ardour; "what are your plans?"

"Yonker Galama will not leave Brabant until he has tried everything in his power to rescue Hans, for without him, he feels himself as a ship without a rudder. The little that I have seen of these two has shown me that the Yonker may be the better educated and the cleverer of the two; but that without Hans to temper him and instruct him with his experience he would long ago have been in our hands. Though unseen by them, I was a witness of the interview between Galama and his cousin Agnes, and I have seen enough to convince me that he will do anything for her sake. With two such baits we cannot fail to hook the fish."

He paused, and looked at the Inquisitor, who had risen and was pacing the room with one hand raised to his chin and his eyes bent on the ground.

" Are you certain he has been engaged in this correspondence with the Prince of Orange?" he asked without looking up.

" I am. Both because of what I heard Peter Blink say and what he said himself to Treslong at the inn where we separated. I found means to engage that fellow Hans, who was watching me, and as I took a good look at Treslong I heard Galama say, 'It was at the express desire of the Prince that I went to Ghent;' so that he must have been in direct communication with him."

" And do you think that if you went to him now, supposing he is in the neighbourhood, that he would believe you, if you told him you had been taken prisoner, but had escaped?"

" He would, I think. It was for that reason that I fell down, when the shot struck me and I am certain all the Beggars believe that I am either killed or dangerously wounded," answered Block.

The Inquisitor paced the room again in silence, during which Block followed the little man's movements with his eyes, as a dog follows those of his master. It was curious to notice how great a difference there was between Gerard Block and Brother Sextus ; between the man who spoke haughtily to Hans and even to Galama, and the man who spoke obsequiously to the Inquisitor ; between the pretended member of the patriotic confederacy, and the enslaved member of the Order of Jesus. The Inquisitor paused, and after some more inquiries he looked at Block, and said slowly :—

"Very well ! Find out Galama. I will give you three days. On the evening of the 7th two carriages shall leave and travel on the road to Ghent, which leads through the forest. One of them shall contain Agnes and Maria, the other Hans. At that spot where the two oaks have grown together, near the Hell-mouth, you and the Beggars must await them and attempt a rescue. A company of light horse shall follow at a little distance, and another from the opposite side shall bar their flight. At the moment they are vainly trying to open the carriages the horse will be upon them. Secure Galama, and the rest may escape for all I care, now that we know their haunt. If you cannot find him you must be back here on the morning of the 7th. Go, and may the holy Virgin protect you. Your reward shall equal your services."

In a few moments the spy had again left the room wrapped in the folds of his cloak. The Inquisitor looked at the door through which he had gone in a dreamy manner, and muttered to himself.

" Once in our power, with his sister and his mistress before his eyes, his secret will be ours in less than a week."

" And Agnes," he continued, after a moment's pause, " so young, so beautiful, so courageous, so pure, who would have believed that she could become a child of the evil one. We must try and save so precious a gem from everlasting destruction."

Chapter Fourteenth.

VIVENT LES GUEUX.

THE Watermael Road ran from Brussels through the outskirts of the large forest of Saigne, and taking a turn to the north, crossed a branch of the Senne and joined the high road to Ghent. It was in those days a lonely, dirty, ill-kept, and melancholy road to travel along. It was only used by persons who had to visit the villages of Berchem, Uccle, and Vlier, to which it was the only access, though even very seldom by those. Part of it ran through the forest, the shades of which often rendered it as dim as twilight. Part ran over heath and marl where, in wet season, it was converted into lakes of mud. Other parts were covered with low underwood, at no place higher than four feet, but woe to the ignorant travellers who knew nothing of the treacherous nature of this portion of the road. It often happened that the inexperienced hunter or the unwary voyager, seduced by a starting hare, or some other attraction, hazarded himself within the bushes which spread their delightful and fresh green before his eyes. A marsh, as deep and treacherous as marsh can be, lay concealed below these bushes. There were indeed paths along which it was compara-

tively safe to go. But one step into the unknown region
beside it, and the slimy and merciless slough engulfed
the victim for ever in its depths.

The peculiar nature of this part of the road was not
known to everyone. With the superstition of those
days people kept away from this spot with perfect horror,
convinced, as they said, that an evil spirit, perhaps the
devil himself, had taken up his abode there. Indeed,
many firmly believed that it was the veritable entrance
to the lower regions, and as little blue lights were often
seen flickering above these spots, their opinion, founded
as it was upon so-called true and proven facts, was
generally accepted as the correct one. The "Hell-
mouth" was dreaded by nine people out of ten, though
its exact position not one would have been able to
point out. The tenth, who was perhaps better informed,
kept his counsel and took good care not to be a heretic
in regard to so popular and universal a belief.

It was not far from the spot where the tall trees of the
forest ended and the low underwood began, that there
stood two oaks, one on each side of the way, which, after
perhaps half a century of independent growth, had resolved to share life together. They stretched their
lofty arms across the road and embraced each other
never to part again. The sort of arch thus formed across
the road was looked upon by the already mentioned
nine people as the entrance to the dark region beyond,
and consequently it was shunned and evaded with an
equal amount of pious and reasonable abhorrence.

Against one of these oaks, in such a manner that they
could not be seen from the road, two men were leaning,

both of whom were dressed in the corselet, trunk hose, and felt hat which usually made up the costume of the wild Beggars. In their belts were a brace of pistols and a sword, while the younger one of the two had, moreover, a large knife at his side.

"I cannot comprehend why they should come this way," said Galama, for it was he who was the younger of the two. He looked considerably pale, and his face showed that he had suffered a great deal of anxiety. He leaned against the tree, and his arms were folded across his chest.

"I can assure you, Yonker," said his companion, who was no other than our acquaintance Block, "that I heard them name this road. I was in the next room, close to the door, which was not shut, and guarded by a soldier, and pretending to be asleep, I heard the voice of the little Inquisitor say that, as the army of the Duke was to move for Friesland on that and the following day, they could not take the main road to Ghent, as it was blocked up with the cavalry regiments, the cannon, and military train. And this, you know, is almost as short and good a road as the main road."

"How on earth did you get clear?" said Galama, eyeing Block with pleasure. It was a clever thing to get away when locked up and guarded by a soldier, in the heart of Brussels, and surrounded by Inquisitors."

"They had forgotten to search my pockets. I had a knife in one of them. The soldier, thinking that I slept, stood with his back turned. I cut the rope by which I was tied, and got up. One blow on the temple did for him. He fell like an ox, and never moved. This is his corselet and his hose ; his helmet I have thrown away. I managed to clear the stairs and gain the house-kitchen, where I saw the servant sitting. I told her if she loved her mistress, to give her a scrap of paper which I wrote in the room, and in which I told Hans to shout if he could see us. I jumped out of the back window, and the sentry on guard saw me, for not very long after half the town was at my heels, and it is a marvel to me still how I got off. But I do not rue my adventure. Though the poor Counts, I suppose, are dead by this time, we have at any rate protested against the bloody massacre, and if one head were as good as another, the two soldiers I killed would weigh against them. But alas ! Egmont was worth a whole army of these foreigners."

"My brave friend," said Galama, evidently moved by his companion's words, " had I not been robbed of my paternal property I would give you a better token of my friendship and gratitude. Accept this gold chain as a remembrance, and whenever you chance to be in the neighbourhood of Brill, go to the widow of Baron Galama, and for her son's sake she will receive you as she would himself."

And unfastening a magnificent gold chain with a Beggar's gold medal attached to it, he hung it round Block's neck.

"And whither shall you go when this exploit is over, Yonker?" said Block, after a moment's silence, during which he had given Galama his own medal in exchange ; "for I should think it is getting dangerous here."

"I do not know, but I may be killed in this affray," said Galama; "but if God and the holy Virgin spare me,

I shall resume my former trade. It is not very lucrative,"
he added with a smile, "but it is honourable, useful, and
hardly anyone else will take it, which is only another
inducement for me."

"I should think our trade is very lucrative," said Block,
"especially when we find a rich parsonage or church to
plunder. But dangerous it is, I confess."

"I do not plunder," said Galama, frowning slightly,
"the letters I carry——but here are all our men returned
from their expedition."

Both looked from behind the tree, and from all points
armed men issued from the bush, and approached the
spot.

"They are coming, sure enough, Yonker," said the bass
voice of the Beggar whom we saw in the Rookery with a
bishop's mantle around him, "now for a good blow at the
cavalry for Hans, and a little innocent plunder for myself."

There were some eighteen men assembled on the spot,
all dressed like Galama and Block. Galama stepped
between them.

"In among and behind the trees is our post," he
said. "Block and I shall each stand behind one oak and
fire the first pistol. But remain in ambush until you
hear me shout, for after all it may be a ruse. Remember,
first kill the horses and then the men, if necessary ; but
no cold-blooded murdering. Whatever the result of this
adventure may be, after this we separate for good.
I do not suppose any of you discovered an ambush ? "

The answers were unanimously in the negative, though
one or two reported that they thought the escort was
very large.

"Well," said Block, "so much the more glory for us. Here they come."

The rattling of wheels in the distance was heard, and in a moment not a single Beggar was to be seen on the road.

The noise of the wheels became louder. At length at the bend of the road there appeared, moving at a jog-trot, four horses and a carriage, with four dragoons at the side, a second one followed with an equal number of horses and dragoons, two dragoons bringing up the rear. There was a driver seated on each pair of horses, and by dint of whipping and spurring, the carriage slowly approached the two oaks.

The first carriage was half-way through, when a roar from Hans was heard. Two well-aimed shots brought the two foremost horses to the ground. A tremendous cheer followed, and in a moment all was a Babel of confusion. The sharp ring of the pistols, the clatter of swords, the shouts, the cries and groans of the wounded, the smoke and the dust were for a moment all that could distinguished.

Suddenly, a tremendous cheer rose up, and Hans appeared hanging half-way out of the door of one of the carriages, and cheering the Beggars on. The dragoons turned tail and fled. Of the ten only four were enabled to escape on horseback, three ran away on foot, and the rest lay dead or wounded on the road. The Beggars had strictly obeyed the command and aimed at the horses first. Almost all of them lay dead, shot or stabbed; but the men had also been aimed at, and that with equally fatal precision.

A scene of plunder now followed. Regardless of

what might happen, the Beggars threw themselves upon the bodies of the fallen, two or three of which belonged to themselves, and began rifling their pockets and cutting away what they could not unfasten, so as to get at their booty.

In the meantime Galama had flown to the foremost carriage, in which he descried the form of Agnes. She had risen from her seat, and while the fighting was going on around her, she had sunk on her knees at the bottom of the carriage, partly to guard herself against the bullets, partly to offer up a devout prayer for the success of the attack.

"Agnes! Agnes! look up! It is I, Karel!" cried her lover in eager tones, looking through the opening in the door, for window it could not be called.

Agnes looked up, and seeing Galama's face in reality, she started to her feet.

"Open the carriage, Karel!" she cried, joyously, and she pressed against the inside. Here, however, they found unexpected resistance. Anyone who has been in museums of antiquities must be acquainted with the form of those clumsy wooden boxes, which formed the predecessors of our neat brougham, or swift phaeton.

It was a four-sided affair, wider at the top than at the bottom. At the front and two sides there were openings about a foot and a half square, too small to let anything but the head pass through. They were constructed of very thick wood, and the doors on each side were fastened in the same manner as the doors of railway-carriages at the present time; a contrivance which even in those days was found a tolerably awkward manner of confining a passenger.

Galama pulled and pushed and called for the help of others, and the door was hammered and kicked and hacked with the sword, but all was of no avail. It remained shut. The lips of Block, who was pretending to work as hard as any, were parted with a faint smile.

Meanwhile our friend Hans was in the same dilemma. He pushed against the door; but as no one seemed to look after him he meant to help himself, and found it answer quite as well.

"Here, van Hagendorp," he roared to the Beggar close by, "cut this confounded rope by which my hands are tied." The rope was cut. Hans laid hold of the door, but it remained firm, and another shake had no better result.

"What!" he cried, "shall I be caught in this little thing after helping myself so far as this?"

He stood on the seat and pressed his back against the top of the carriage. He had attacked the weakest part of the fortress. It flew off, and in two leaps he was by the side of the carriage in which Agnes was confined.

"There is cavalry coming," he roared out, "so make haste, for God's sake! Who has a loaded pistol?"

Three or four were offered him. Placing the muzzle of one against the resisting lock, he cried,

"Take care, Mistress Agnes," and fired.

"Hans is the boy for a bad lock," he said, triumphantly, as the bullet, weighing nearly two ounces, smashed the lock. Galama at once tore open the door, but started back, for a large splinter had flown up and hit Agnes's fair white neck. A stream of blood immediately began to flow, and coloured her dress. She uttered a slight shriek and fell fainting into the arms of her lover.

The consternation of those around when they saw Agnes lying on the ground, with her beautiful head resting on her lover's knee, while he with frantic efforts tore up his linen collar and endeavoured to stop the blood, was almost tragic to witness.

" Do not be alarmed," said the calm voice of Block, as he pushed two men aside. " I have studied medicine, and will cure this in no time. Allow her head to rest on my knee. " And very leisurely and slowly he proceeded to place the girl's head upon his knee, and tear a bit from a kerchief of his own.

" Agnes, Agnes ! " cried Galama, seizing the girl's hand and covering it with kisses, " speak to me."

" Yonker," said Hans, seizing him by the shoulder, " the dragoons are coming, let us fly, else we shall all be cut to pieces."

" Yes, " cried the Beggars, " let us fly, some of us will carry this young lady."

" Fly ! " exclaimed Galama, scowling at them. " I shall remain here. This lady cannot be removed, she is dying."

At that moment, as if to contradict his statement, Agnes opened her eyes. " Fly !" she whispered, and she fell back into unconsciousness.

" Do not be alarmed ! There is *no* fear of cavalry," said Block, speaking decidedly and slowly, and proceeding to dress the wound at his utmost leisure. He had listened with intense application, and his face became every moment more anxious. At last, a gleam of pleasure crossed it, and he said leisurely, " We are some ten miles from town here, and before the fugitives could bring help we shall be far away. This maiden is dangerously ill."

" You lie, you blackhaired cur ! " cried Hans. " Do you think they would move *me* from Brussels to Ghent with no greater guard than ten men ? Come, Yonker, for God's sake, I've seen a hundred of them, and why they are not here yet I don't know. Come ! you are wounded yourself and bleeding. Fly ! I hear them coming, I shall carry Mistress Agnes." And the faithful fellow made a move as if to take her up.

Galama hesitated, but Block held up his arm.

" Don't touch my patient, " he said, " unless you want to kill her."

" Leave us to our fate ! " cried Galama, jumping up and drawing his sword.

But he staggered and fell on the ground, and the blood trickled from his knee and along his hose, and coloured it blood-red. " Ah," he said with bitterness, " fly, since you wish, but leave me here with Agnes." A bullet from one of the troopers had hit him, though in the excitement he had not perceived the wound.

At this moment a Beggar, who had strayed towards the bend of the road, came running back with all his might.

" The dragoons, " he shouted, " *sauve qui peut!* "

" At last ! " sighed Block, almost inaudibly, as a heavy noise was heard rapidly approaching.

But, softly though he had breathed it, his words were caught by Hans.

"Ah!" he cried triumphantly, 'At last,' is it? Here it is then."

A tremendous blow with his fist sent the Jesuit insensible to the earth. Hans stooped and took Agnes in his arms as if she had been a child. At that moment, a troop of cavalry turned round the corner, and with a tremendous cheer as they discovered the party, they clapped their spurs into the horses' flanks.

The Beggars turned on all sides. But the underwood which grew between the oak and pine trees resisted their violent and misdirected efforts. At once, the voice of Hans was heard.

"Follow me into the 'Hell-mouth,' and take care of the Yonker! *Vivent les Gueux !*"

He turned before the cavalry, which came thundering on, and was followed by van Hagendorp, who supported Karel. A few yards brought them to the marsh. Just at the moment that another troop of horse came galloping on from the opposite side of the road, Hans flew into the bushes and ran along the path which was so well known to him. It was hardly broad enough for one man, but running quite close to each other, and bending as low as the bushes, the Beggars followed Hans in his swift course and heard the bullets whistle over their heads.

"They cannot follow us here boys," chuckled Hans. "See how they jump. By the holy Virgin, that's the fellow that called me a black-looking cur, just disappearing. Serve him right."

The Beggars turned their faces and beheld a frightful scene. When the dragoons saw their enemies disappear in the low wood, they gave a tremendous shout, deeming them now caught beyond doubt. Few among them knew the dangerous character of the soil, and the warnings of those few were unheeded. Almost at the same moment both parties dashed into the bushes. In another shrieks, oaths, curses, cries for help, and broken prayers filled the air ; every moment some head was seen to sink, some helmet or hand to disappear. Those who had stayed behind gazed with fearful agony and gnashing teeth at the inglorious death of their comrades. And their rage became greater still, when far away over the tops of the bushes a felt hat was raised on a sword, and a cry resounded through the evening air of—

" *Vivent les Gueux ! Vive Yonker Willem.*"

Chapter Fifteenth.

AT DEATH'S DOOR.

IT was with difficulty that the wounded Yonker managed to limp behind Hans, and scarcely had they reached a place of comparative safety when he fell down exhausted, and was soon in a state of unconsciousness. The sudden exertion of their flight through the marsh, the effect of what he had experienced during the last few days, and, most of all, the melancholy end of the two Counts, which he knew must now have come, had told sadly upon his health. The bullet which struck his knee, though at the moment it caused him no more than a sharp pang, now threatened to finish what the other had begun.

For some time the fugitive Beggars were at a loss how to act, charged as they were with the care of a delicate girl, and their wounded chief, and being in constant expectation of a renewed attack from the remaining dragoons. But here Hans, who was best acquainted with the marsh, shone out in his best qualities. Cheering up the men's spirits with jokes and pleasantry, he first of all made them conduct the two invalids to a spot which, being situated a little higher than the surrounding marsh. afforded at least a dry and perfectly unobserved place of shelter.

With one accord the men here chose him as their temporary chief—a choice to which even van Hagendorp gave his consent without hesitation. After the unsuccessful adventure upon the wall, Seigneur de Treslong and two or three others had resolved to take to their horses and join Count Louis. In vain they had entreated and almost prayed Galama to come along with them. Resolved to do all he could for the rescue of Hans, by whose noble sacrifice he now acknowledged himself to be saved, their prayers had no effect upon his Frisian determination of character. They separated and left him behind with most of the Beggars, who preferred their roving and adventurous life to the somewhat duller routine and strict discipline of an army.

The first thing Hans did in his new capacity was to send half his men into the forest again. Two were to go to the Rookery and see whether it was still safe to repair thither. The others had instructions to "pick up" what they could get—in other words, to get provisions of any kind, and find out at the same time how matters stood. In an hour's time the two men who were sent to the Rookery, came back with the intelligence that the place was dangerous, the warning cry having been given. On the return of the others with provisions, consisting mainly of wild fowls and rabbits and a few loaves of bread, a council of war was held. Agnes had recovered her consciousness soon after she reached her present shelter, and though greatly shocked by the late events, she yet took active part in the debate. For some time there reigned a great diversity of opinions. That the Yonker must be removed to a place of safety, all admitted. That this place ought to be as far away from Brussels as possible was equally clear. But where to go? and how?

Some mentioned Friesland, where he had many friends, others were in favour of France, until Agnes in a momentary pause, said that if he could be removed thither no place in the world would be better for him than Brill, where his mother lived and where the municipal authorities of the town were more lax in their religious and political persecutions than in most towns of the. Netherlands. Hereupon one Beggar, who had brought a bottle of beer, informed the assembly that he had fallen in with a friend of theirs, a certain Jan Skipper, who was engaged in cutting wood from the forest, to load his barge, which lay in the river Senne hard by. This man was a secret friend of the Beggars and had often done them great service. He plied with his barge between Holland and Brussels.

Immediately two men were sent out to find him and treat with him. It was not long before they came back with satisfactory intelligence. When the skipper heard that it was the well-known Yonker Galama who would be entrusted to his charge, he gladly offered to take him to Brill and run all risk. In the dead of night, a litter having been constructed, Galama was conveyed through the forest to the banks of the Senne, and thence to the barge. A sort of secret cabin, made by piling wood all around and above it, was formed in the hold of the ship, and here Karel was laid upon as soft a bed as could be made. Hans procured for himself and for Agnes some peasant's clothes, and thus—she as the skipper's daughter and he as the skipper's mate—they set out on their perilous journey, after a cordial farewell from their courageous and faithful confederates.

It would be useless, nay tedious, to relate the particulars of the journey to Brill. Suffice it to say, that after a few hair-breadth escapes and a tedious voyage through canals and rivers, the skipper arrived in the haven of Brill, where he was well known.

The town of Brill was a small but strongly-fortified place at the mouth of the Meuse, situated at about half a mile off its southern bank, and connected with it by a canal or haven, the water of the river was admitted. Through this into two large canals running through the town at an angle of fifty degrees to each other. The longer of the two ran from the water-gate in a south-easterly direction, and in the form of a crescent, towards the south gate, close to which it discharged its water into the fosse which surrounded the city. Part of it was called "The Spuy," an old Dutch word, which means a sluice or water-gate, and part "The Quay." The other, which was only half its length, and bore the name of "Maerlandt," ran to about the middle of the town, where it made right angles with "Long Street," the principal street of the city. The Spuy, the Quay, and the Maerlandt were occupied by the residences and warehouses of the chief merchants of the little town, whose goods were stowed up in the garrets and upper floors of their dwellings.

It was a simple and homely way in which these ancient Dutchmen earned their money. You might see them sometimes in their doublets and hose, their blue silk stockings and low shoes, at their desks or in their warehouses, or refreshing themselves with a tankard of wine or ale in the family room. Or they might be standing on the quay superintending the unloading of the goods

which some newly, arrived broad-bottomed barge had
carried to their doors.   For in those days of bad roads,
and highwaymen, of robberies in which, even the authorities sometimes had a hand, and of unfordable streams
over which no one had ever thought of throwing a bridge,
it was both safer and quicker to have one's goods sent
by a ship, which, gliding slowly ands urely along the
innumerable canals and rivers which even at that period,
intersected Holland appeared in its own time in the haven
and before the sluices of the town, whence it was pushed
along until it had arrived in front of the merchant's
house, where it deposited its freight and departed as
leisurely and comfortably as it had come.

Most of these houses had large gardens behind them,
especially on the Maerlandt, which was considered the
more aristocratic of the two canals.   One of these
houses was occupied by the Baroness Galama, the mother
of Karel and Maria, and the widow of one of the earliest
sufferers for Dutch independence.   One look at the widow
was sufficient to reveal the relation borne by her to
Karel and Maria.   There was the fair complexion, the
light hair, the blue eyes, the noble forehead, with which
we are already familiar.   But the mouth, that index
of character, was not like that of either.   If it was not
so decidedly set as Karel's, it certainly wanted that
softness and those lines expressive of meekness and
timidity which were apparent in Maria's face.

If her brow was less frequently contracted, and if her
tones were less imperious than those of her son, her
commands were yet as regularly and as dutifully obeyed
as his.   Hers was a face upon which it was pleasant to

look, presenting to the observer many traces of interest. It possessed all the dignity, verging upon haughtiness, of one accustomed to command, but blended with it were shades of sorrow, of meekness, and of sweet compassion.

She had been the daughter of a wealthy merchant in Flushing, her education as such had been tolerably good, and a residence in Brussels, the centre of fashionable life, had completed it. There she met the poor but noble Baron Galama, who could proudly talk of the deeds of his ancestors of ages back, and was a descendant of those sturdy and unbending Frisian podestas, who, with their little castles and commonwealths, defied the proudest and mightiest of tyrants. He was, however, no lineal descendant of the reigning family of the Galamas, and as such his property was very small; no wonder therefore that he was not averse to a match with the rich merchant's daughter.

But their happiness did not last long. By a succession of disasters at sea, her father lost the greater part of his fortune, and died leaving her and her sister not more than a fifth of what they had expec ted. Baron Galama, now that he could no longer ho ld his own amongst the other nobles, and by the side of his wealthier cousins, wisely determined to withdraw to some smaller place where he might still be an important personage. He went to his native land, Friesland. There, however, he soon became too important, was seized, tried, and executed. His widow, who felt herself less at home among the Frisians, returned to Holland, and settled with her two children in Brill. From time to time she was here visited by her cousins, who were in the midst of the political turmoil of the day and who, patting young Karel on the head as he proudly paraded about with their swords or helmets, promised to take him under their protection and make a real patriot of him. The Baroness had inherited from her father a strong love of liberty and of country, her husband's disposition had run in the same direction, so that she now occupied her time in educating her two children, and especially Karel, in all the principles which she held as a pious and faithful Catholic, and as a free-born and freedom-loving Dutchwoman.

When he was old enough, Karel was sent to the University of Louvain, while Maria, at the urgent invitation of Agnes Vlossert, the daughter of her sister, was sent to Brussels. Six months later, Alva arrived in the Netherlands, and notwithstanding his mother's prayers and tears, Karel snatched up the sword. And she afterwards confessed that she was proud of her son. While at Louvain he had often visited Brussels to see Agnes and his sister, and he thus became fully interested in the political questions of the day.

His first act of rebellion was on the occasion of the departure of the Prince of Orange for Germany previous to Alva's arrival. Galama, who was a fervent admirer of the Nassau family, charged himself with a letter from the young Count de Buren, the son of the Prince—who was also studying at Louvain—to his father. This fact got known, and endeavours were made to intercept the letter, but thanks to his own valour and sagacity, as well as to those of Hans, he reached the Prince in Flushing. The Prince immediately took a liking to him, and with that wonderful talent which he possessed of judging men's characters and capacities, he saw that Karel was a man he could use.

Ever since that time Karel was as devoted a servant of the Prince as could be found. He was happy, but not so his mother, his sister, and his cousin. They feared every moment that he might fall a victim to the tyrant, like his father and his uncles ; for they knew that every escape which he made, every successful journey which he a ccomplished only enhanced the danger of the next. Day by day Karel's mother prostrated herself before the image of the Virgin in her bedroom, imploring protection for the darling of her heart. Each time that some traveller or friend brought intelligence from Brussels, or from other parts of Holland, and spoke the bloody deeds of the Spaniards and the bold behaviour of many of the patriots and Beggars in the land, her eyes would be dimmed with tears, and she would creep away to her own closet and weep half for grief and half for joy. For the good woman, though a pious Catholic, was as decided a patriot, and when the deeds of the Beggars were related she was proud that her son was amongst them and upheld the honour of his country and his race. I am afraid that some of my readers would smile were I to tell them how many pounds of wax-candles the Baroness presented to the Madonna of her favourite church, for her son's safety ; but certain it was that she often pinched herself in many little conveniences for the sake of these candles. Poor soul ! her piety was none the less sincere because it was worthy of a better object.

O

She was sitting in the large room on the first-floor which looked out upon the *Maerlandt*. The room looked as if it had been prepared for some visitor. It was for those times well furnished, and the snow-white sheets on the large bed spoke of the cleanliness of the mistress of the house. She had received a visit from the skipper that morning, who had cautiously made known to her that her son was in Brill, and that he would towards evening come with his ship alongside the canal, when at the most convenient hour her son could be removed. Great caution it was necessary to be observed, for the authorities, though lax, would certainly not allow such determined fellows as Hans and Galama to escape if their presence were known. Evening came and with it the ship. The skipper, for appearance' sake, began to unload some wood, but when it had grown totally dark, the sick and feverish Yonker was removed by him and his mate, our friend Hans, to a comfortable bed and a mother's care. And Agnes, who had nursed him and kept him alive during their confinement in the ship, found a place of shelter in Maria's neat little room, and a place of refuge in the loving heart of her affectionate and tender aunt.

Chapter Sixteenth.

GREAT EVENTS IN A SICK-ROOM.

AND now the two women set themselves with a determination and patience such as only women can show, to watch the sick youth. When he was carried into the room and laid upon the bed, his mother started. He had left her a blooming, strong, rosy-cheeked lad ; she found him now pale, worn out, unconscious, all but dying. Much as she was prepared for she had not expected this, but she restrained her grief, and hidng her feelings which well-nigh despaired of his ever recovering, she showed Agnes a hopeful if not a cheerful face. But as that little hypocrite was doing exactly the same thing, there is no wonder that between the two, the truth ere long came out.

Their faint hope was not augmented by the doctor, or rather barber, for in those days the professions of barber, surgeon and physician were all practised by the same individual. He, however, had his own reasons for pronouncing the case to be very bad, that he might gain all the more honour by his cure and therefore we may as well state that dangerous though Karel's condition was it was by no means hopeless. The damp marsh and his confinement in the hold of the ship, together with his loss of blood, had certainly not improved it, and probably a few more days of it would have finished him. As it was, however, it was nothing more than a bad flesh-wound, the principal danger consisting in the fact that the bullet was in it still.

What with lancing, and nipping and bleeding, and inflammation, however, it seemed as if the experimentalist and nature were working hand in hand to bring our hero to his last resting-place, for he relapsed into a state of total unconsciousness. Each time the doctor approached the bedside, and looked at the pale form as it lay upon the bed, he shook his head gravely, and to judge by the different Latin names which he uttered with an air of importance, it seemed as if each time the disease had entered a new phase. And one day, some two weeks after Karel had been brought into the house, he informed the Baroness in a low voice that she had better send for a priest for that the young man's last hours had come.

It was then that the Baroness began to feel all the danger and distress of her position. The doctor, who was an old man, a sort of sceptic, and moreover a secret friend of the patriotic party, had faithfully promised to let no man know that Karel Galama the outlaw was in the house, and had kept his word. But now that he advised, as was his custom, to have a priest sent for, the mother's mind became swayed to and fro by doubts and thus once or twice, it is true, she had had her confessor in the house, while her son was there, but she had kept him downstairs, and he had seen neither Agnes nor

Karel. Now, however, her only son, and perhaps her only child— for having had no intelligence from Maria, it was almost certain that she had fallen into the hands of the Inquisitor—was on the verge of death, and the question arose within her, whether she could allow him to die without receiving extreme unction and thus be lost for ever. On the other hand, the danger not only for her son, but also for herself and for Agnes was but too apparent. She thought how the priest would rave at her having Karel Galama in the house, and that for a fortnight without his knowing it ; and thus perplexed she sank down before the crucifix in her little bedroom in an agony of mind which we will not attempt to describe.

As Agnes witnessed this struggle, she too went into her little bedroom, and knelt down, but before the crucified One, not before the crucifix. A strong attachment had sprung up between Agnes and the Baroness. The more they began to know each other the more they loved each other, and the latter could not but applaud Karel's choice, of which she had been made the confidante long ago. It was therefore with the greater earnestness that Agnes prayed that her aunt might not commit so foolish and dangerous a deed, and that the object of their fears might yet recover. Her prayer was heard. The next morning, as the Baroness was, still in great uncertainty, Karel opened his eyes and asked for something to eat, thereby putting to flight all their cares, doubts and fears. It appeared that what the doctor had looked upon as his last slumber was a healthy sleep, and that instead of going slowly backwards, as the medical man thought, he had imperceptibly advanced.

A happy time now began for the three, and the only cause they had for grief was the uncertainty of Maria's fate. Hans, like a faithful fellow, had volunteered to remain the skipper's mate for some time, and made many journeys to Brussels and back ; but he could only get at the most scanty intelligence regarding her, as the Beggars had abandoned the Rookery, blown it up, and retired to Dirk's Castle. As Karel began rapidly to gain strength, and to grow interested in the things about him, the two women took their embroidery or their spinning-wheel up to his room and enlivened him by talking and reading. It was to this time, that he ever afterwards attributed the great change which took place within him ; for in the conversations which ensued, religion was frequently the topic, and it was to be expected that Karel, who had read far more at the University than laymen were generally allowed to do, and who, young as he was, had already passed through many experiences, would ponder all that he knew, and all Agnes' arguments—as he lay upon his bed, and could do nothing but muse and think. And at length when he learned one evening what the women had resolved to keep secret from him, namely, that the Baroness had very nearly sent for a priest, his mind became decided.

This took place one beautiful evening in the latter part of July. He lay asleep in bed, and his mother and Agnes had taken their work up to his room where they had a view of the ramparts, and in the distance, the Meuse, upon which the rays of the sun were dancing merrily.

As he was asleep, the two women conducted their conversation in an undertone,—

" Yes, blessed be God," said the Baroness " you are right, Agnes, we have as it were received him back out of the jaws of death."

" I shall never forget that night," said Agnes, " that Thursday night, when we thought that all hope was lost. It was the most fearful moment of my life. How he lay just like a corpse ! For myself, I had already given up every thought of seeing him again."

" So had I," said the Baroness, " and my greatest pain was the uncertainty as to his dying within the arms of our only saving Church."

There was a pause, not because Agnes had nothing to say, but because on account of the sleeping invalid, she did not know whether it was the right moment now to say it. Hitherto, as if led by some instinctive agreement, the two women had avoided entering upon any directly religious discussion. The Baroness knew very well that Agnes had adopted the new religion ; and she regretted this change in the girl's mind all the more, because she loved her so dearly. She could not but look upon her niece as a soul for ever lost, and though her loving heart continually revolted against this distressing conclusion, she was too devoted a daughter of the Church not to submit her human feelings to its dogma. But agree as she might with the priests in judging of the state of Agnes' soul, she did not agree with them in the means chosen to bring her back from the way of everlasting destruction. She abhorred persecution with all her heart. Of course, she could not but acquiesce in it, if carried on by the priests, but she could never be prevailed upon to practise it herself. She hoped to gain the lost sheep back by means of gentle persuasion and kind admonition, though knowing that Agnes was well instructed in the fundamental principles of the new religion, and that she was not easily conquered by argument. She wisely abstained from directly attacking her niece's opinions, but would, ever and anon, throw out serious hints, or make inci-incidentally some grave observation which she hoped the Holy Virgin would carry home to the heart of the poor stray-heretic.

Agnes was quite aware of her aunt's intentions, and understood her tactics completely. To avoid anything like controversy, which, during the sorrowful days of Galama's unconsciouness would have led to nothing good, and have been altogether out of place, she had received the Baroness' hints as if she did not notice them. But the reason of that precaution had happily subsided, and she thought that she would be doing violence to her own conscience if she neglected to enlighten her aunt, whom she regarded as walking in a way from which she herself had fled with horror.

So feeling summoned as it were now to speak her mind, she said in a gentle voice : "My greatest pain was dear aunt, the uncertainty whether he was falling asleep in the arms of Jesus."

"Why, yes, of course," replied the Baroness ; "but it is only the Church that lays the poor sinner on the bosom of Jesus, is it not ?"

"Quite true," said Agnes, "but I hope you agree with

me that every one who believes in Jesus is a member of the Church."

"Well—yes," said the Baroness, hesitatingly, "but explain yourself. What do you mean by that?"

"I mean to say," answered Agnes, "that every one who believes in Jesus has the right and the power, nay, that it is his duty to commit the soul of an unbelieving friend to Jesus, to implore Him on behalf of that lost soul, to speak to that soul about its lost condition and about Jesus, and that thus he may be said to lay a poor sinner on the bosom of an all-merciful Saviour. And when he has so done, it may be said that the Church has done it through him, because he, as a believer is a member of the Church."

"Oh, I see," said the Baroness, "well, yes, that is quite true in one sense, but it is not enough in another. You know that Christ has ordained the priests of the Church to absolve us of our sins, and that we are not received by Him unless we go to Him through them, whom He has appointed. Therefore it was that I was so anxious to have them at our dear Karel's sick-bed when we expected the heavy stroke."

At this juncture a rustling was heard in the direction of the bed. In the fervour of their conversation the women had gradually raised their voices so that Galama could catch every word. Involuntarily they turned their eyes towards him, and saw him in a reclining position, looking at them with an expression of great attentiveness.

"What? have you really had the priests about me?" he asked with a sarcastic smile. "How could you do

such a thing, mother ? I thank God that I need not trust
my soul to their hands."

"No, Karel, we have brought no priest to your bed,"
answered the Baroness. "It would have been risking
too much; but I hope our good Lord will vouchsafe better
days to dawn upon us soon, when you will be able to
kneel down at the confessional, to speak of the concerns
of your soul to the priest of the Lord, without being in
danger of your life."

"A sad religion, dear aunt," said Agnes, "which re-
quires a poor sinner to wait for better days, before he
may approach his Saviour. We must have gone down
fearfully indeed. Sixteen hundred years ago a poor
dying thief, though he found himself in the most wretched
condition was helped at once in the twinkling of an eye.
But he did not apply to priests, but to Jesus himself, and
that makes all the difference."

"Ay," said Galama, in a grave voice "that is what I
call true salvation, ' To-day,' He said, 'thou shalt be with
me in Paradise.'"

"Just so," said Agnes "that is salvation by grace,
without works, solely by the blood and the work of
Christ."

Much as the Baroness regretted the spirit which
her son revealed by these words, she deemed it not
wise now to remonstrate with him about what she would
call profane language. She not only perceived that he
was too weak for controversy, but she was also afraid
that she herself would not prove strong enough to defend
her position against two such opponents. So she kept
silence, and being aware of the rather unpleasant position

in which she was thus placed, she tried to make a pretext for leaving the room. In this she was unconsciously aided by her son, who said to Agnes:

"Oh, do read that third chapter of the Epistle to the Romans, in which it is so clearly shown that we are justified only by faith."

"Then I will meanwhile go and look after that broth for you," said the Baroness, rising. "I will be back in a few minutes."

While she left the room, Agnes took her New Testament, and read the desired chapter to Karel.

"Great, glorious truths," he said, when she had finished the reading, "is it not just what we want, and is it not just like God?"

"Oh I am so thankful that you see it," said Agnes. "I now praise God with the deeper gratitude because you are given back to us, not only to defend our political liberties, but the most precious treasure we have on earth, our religion, the saving Word of God."

"Well," he answered, "you see Agnes, a man learns a great deal at death's door. I have found that I was a fool trying to be a saviour to others, while I was without a Saviour myself. I saw that you were right when you said to me at Brussels, sin is a more terrible evil than the Inquisition. It kills the soul, and who can save from it but the crucified Son of God?"

"Oh would to God all the people who are now in arms against the Pope and the Inquisition saw that truth," said Agnes, "as I believe the Prince does; then I am assured that God would speedily give us the victory. But, as it is now, I am afraid our poor country will for a long time be bathed in blood and tears, because so many make flesh their arm, relying upon their own strength instead of making a covenant with the Lord of Hosts."

"I believe you are right," said Galama, "but we must allow those people to swell our band, though they do not fight from the right principle. It cannot be helped, and I trust God will even use them as a means to destroy the work of iniquity, that those who love His name in sincerity and truth may be delivered out of their distress. I must confess that now I dread very much returning to the company of the Beggars. Their conversation was never very much to my taste."

At this juncture the Baroness again entered, and the conversation took another turn. But the words which had then been spoken sank deep into Karel's heart, and produced their fruit in due season.

Chapter Seventeenth.

A SAD STORY.

THE Baroness had not been seated long when a knock was heard at the door, and a gruff voice asked for admittance. The door opened and to the eyes of the somewhat astonished party was revealed the broad figure and smiling face of our old acquaintance, Hans. He was dressed in the attire of a servant of those days, which generally consisted of a doublet and trunk-hose of dark cloth without collar or other ornament. The servants of the nobility, however, and of those who were entitled to the privilege, wore the livery of their masters, and then as now the arms of the family were emblazoned upon the buttons of the dress. To the astonishment of Galama and his mother they perceived that Hans had assumed his old livery which he used to wear when waiting upon Karel in Louvain, but which he had laid off when he changed his cloth doublet for a steel corselet. He entered the room with a parcel under his arm which he deposited in a corner, as soon as he saw the two women, whose presence he had apparently not expected.

Hearty was the welcome which Galama gave to his servant, for it must be mentioned that he had not seen him since the rescue, and he extended his hand to press that of his faithful follower. But Hans had always prided himself upon knowing manners, and before he deigned to accept Karel's hand he gravely made his bow to the ladies. The Baroness answered his salute with a grave and pleasant movement of the head; but Agnes, who could not be so cold towards her prison companion stretched forth her hand, at which Hans went down upon one knee and impressed a most respectful kiss upon her fingers.

Then turning to Karel with the seriousness of an old lackey he said:

"Good morning, Baron! When would you like to dress."

The comicality of this speech, addressed as it was to the youth who could hardly sit up, set all three laughing.

"I do not think I shall dress for another month yet, Hans. You see how thin I am. In fact, I think I should hardly find clothes to fit me. But surely what I have lost in appearance you have won. You look better than ever. What have you been doing all this time, for I hear that I have been ill very long?"

"Well, you see Baron," said Hans, "I've turned skipper for some time, and it isn't a bad trade, I can assure you. It has suited me excellently."

"I seem to have risen in your estimation," continued Galama, shutting his eyes, languidly. "I used to be plain Yonker before."

"Ah," said Hans with a grave shake of the head "don't you know? You're the heir of the family now. You're the Baron now, since your poor father died."

Karel smiled ; for his father had been dead for years, and Hans had never thought of giving him the title before.

"According to that argument, I have been Baron for some time, Hans."

"So you have," answered Hans, significantly, "only don't you see, I came to think as how when your uncles were yet alive, and you hadn't over much money, Yonker wouldn't sound so high as Baron. But now you are heir to all the estates, and that is something."

And he accompanied the suggestion with an expressive wink. But Karel shook his head and said, slowly,

"You are mistaken, Hans. There's my great-uncle in Friesland, Igo Galama, and his son. They are both alive. And then do you not know that our estates have all been confiscated?"

"Oh, that makes no difference. We'll get them back quick enough," observed Hans, as if he had a whole army at his back. "I'm thinking Baron, that we are something like Alexander the Great who could only be killed at his heel, eh ? I was rather too sharp for the Duke in the Broodhuys. *He* couldn't keep me."

"Oh yes," said the Baroness "tell me how you managed that Hans. How did you fare in the Broodhuys ?"

Hans made a polite bow to the Baroness and began:

"I went through the gate well enough. I frightened the soldiers on guard with my Latin, but my difficulty was to get inside the Broodhuys, where I was pretty well known. You never told me what arrangements you had made. So when I saw a sentry at the back door I waited on the opposite side of the way. Presently Gritta comes out and begins talking to the soldiers, and

taking my chance at that moment I opened the window
of the sitting-room and jumped inside. I had seen
beforehand that no one was there but Mistress Agnes;
but she, Baron, upon my Beggar's oath, was all of a
tremble at first and———"

Here Agnes cast a beseeching glance at Hans, which
however he pretended not to notice, the more because
the eyes of Karel were now wide open.

"And," he continued, "the first thing she said to me
was, 'God be praised it is not Karel.' And I said 'Amen,'
Yonker—Baron I mean."

Karel threw a look of intense love at the girl who
bent blushing over her work. The widow wiped her
eyes and Hans proceeded:—

"I am sure it was my Latin that frightened the fellows
on the stairs, for they let me pass with hardly any moles-
tation, but when we had arrived in the little room both
doors were locked and we were caught."

Here Agnes looked up again, and pressing her finger to
her lip, cast a look at the Baroness. Hans took the
hint this time and was silent about Maria.

"They took me up stairs to the third floor into a dingy
little place in the front of the house where I could see
right over the square. Here I had a visit from the
original Father Florisz, who came out of compassion for
my garb, for he still believed me to be one of his order
led astray by heresy. I kept him in that opinion for a
couple of hours, but as I knew only five sentences in
Latin and had to repeat them constantly, he began to
smell a rat I suppose; at least he ended by excommunica-
ting me, and delivering me over to all the devils in hell."

"Ah, Baron, I shall never forget the morning I passed in that room. I don't know whether they arranged it on purpose, but I could see everything as it happened. First, at daybreak, I saw the dim figure of the black scaffold, and as the sun rose and ascended higher, a crowd collected around it and became larger every moment. At last, I do not know exactly at what time in the morning, I saw about two or three thousand soldiers march into the square, and take their position around the scaffold. I soon made friends with the soldier who was guarding me, and who had immensely enjoyed my taking in of the old priests. He pointed out to me the different regiments and the officers, and where Alva sat, just opposite me in the town-hall. At last I heard a stir in the house below, and I could see the crowd pressing and pushing the soldiers. 'Oh,' thinks I, ' now the play is going to begin,' and sure enough it was, for a moment afterwards Count Egmont walked up the steps, followed by a bishop, I forget his name, and that fellow Romero. The Count was dressed beautifully, and he looked a fine fellow and a hero to the very last.

"He walked up and down the scaffold with his head bent down, and stopping, said something to Romero, who shook his head. He then knelt down and prayed while the bishop knelt down beside him. Oh, I thought when I saw that, I wish I were in front of that scaffold with the Yonker and some of our men, I would have made an attempt at any rate. But he got up again and took off some of his clothes, and then he knelt down on the cushion and drew a little cap over his head. I have seen a good many executions in my time, and there

P

have been some amongst them that were very touching and awful to look at, but I never saw anything like this. You might have heard a mouse squeak, so silent were the people. It was just one white mass of faces, most of them with their kerchiefs or hands before their eyes, and some with open mouths, staring when he knelt down there in expectation of the blow, and looking as if they expected to receive it themselves. Suddenly, a fellow stepped from behind some drapery and raised a tremendous sword. Several women lifted up their hands, others shrieked and hugged their babies to their breasts, and cried over them. Then the fellow gave one blow with his sword, and I saw the head rolling away, and the blood flowing. Ah!" he continued, with a shudder, " I thought I would see both of them die, but when I saw that I turned away from the window, and so did the soldier, and I could not look at Count Horn. It was horrible, horrible."

And as if the recollection of that tragedy had not lost its effect upon him yet, he wiped a big tear out of his eye with the back of his hand. There was a silence in the room, during which all were occupied with the melancholy deaths of the two noblemen. Karel lay upon his bed with his eyes closed, and a dark and gloomy expression upon his face.

"They have died as martyrs to Spanish treason," at last the sweet voice of Agnes said ; "they have died for the best, and may God in His mercy have pity upon their souls."

"Amen," whispered all three.

"What puzzles me most of all," said Karel, after a

moment's silence, "is that they should have thought of transporting you from Brussels to Ghent. Surely you were not such an important prisoner as either of my two uncles, or Treslong's brother, who were kept in Brussels."

"Well, I don't know," said Hans, in a tone somewhat offended, "there was not much to be got out of them, you know, Yonker. At least, they did not know as much about everything as I do, that's certain."

The point did not seem quite so clear to Galama as to Hans; but not wishing to disturb his servant's harmless conceit, he said,—

"But Agnes? why should she be taken away? I do not suppose she knew anything, and does not now. I cannot understand it."

"Nor can I," said the Baroness. "It seems to me so unlikely that you should be removed from the headquarters of the Inquisition unless it were for some deep reason or other."

"Ah, my lady," said Hans, with a knowing wink, "*you've* hit the nail, to my thinking. Look here, Yonker. These priests, you know, are just like that there marsh, the Hell-mouth as they call it; they are very deep and very dirty, but when you know the way, you can go through them as we went through the marsh."

Galama cast a rapid glance at his mother, who was bending over her work, and said nothing.

"I think it was this way," continued Hans; "they wanted to catch all the Beggars while they were at the rescue, why else should they have had cavalry on both sides? I saw only one party when I was put in the coach, and the other must have been sent round beforehand. I knew the cavalry was coming, though why it stopped away so long I do not know. But that that arch-traitor Block had a hand in it, I will swear."

"He had not, Hans. He was wounded himself, and escaped with difficulty to inform us what he had heard; but for him you might now be a mangled corpse."

Hans was going to reply, but the Baroness glanced at him as if to stop him, for she saw that the conversation was not pleasing to her son, and the doctor had told her that anything that might ruffle his spirits should be avoided.

"Never mind, Yonker," he said, therefore, in a light tone, "we'll pay them out soon. I saw Jonathan a week ago, and he told me that he was watching near the Rookery in the oak, when he saw soldiers approaching. He gave the cry, and the other sentry had his match ready when the soldiers, about fifty of them, surrounded the old tower, and half of them went into the vault and began drinking our wine. All at once bang goes the powder and down comes the tower on the top of them. Half of them at least killed."

"A lucky thing the Beggars were not there," said Galama; "the place was suspected for a long while. How sad it is that thus we must obtain our liberty. I am almost sorry to get well again, and if it were not for the sacred cause, I would have loathed this work long ago."

" I thought there was a letter, which you got from the Prince, Yonker," said Hans directing his thoughts into another train; " has it been delivered?"

" No! by all that's stupid! Forgotten." Then turning to his mother, he asked her whether she could give him his doublet, in which Hans would find a letter. " You can deliver it, I suppose, Hans ? It is to Master Buys in Leyden."

" All right, Yonker," answered Hans, cheerfully.

" Have you heard anything from Maria, Hans ? " asked Agnes anxiously, as soon as the Baroness was away.

" Ay, that I have. The skipper went to the Broodhuys and told her where we were, and she was ready to cling to his neck and go off with him then and there, only that it could not be. It was a great danger for him, you know. But she is to come next voyage, when he is going to take his wife with him ; or if she can she'll come over before that. Maybe she is on the way now. And then we'll all be here, Yonker. Your mother and your sister and your—h'm—your-a-cousin," he said, with a wink to Agnes, "and your humble servant, Hans. And then we'll call this Galama House, and you must be the Baron."

Agnes smiled, but Galama shook his head and said,—

" No Baron for me, Hans. A Baron with a little house and a garden to boot will not do. We would get the oil merchant over the way calling himself Duke if he heard of it. So, if you please, let us wait till we have carved out for ourselves another barony out of some province or other," and he smiled ironically as if he were of opinion that that time would never come.

" Ah ! " said Hans, fetching a deep breath, his face which had fallen considerably during the Yonker's speech, lighting up with pleasure. " You'll be strong soon, and then we'll go at it again for a count's coronet. Count de Galama won't sound bad, will it ?"

" It does not depend upon me now," said Karel, casting a significant look at Agnes, who had looked sad when Hans broached the warlike plans of the future. " I shall thank God if we can emigrate, and live peacefully and quietly in England."

" And leave this unhappy country to its own fate ? " said Agnes in a low voice, bending over her work so as to hide from Karel the trouble which it cost her to utter words so contrary to her own dearest hopes.

Karel looked at her, and his eyes seemed to endeavour to pierce her bosom and read what was hidden in its inmost recesses. It was clear that two feelings were dividing his heart, one of duty and one of love. He too, acknowledged it his sacred duty to fight for his country, but opposite him sat the girl whom he considered it would be his greatest blessing on earth to make his wife, and how both could go together he saw not. In the perplexity of his heart he sighed :

" I wish I had died instead of Count Egmont."

" I wish I had, " said Hans, " that's what I said to the soldier, and he would not believe me. But I know that if old Egmont had been in Friesland, Alva would never have been able to make such a mess of Count Louis's army."

" What ? " cried Karel, " What ?" and he tried to raise himself up in bed, but fell back. " Count Louis's army ? Tell me, Hans, you stupid fool, why did not you tell me before ? What has happened ? Answer me. "

The reason why Hans did not answer was simply this. The news of the fearful defeat which Louis of Nassau's army had suffered had flown through Holland and

spread a gloom wherever it flew. The two women had
heard it also ; but they resolved with one accord to keep
it a secret from Karel until he should be strong enough
to hear it, or until some splendid piece of news should
counterbalance it. It was but newly that his concious-
ness had returned, and Agnes, who had started the
moment Hans mentioned Louis's name, now lifted up a
terror-stricken face to Hans, upon which it was plainly
written that she implored him not to tell any more.

But the dam was broken and the river rushed impetuously through the breach. The Yonker had recovered so
much of his strength as to show some of his old imperi-
ousness, which, as a rule, proved irresistible to Hans.

With a sulky voice, and very reluctantly, he began,—

"I'll tell you all I have heard, Yonker, for I know you
would not be content with anything less. The Count,
like a fool, posted his army with its rear resting upon the
Ems, quite near the Dollart. Now his army was not
only smaller than Alva's, but consisted of hired troops
without pay, and as I said to Hoofd, who told it me,
I would like to see the man that could make me fight,
if he did not pay me for it, nor allow me to pay myself. Now then, here was the Count with his troops all
in mutiny, because, as I said, they were not paid, and
the Count would not allow them to plunder, for surely
he could not allow his own countrymen to be robbed.
If they had been Spaniards you know, it would have
been quite a different thing. But if I had been the
Count I would have taken boats and crossed the Zuyder
Zee, for Alva could not have followed so soon, and "—
He stuck in the middle of his sentence and looked con-

fusedly at Agnes and then at Karel. The poor fellow had attempted to fabricate a tale while he was holding forth, but his usual talent forsook him, and he broke down.

" In heaven's name tell me what has happened. Cut down,—dead,—what ? " said Galama in a terribly anxious voice.

" Ay, Yonker, " said Hans, savagely, " beaten. The cowards wouldn't fight, they wouldn't even fire the guns. The Duke was upon them in a moment, and chased them into the river or killed them. Every man-Jack of the whole army has been killed except the Count and a few others. But Treslong and the whole batch of them are dead. That's all."

" Great God," cried Karel, growing deadly pale. " Count Louis defeated !—Treslong———."

Agnes rushed to the bed. Karel had fallen back in a swoon.

At this moment his mother came into the room again with his doublet which she threw over to Hans, and ran to assist Agnes at the bedside. Hans soon found the letter which was addressed to Master *Borsels, Mercurius,* the assumed names for Paul Buys and Leyden.

"Ah !" muttered Hans to himself, "I shall go with this. They know how to manage him better than I do. What a fool I was ; I only hope he is not seriously ill, and I'll have to take these clothes away too. Well, I don't know but they would be somewhat too large for him now, seeing that they belonged to the old Baron, his father."

And taking his bundle, Hans was soon in the disguise of a hawker on his way to Leyden, whither we shall no follow him.

Thanks to the care of his mother and Agnes, Karel was soon brought to life again, and found himself none the worse for the sad intelligence, as far as his body was concerned. But he acknowledged that the affairs of his country were now in a far more desperate state than before, that it required his help more than ever, and that the first step towards being enabled to give that help was to lie perfectly still and become strong. Still he lay, therefore, and soon fell into a healthy sleep.

When he awoke, it had grown quite dusk; but in the evening twilight he could see the figures of Agnes and his mother engaged in earnest conversation. They spoke in a whisper, that they might not disturb his sleep, out of which he had awoke without their perceiving it. The Baroness held something glittering in her hand, but what it was he could not distinguish.

"This is my husband's chain, I am certain," said the Baroness, looking down upon the object in her hand. "I cannot conceive how it got into that man's hands."

"I do recollect his face," said Agnes, musing, "but where I have seen it I cannot say. The moment I saw it I recognised it; where have I seen him?"

And she put her hand to her forehead as if to bring some old recollection back to her mind.

"Let me look at the chain mother," sounded Karel's voice. The widow started, and after a moment's hesitation handed the gold chain to her son. It was the one Karel had given to Block previous to the rescue. He recognised it at once.

"What, he cried out joyously," has Block been here? Who gave you this mother?"

"Be quiet, Karel, and I'll tell you. About two hours ago the servant told me some one desired to see me. I went downstairs and found a tall dark man, dressed as a Spanish soldier. He told me that he had had the honour of your friendship in Brussels and that he once saved your life. That you gave him this chain and told him that at any time, if he happened to be in Brill, I would welcome him. He said he was a fugitive and wanted a few days' shelter. Could I give it him? I told him that you were lying ill upstairs, which he seemed to know. That I could give him no answer till I had spoken with you, but that I would be very glad to entertain him for the moment. He politely declined my offer and said he would come back in three hours and bring me a pleasant surprise. What is his name do you say, Bock?"

"No, Block. Gerard Block. One of the Beggars, and one of the best too."

"What will you do?"

"Take him in here, of course, if it be for a year. Where there's room for one there's room for two, mother, that's our old Frisian proverb, is it not?"

"I cannot say that I like his face," said the Baroness. "There is something decidedly unpleasant about it."

"Are you going to take him in here, Karel?" asked Agnes. "That traitor Block."

"Traitor? who calls him traitor, I would like to know?"

"Hans does. He says he is sure the whole attempt to rescue the Count was betrayed by him. Hans hates him with deep hatred."

"Hans is a great ass. He hated him from the very

first because he wanted to give himself airs before Block,
who is a gentleman, and who showed it too. A traitor
indeed! The man saved my life and was wounded in
the rescue which Hans says he has betrayed. Don't let
him say it to me."

"But was not his conduct very suspicious at all
times?" asked Agnes.

"Suspicious! Agnes! I am astonished to hear *you* say
so. He rescued you too and dressed the wound, which
that fool of a Hans gave you. I see the mark on your
neck yet. You will have an opportunity now for thank-
ing him. Did you say you had seen him before? You
saw him then, in the forest."

"I did not, I am positive, but——" She paused, for her
heart spoke against her offering any more objections to
the preserver of her life and that of her lover.

Here the servant announced that the same soldier was
again downstairs.

Agnes left the room, and a few moments afterwards
Block appeared, and having made a low bow before
the lady of the house, he kneeled down by the bed, and
grasping Karel's hand, cried out,—

"My friend! Yonker Galama! The holy Virgin be
praised I find you still amongst the living."

With as much strength as Karel could master he returned the cordial pressure of Block's hand, and expressed
in words what he felt indeed, a sincere joy at seeing him
back.

"I think, madam," said Block turning to the Baroness,
"you will find some one downstairs whom you will like
to see. It is the surprise I spoke of."

At this moment a sort of shriek or exclamation was heard downstairs.

"What," gasped the Baroness, "is it——my daughter, Maria!" and rushing downstairs she soon found herself in the arms of her sobbing and trembling daughter.

"We made the flight from Brussels together," said Block smilingly to Galama, when they were alone. "And it was tough work too. But how, when, and where it all happened, I hope to tell you to-morrow, if you will allow me shelter here for a few days till I can get a chance to go to sea."

The request was granted with every readiness and cordiality.

The serpent had been taken to the bosom, and immediately set about coiling itself round the heart, which it intended to explore and then sting to death.

When Block recovered from the blow which Hans had dealt him, he had returned to Brussels once more to report his failure, which was this time the fault of the officer in command of his horse, who had waited too long ere he came down amongst the rescuers.

Both Block and the Inquisitor resolved to wait, since all researches for Galama had remained fruitless. They had at any rate a sister of his still in their hands, and they rightly conjectured that ere long she would be made acquainted with Karel's whereabouts. Both, however, had come to the conclusion that violence should only be used in the greatest extremity, and that Galama was more likely to betray the secret of the correspondence to a friend than to a foe. How their plan has already partly succeeded has now been shown ; how that master in the art of deception, Block, succeeded farther will be shown hereafter.

Chapter Eighteenth.

A BAD NAME FOR THE DOG.

A FEW days after the above occurrence we find Gerard Block pacing with cat-like steps up and down the room in which Karel Galama was still confined to his bed. He slept, and the regular heaving of his breast showed that his sleep was calm, and in no way disturbed by the presence of the vampire who hovered around him. The reception which Block had met with had been cordial in the extreme, as far as Karel was concerned. He would not hear of anything but that the saviour of his life should sleep under his roof, nay, in his own room. His mother, who could never resist his obstinacy, and would not even have done so now had she been able, because of his illness, granted the request, and Gerard was from that hour an inmate in the house.

Nor could it be said that he made himself anything but agreeable and useful. It appeared that he had practised medicine, for he prepared a draught for Karel, which, as the latter declared, did him much good. He treated his wound too, and with so much success, that, to everybody's comfort, the patient became better every day, and the barber could be dispensed with. He was, at the same time, of very little inconvenience to the household, and excellent company for Karel. In the evening he rolled himself in his mantle, and slept on a simple mattress as soundly as anyone. The Baroness was soon entirely won in his favour by his great piety and extensive reading, as well as by his patriotism. Agnes lost her antipathy in a great measure, by his politeness and his evident love and admiration for Karel. Maria, who had arrived with him, seemed to look up to him with an amount of reverence, nay of awe, which could easily be explained by her mother and cousin, seeing that he had been instrumental in delivering her from Brussels.So the women were thankful, on the whole, that Karel had such a good and faithful nurse, who was at the same time his physician. It happened sometimes that he went out after dark and returned late at night, when he always had some curious piece of the latest news of some of the little pamphlets which, despite the terrible punishment that followed their sale, yet found their way by thousands into the families of the land.

So Galama slept calmly, and the women below span and embroidered and chatted, and were very pleasant together. But if any of them had been in the room where Block was, as unseen spectators of his actions, it is probable they would have felt a little more uneasy. For why should our honest friend Block, open every drawer of the large oaken cabinet which stood in the room, and shuffle and sniff into every corner of that extensive warehouse of linen, the wealth, the comfort, and the pride of every Dutchwoman in those days ? He surely did not want to set up a house himself, and take an inventory of what would be required beforehand ? He hardly looked at the linen, but snatched with eager movement at every bit or scrap of paper or parchment he could find, and after having read it threw it away with an exclamation of disappointment. His work did not seem to prosper, for after having ransacked everything in the room, chairs, pictures, the hearth, nay the bed upon which our patient lay, he folded his arms and looking thoughtfully at Karel, said to himself,—

"He will not awake for an hour yet ; my draught has worked well this time. Where can that letter be ? I am sure he had it in the Rookery, and he cannot have delivered it himself. I wonder whether Hans has gone with it. I have not seen him at all. If I had that letter it would explain a good deal, I am sure. But it is not here, that is clear. Now let me see what I have to do here. Above all things I must get Hans away. They must quarrel. The Yonker, I think, suspects him a little already. Then shall I put the girls away too ?—Dangerous. He might grow suspicious. Let me see," and he began pacing up and down the room. "Yes," he continued at last, "that's the way. If they do not grow suspicious they can remain, for if, after all, I can get nothing out of him by talking, I will seize him and put him on the rack, and then they'll come very handy, for I have seen enough of him to know that he would not breathe a word to save his own life. I must be cautious, though, for he's not a fool. Let me think it over again."

The sun was sinking in the west when Karel awoke out of his deep sleep. It had been a magnificent day, and the heat even at that hour of the evening was oppressive.　But a deliciously cool sea-breeze played through the open window, and brought with it the perfumes and odours from many a tarred bottom, laden with the spices and fruits of every land.　It carried along with it the sweet smell of the hay and of many flowers.　It wafted across the little town the various sounds of a summer's evening.　The ploughman shouting to his beast to turn homewards ; the merry lasses and youths haymaking in the fields, the boatmen calling to each other across the broad and stately Meuse, or the sailors singing a simple ditty to accompany their united efforts at the anchor.　In that little corner of Holland, everything breathed peace and quiet.　And but for the soldiers, who loitered about the streets, and gazed impudently at the women as they walked past or sat in their houses, and but for the hurried and almost reluctant salute which their officers received, one might have fancied that those stout and stalwart men, who sat and drank their beer in front of the alehouses, dressed in their wide baggy trousers, tied up a little below the knees, their closely-fitting jacket, and the straw hat with broad brim, were nought else but the free and independent burghers of Holland a hundred years ago.

It was to be expected that such pleasant sounds, so delicious and cool a breeze, should gladden the Yonker's heart, and stir the awakening life within him.　But his brow remained clouded, and an expression of sadness played around his mouth.　He looked round the room. He perceived Block standing before the open window, but so that he could not be seen from without, with his arms folded and apparently lost in deep thought.

"The evening seems to have but little charm for you, Gerard," said Galama leaning upon one arm.

Block started. "And no wonder," he said, "when all around us seems so smiling, and I consider what is really hid under that smile. When I think that I shall soon have to leave again to fight against our common foe, instead of waiting that we might brave him together, it is no wonder that I should look melancholy."

"But who, my dear Gerard, has said that you should leave? Are the Spaniards suspicious of your being here? Surely it will be time for me to leave too. Has my mother told you, or have I perhaps muttered it in my dream?"

Block shook his head.

"Then pray who has ventured to talk about your leaving us?"

"I did not say any one had, my dear Yonker," answered Block.

"Then why leave? You are safe here, wait till I am well again, and we shall go together."

Block shook his head again, and said with a sigh, "It cannot be, Yonker."

"And why?" Then, after a pause. "Is anyone in this house against you?"

"No," said Block, "not yet; but————." He hesitated and stopped.

"But what?" fiercely asked Galama, who began to feel himself the head of the house. "But what?"

"Well, Yonker, since you insist upon knowing it, I fear they may be turned against me, and sooner than remain in a house where I am looked upon with unfavourable eyes, nay, perhaps, with suspicion, I would rather

Q

throw myself upon a hundred sentries on the walls of Brussels, or die sword in hand for the King and my glorious country."

"But who would turn us against you?" asked Karel. "We see no one; indeed, no one but the old surgeon and our servant know that you are here, and neither of them would think of saying anything against you."

"Oh, it is not from that quarter that I fear anything," said Block, "my foe has not arrived yet, but in the kitchen this morning I accidentally heard that Hans was coming home to day. If that be the case I must leave you."

"Hans? what would Hans do to you?" He will not be disagreeable. He is a very fine fellow when you know him well. You should make friends with him."

"With all my heart," said Block cordially, "but I am almost afraid *he* won't. You know, Yonker, there are some minds more disposed to jealousy than others, and it seems to me that good Hans fancies I have no right to be your friend."

"Now, is it not curious?" said Karel, not a little flattered at finding himself an object of contention. "I have often heard my uncles talk about this feeling, and what misery it can bring into the world, and I never felt it. Even the soldiers and captains round the Prince are jealous of each other."

Block pricked up his ears, but the Prince was no more mentioned. "Ah," he said, "perhaps you have never had anyone who stood between you and the object of your affection. I must confess I have but little of that feeling either, but Hans has a good deal. He thinks, because you have been very fortunate in your expeditions, and he has constantly been with you, that a great part of the merit is due to him, and that since his advice was not asked in our last undertaking, its failure is to be attributed to me."

"Oh, that is ridiculous," said Karel, "now when I reflect upon it, I must confess that it was a mad undertaking and the most startling thing of all would have been its success. Never mind Hans, Gerard. He will not be so foolish, and if he is, tell me, and I'll make him desist."

"Well," said Block, "I tried before to make friends with him, but he seems not very well bred, and he might insult me ; a thing which I can never brook. I have nothing against him ; on the contrary, I think he is a splendid fellow. But he seems to be my sworn enemy, and I would rather leave you for ever than be a source of discontent between you and so faithful a servant as Hans appears to be."

"Faithful or not faithful," said Galama, "he is my servant, and he shall honour whomsoever I choose to accept as friend. Of course if you must go, go. I shall be the last to keep you. But be assured that the first impediment which Hans puts in your way shall be the signal for his dismissal. He ought to be here by this time. I wonder where he is." And then changing the subject he said : "But you never yet fully told me how you managed to escape unhurt after the rescue. I thought you must have been killed."

"No ; I have to thank Hans for that," answered Block. He gave me such a good knock on the pate, that I lay as dead, for some time ; I suppose all the cavalry must have gone over me, for when I woke I found they had all passed me and were trying to get into the marsh. All right, I thought, and I cautiously crept off the road and as far into the bush as I could. In the night I got to a woodcutter's hut, where I procured a disguise and went into the country next day, thinking all of you had been killed or caught. About a month later I ventured into the city again, all the soldiers then being away, and got shelter with some friends. Fortunately, I found out your sister who was desirous of fleeing too, so being afraid, indeed all but certain, that I was watched, we made our escape and came here."

"Ay," Galama said, "you must remain. Here, I suppose, comes our friend Hans"—he added as a knock was heard at the door—"now for the opinions of this mighty foe of yours, Gerard. Come in !"

It was indeed Hans. He was dressed in the same disguise of a hawker in which he had left Brill, and to judge by the bespattered and dusty state of his clothes he must have newly arrived from his journey. He seemed prepared for the presence of Block, for he looked unusually grave, and the dark look which he gave him as he stood at the window farthest from the bed, boded him no good. With that exception, however, he proceeded as if nobody had been in the room but his master. He passed by Block without as much as turning his head, and halting before the bed said in a voice of gaiety which was plainly forced :—

"Good evening, Yonker. Still in bed and that in this glorious weather ? It would have been far better for you to have been outside, methinks."

" I can dispense with your thoughts, Hans, and would have a little more of your good manners. See you not a friend of ours behind you, and you greet him not ?"

"A friend of ours ?" repeated Hans, slowly turning round and eying Block from head to foot, "oh indeed Master Block! Come to life again ? Have you come to tell us that there was cavalry after all ?"

"I have come to thank thee for thy timely blow, friend Hans," said Block in a condescending tone, "for though it was ill-meant, it was certainly the means of saving my life. And I would feel pleased by thine acceptance of a couple of ducats wherewith to drink my health the first time thou canst get a chance," and he held out two silver ducats between finger and thumb.

"Nay, friend Block, thou'dst better drink thine own and pay for it with honest gold," said Hans, coolly extending two pieces of gold between his finger and thumb.

"None of thy impertinences," cried Galama, his cheeks flushing with passion, "give this gentleman a good evening, or hold thy tongue and do not insult my guests."

"Nay, Yonker, we are equal," said Hans, in a respectful tone turning his back upon Block, "since he's no more than a Beggar, and I'm no less."

"You have been long gone for so short a journey. Where have you been ?" said Galama, keeping down his anger.

"I've been to Brussels and back," said Hans.

"To Brussels ? Why there ? And what's the news ?"

"Oh, news enough. The Duke as usual has mixed

the foolish and the wise up together. He has done a
wise thing in hanging a great rogue, provost-marshall
Spelle."

"And what's the foolish thing?" asked Block.

"He's left a greater rogue unhung," answered Hans,
speaking to Galama. "I was told by our confederates
that one wretch of a jail-bird, who, like Tittlemann in
Flanders, was condemned to the flames has saved
his miserable life by turning traitor. And the blackhaired cur seems to have entered among us confederates in order to betray our secrets." Hans spoke
slowly and turned half round to Block behind him.

"I tell thee once more, Hans, none of thy insolent
insinuations in my hearing," said the Yonker, "or thou
shalt leave me on the spot. What has come over thee that
makes thee so untoward? Thou comest from Leyden.
"What is the news?"

"From whence?" said Hans in great astonishment,
while at the same time he sounded a very soft "hush!"
through his teeth.

"From Leyden! Treat me not as if I were a child.
Tell me the news at once. I have no secrets for my
friends!"

"Ay, for a friend Yonker, I should not. But for a
stranger hardly two months old, I——"

"Come, Hans," said Block, stepping nearer, "let us be
friends too. You have always looked upon me with suspicion. At first that could be pardoned, nay, it was
laudable. But now, we have surely seen enough of each
other to cease doing it."

"Ah," said Hans, stepping aside as if shrinking from

his touch, "I have seen enough of you indeed to continue doing it, and to make me believe that you are the most damnable traitor on earth."

Block's face flushed deeply and he made an involuntary movement to his sword. But Karel who had half risen from his bed, ·motioned with his hand to desist. The slow and fearfully earnest manner in which Hans spoke seemed for a moment to awaken his suspicions. With one effort almost too much for his not yet fully recovered strength he suppressed all anger and said to Hans :—

"Hans, your suspicions of Master] Block are terrible, or perhaps they appear terrible because you hide them behind insinuations. Give your grounds. Speak out and either you or he shall leave this house to night."

"They are hardly suspicions now, Yonker," said Hans, gloomily, "but certainties. What but ill-luck and defeat has been our share since that man came to us recommended by a false name? Ever since I have seen him he has watched you as a cat watches the mouse with his eyes that gleam like the devil's. That some one has betrayed our enterprize in Brussels there's no doubt. And he who knew so much about the news, who took one of the leading posts and escaped twice unhurt, he is the traitor I'll lay my life. All the Beggars were known to each other, but he was known to none, and he is the one we all suspect, because he is the only one that could have betrayed us."

"Ha, well have you said, Yonker," interrupted Block, "that his suspicions are terrible because they are hid behind a cloud of insinuations. But since you choose to speak such language, fellow, let me say that your own conduct is far more suspicious than mine. How did you spend the hours we were inside the city ere we came to the Rookery? We do not know; but the Yonker was beset by soldiers and it was with difficulty that I saved him from their hands. And pray how was it that when the noblest bird of our flock, my Lord de Treslong, declined to go to the Broodhuys that you went slyly so that you might receive no harm upon the wall. And who, I pray you, procured such tremendously thick carriages that would take a long time in opening; your carriage was open quick enough though, to your great disappointment I suppose, you failed in killing Mistress Agnes, who but for my help, which you grudged her, would have bled to death there and then. And who knew all about the cavalry coming, and urged us to fly, whereas, as I afterwards found out, the whole forest was full of soldiers. And who laid the Yonker in the wet hold of a leaking ship where assuredly he would have died but for his mistress's nursing. I do not relish being an apple of discord in any place, but when I am thus taunted and insulted I must spurn the accusations from me. I do not mean to say that you did any of these things. On the contrary, I believe you were quite honest in all you did, but what I want to show is, that anyone's conduct may be brought under suspicion and yours as much as, if not more than, mine."

Hans had listened to these words, calmly and benevolently as they were spoken, with a feeling of rage and astonishment, and when their sounds had died away, he turned to his master, and said,

"A sad rascal that! is he not Yonker? Shall I just———?"
And tapping on his dagger he gave a mysterious nod in
Block's direction.

But Karel's face wore a sad and troubled expression. He shook his head decidedly and said in a tone of
grief :

"Why should you be so silly, Hans? You have
been with me now as long as I can remember, and
you know I am not in the habit of making friends
quickly, shake hands with Master Block, and go and
fetch some wine."

"Never," said Hans with energy. "Shake hands? Never.
I did not tell you Yonker, that in the forest at the rescue
when the cavalry was coming, this friend here said to
himself 'At last they are coming,' and that's why I
knocked him head over heels. That shows that he knew
they were coming."

" My dear fellow," said Block, in a merry tone, " you
deceive yourself. If I knew they were coming, I
should have been the last to sit there quietly, as if they
were not. I should have made away quick enough, I
assure you, having only escaped from them two days
before."

"Look here, Yonker," said Hans, who was not experienced in sophism, "this is what it comes to, I will
not be here while that fellow remains. So now you must
chose. Will you tell him to go, or shall I silence him?"

Karel loved his servant sincerely, and it was but
seldom that he refused him anything when he spoke in
such earnest. But, as in all his race, the feeling of gratitude was very strong. He could not insult or even

grieve the man who had saved his life. Moreover
Hans's decided tone somewhat irritated him, and thinking that his servant was not in earnest as to leaving, he
said curtly:

"Do not be a fool. Go down stairs and get us some
wine, and we'll talk about old times."

"No, Yonker, I must have a definite answer. You
must send that fellow away or I'll——"

"I'll go," said Block, suddenly. "Good-bye, Yonker.
I have not much luggage with me. My mantle and my
arms are all. I shall sleep in the hay, and may——"

"Stay, stop Gerard," he cried out as Block made a
movement to the door. "Look you Hans. You must
cease that conduct; Block remains here, and if you do not
like him, you must remain downstairs till I'm better.
So."

Hans had hardly heard a word .of this speech.
He had intently looked at Block, who stood before the
window. The sun had sunk, a grey twilight hung over
the town, and the sharp outline of his face could be distinctly seen against the dusk, revealing its sharp and
angular proportions to the full. His lips were parted
with a sort of diabolical smile of pleasure.

"Block, Bock, Block," muttered Hans as if lost in
thought. "I'll find out Peter Blink and see what he
says, that is the thing."

Then hearing his master's injunction to go he turned
to the door. With the opened door in his hand, he
paused, and once more approaching Block he stretched
out his hand, and said:

"Good evening, Master Block. *Good* evening. You

have not seen the last of me yet," and the door shut behind him.

Agnes and Maria were alone in the sitting room, the Baroness having gone to vespers. Having changed some of his clothes, Hans went into the room to bid them good bye. Both looked up.

"What is the matter? You look disturbed," said Agnes.

"And well I may be, Mistress Agnes, I am going away for some time."

"Going away, Hans? You have only just come," said Maria.

"Ah," said Hans, with a significant look. "I want you two young ladies to take particular care of the Yonker. I've had a quarrel with that fellow upstairs, and now my master is angry with me. I told him he was a traitor, and I think he is trying to do something with the Yonker, so be on your guard and do not leave him. I'm going to find Peter Blink, and then we shall see what he is." A moment later he had left the house unnoticed.

Chapter Nineteenth.

AN OLD FACE.

Two nights after Hans had left, Agnes and Maria were sitting alone in the room below. The two girls loved each other dearly, and as they were the whole day together, they told their secrets and laid their hearts open to each other. The Baroness, who always looked back with regret upon the splendid past which she longed to see restored, though she was proud of having lost it in the manner in which she had, could not enter into the spirit of the girls so fully as they did. She was moreover occupied with her household, which needed all her careful superintendence, and though she had but few acquaintances in the little town, between them and the observance of her masses she spent the greater part of her leisure. This evening she had as usual gone to the cathedral to attend vespers, and as Maria was not well enough to accompany her, she left her behind with Agnes.

Agnes sat with her arms folded in her lap, in a musing position. There was an expression of sadness in her beautiful eyes as she looked at the figure of her companion. And it was a sight well worth looking at. The golden light of the departing sun, reflected by the clouds, surrounded Maria with a soft ethereal light. It shed a kind of halo around the fair locks that dangled in profusion over the bodice of spotless white, which vainly strove to hide the whiteness of her bosom. The red eyes, and the nervous manner in which she worked at her spinning-wheel as if by rapid work to stop the thoughts which came crowding into her little head, told a tale of inward agitation and restlessness. The bright spot upon her cheeks, the brightness of her eyes told a tale even more sorrowful and more disquieting.

As the light grew dimmer, she bent more closely over her work, and one or two silent tears which she wiped away as quickly as they came, were the only language she spoke. But they spoke to Agnes with a deeper meaning than words. She laid her hand gently upon Maria's arm, and when the latter raised her head with a shy and nervous movement, and looked at her cousin as if to ask her meaning, Agnes said in a tender tone:

"You will spoil your eyes, dearest Maria, it is getting too dark. Lean your head upon my shoulder, and let us have a talk. I have to ask you something and I want all your attention."

Maria did as she was bid, and silently laid her head upon her cousin's shoulder. There seemed to be a mutual understanding between the two. Maria looked up to her cousin's high-minded piety and courage with admiration, while Agnes regarded the weak trembling little bird with feelings akin to those of a mother. She felt that it was her duty in a great measure to lead, and as she knew that the other would follow, she fulfilled her duty with prayerful conscientiousness.

For some moments she looked lovingly at the fair head that rested against her, and bending down she imprinted a tender kiss upon her forehead. It was hot, and so was the little hand that stole into her's at that moment.

"When I sit on a summer evening," said Agnes, "and see the sun setting, and hear the various sounds that come to us through the quick air I always call to mind the days of my childhood when I used to play the whole day in happy ignorance. I see the same things, I hear the same things, but with what different eyes, with what different ears. I remember one day, when I could not have been older than five years, a scaffold was erected the square in front of the Broodhuys to execute some malefactor, and I remember well how I played around it with some other children of my age, and asked my mother whether we could not always have it here as it was so nice for hide and seek. Little did I think then that some years after I would look upon another scaffold, such as I saw two months ago."

"I wish we could always remain children Agnes, dear," said Maria with a soft voice, "I often wish that we might play together such as we were then, and never, never alter."

"But Maria," said Agnes pensively, "if childhood has its charms, it has also its drawbacks. I think that to be entirely ignorant and careless of what goes on around us; to know little or nothing about the Word of God and what He did for us, and to have others bearing that responsibility which properly and justly belongs to us only, are surely not the reasons that should make us wish to return to childhood.

"But is it not unjust," said Maria, "to give us duties and responsibilities greater than we can bear? We are in this world and we must do something, but when we look up to what we should do and what we must do, it looks to me as if these were as high and as insurmountable as the tower of the church our Blessed Lady."

"Maria, Maria," answered her cousin, in a grave and yet loving voice, "do you believe in Jesus Christ? Do you believe that He died to bring you to heaven, and do you believe that He would make the entrance to that heaven an impossibility for you? Has He not promised to help you in everything, however difficult it may be? I know that if we were left to ourselves we would do nothing. If the burghers of Holland could remain rich and free by sitting still they would not fight. And so it is with you and me. We *have got* heaven, we are saved, but we must work and suffer to keep what we have, and if Jesus suffered and did so much for us, our part is surely little in comparison. But then, my dear Maria, you should not look at what you are required to do first. Look at Jesus, look at the glorious things which are ours, and after that, all things else, imprisonment, suffering, torture, death are nothing. Oh, I wish I could read to you a part of the little book written by Dr. Luther at Wittemberg. He says so plainly and yet so truly that if we look upon our own little cross first, our eyes get so dimmed with tears that we cannot see anything else, while if we look at the big cross at once and at the immense sufferings of Jesus, our little crosses dwindle away to nought. Take courage Maria, and go to Jesus at once. Not to His mother for she did not suffer for you, but to Jesus, and He will help you."

Maria had listened to Agnes with suspended breath. It was plain that the words made a deep impression upon her. She was silent for some time. Then she said with a sigh, which sounded almost like a sob :

"Oh Agnes, I shall never forget what I did in Brussels that night. Do you think I can still be forgiven."

"My dear girl?" said Agnes, "Peter denied it three times and he was forgiven. Your greatest sins will be forgiven if you repent. Go to Jesus."

"Ah but it was so very wicked of me, just after we had read in the book, too," said Maria. "But I cannot tell you how much I have suffered from the thought of it. When I became conscious again, you were away and I was told that I must go downstairs ; I went into my bedroom and I never came out of it until Gritta told me that you were to be removed. And when I saw you taken away, Agnes, for they would not allow me to speak to you, my heart sank within me, and but for that kind skipper and Gerard Block who helped me to escape, I should perhaps have been dead now."

"I do not know," said Agnes, "but I can never look at that man Block but a strange feeling comes over me, a something which I cannot name. I have seen his face somewhere, I am certain, but where, I cannot recollect. I do not like him, I——"

A cough behind them made both girls start with a slight cry of alarm. In the doorway, and hardly visible in the indistinct twilight stood Block wrapped in a mantle.

"What do you want, sir?" said Agnes haughtily, rising, "know you not that you should not enter this room without previously knocking ?"

"I crave your pardon, madam," said he, making a step forward, "I knocked thrice and receiving no answer I made so bold as to enter. I assure you I would not have done so had I known that it would be unpleasant to you, but I wish only to tell you that your cousin the Yonker is sound asleep, and I am going out in the dark to see whether I can gain any intelligence about our cause."

"Very well, sir," said Agnes, and Block withdrew. A moment afterwards the front door was heard to close, but Agnes remained in the same postion, as if she had all at once been struck by some thought.

"Can it be possible!" she said to herself "can it be the same face? Let me remember it again."

"Agnes," said Maria, anxiously, "what is the matter? You are quite cold, and you tremble all over, and you are breathing as if there is something that terrifies you;—what is it Agnes?"

"Maria," said Agnes in a trembling voice, "I know now where I saw that face before. I am sure of it,—certain. It was on that evening that Karel came suddenly into our room—you know the night previous to the one that everything happened—I saw him looking through the window. He drew back when he saw me, but I saw his face for all that. And it looked exactly as it does now, in the same light and I remember the same mantle too."

She stopped and there was a silence in the room.

"Hans, too, has warned us against him. Who can he be, and what does he want?" said Maria in a terrified voice.

"I do not know. Let us go and awaken Karel and ask him. To-morrow night after dark we are going to Van

R.

Alphen, the grain-merchant's. Wouter Barends will preach and there will be a good many friends there. We shall ask them for advice.

"Will Wouter Barends be there?" said Maria, in accents of pleasure, "O do let us go. But let us go to Karel now."

And the two girls rose. At the same moment, Block slipped away from the door of the room and disappeared through the front door which was ajar, for though he had shut it, he had not gone out but opened it again softly.

"Aha," he muttered, "she's found me out has she, and she's going to Van Alphen's to-morrow night. Very good. *Very* good. She will get very little out of Galama to-night."

So it was. They tried in vain to awaken Karel whom Block had drugged, and that evening and the next day they were in a fever of suspense. They resolved not to speak to the Baroness until they had been to Van Alphen's. No sooner was it dark, therefore, than they set out, and left the house before the Baroness had returned from vespers. Little did they know that they would never see her again.

Chapter Twentieth.

A CONVENTICLE.

"Come Dirk, make haste with that cart. It is past six o clock now by the bell of the cathedral and we have not half done our work."

These words were spoken by a buxom lass of some five-and-twenty summers whose dress revealed her to be a servant girl. She was engaged with another servant girl and three men in clearing a barn, which seemed to be used as a warehouse for grain, for sacks and bags of every size and description were piled upon each other and one large waggon full of flour-sacks was standing half way in the open door. It was the barn of Van Alphen, the corn-merchant, and the secret favourer of the new religion, in which that evening its followers were to come together. Its position for this purpose was exceedingly favourable, situated as it was at the back of his house and separated from it by a yard. It could be approached by this yard, through the house and also from the other side, where a small path, which led through Van Alphen's garden, allowed people to come to it from the walls of the town unseen by anyone. They were just engaged in putting three carts before the back door so as to hide any gleams of light that might shine through that night, and in arranging seats for the expected visitors.

"I hope there will be a good many coming to-night," said Dirk, a tall broad-shouldered fellow who was throwing the sacks about as if they had been empty. "There's no doubt about it that Master Barends is *the* man for us. He gives us good stuff, I can tell you."

"Yes, Dirk," answered the girls, sweeping up the floor, "you are right there. And I hope you'll listen to him to-night and take to heart what he says. For you know Dirk, that you like a little bit of fighting now and then, and that's not right, you know."

"Ah, dash it all," said Dirk, pitching a heavy sack on one side, "you women you do not know anything at all about what we men have to go through. Hand us that iron hook. Thank you. When I hear the Spaniards or the Catholics talk against the Prince, my blood gets up you know, and I do not mind giving them a clout on the pate for it."

"But you should not, Dirk," answered the girl. "Does not the Bible say that you should overcome evil with good, and that vengeance is the Lord's? If you acknowledge the word as true you should do what it says."

"Yes, Alida," said another of the men who was a good deal older, "that is what I am continually saying to Dirk, but he will not listen. I say if the Lord wants to revenge himself He'll do it without him."

"Just help me to lift this board here on to this stone. Now I will tell you what it is," said Dirk after they had adjusted a board so that it formed a seat for some four or five persons. "It's just this; I know very wel that Master Barends is speaking the truth, and I do not believe any more in priests, and absolution, and the Pope and the Holy Virgin than any of you. But if that Bible tells me that I must not fight against the Duke of Alva, and that the Prince of Orange is a scoundrel, I say it is wrong, that's all."

"But it does say that you must not fight, Dirk," began the girl when he interrupted her.

"Give me the text then. Chapter, how much, verse what, eh? There you are, you see. Paul did not say so, and Peter did not, and I tell you what," and he paused to adjust another board, "if any of these soldiers come to night and molest us, I'll——," and he flourished a formidable crowbar.

"Know you not that Jesus chided Peter for using the sword and cutting off the man's ear?" asked the elder man.

"Doest think we want more than four rows of seats? We will not get many people; for the bloodhounds are sniffling," said Alida.

"I think it is enough," said Dirk. "Now I tell you how I always looked at that story of the sword. Suppose you and I were walking together and some soldier was wanting to take you, and I was to pull his nose, and then run away. Why, you would say, what is the use of that, either kill him or let him alone. Now what was the use of Peter cutting off that man's ears. That would not stop them from taking Jesus. But if he had taken and put them all to flight so that they dare not come back, may be the Lord would have said 'Right.'"

Here their help was invoked by the others, and their

conversation ceased.   But it may be remarked that Dirk
was a sort of type of a great many of the inhabitants of
the Netherlands, who had abandoned Popery and clearly
saw its errors, but who, while they embraced Protestantism
because of its truth, lacked either the inclination or the
conviction to put all its injunctions into execution.

When Van Alphen's servants, who were all adherents
of the new religion, had arranged the barn,—and the
arrangement was very simple, consisting of a table with
a chair before it and four rows of seats—they went into
the house till dusk should come. When at last it came the
seats gradually filled.   One by one the hearers crept in
through a little side door and took their seats, and the
warmth with which they were welcomed showed that
the saying still held true, "How these Christians love
each other."

Rich and poor, old and young, were mixed up without
distinction, and conducted their conversation in a low
tone, and when at last Van Alphen and the preacher
Wouter Barends appeared, they were surrounded and
almost overwhelmed with affectionate questions and
greetings.   They were both in the prime of life ; Van
Alphen was a tall fine man, undaunted and honest in his
appearance, while Wouter Barends was a thin man who
looked as if he had suffered much, with a face full of
sorrow, and yet with a marvellous expression of bliss
and benignity in his clear bright eyes.

The meeting between him and Agnes and Maria, who
had come among the earliest, was very touching, and
the hearts of many were softened when they saw the pious
man greet his daughter in the faith with a holy kiss.

At last, when he had shaken hands with all present, he took his seat at the table and opened the Bible before him. The table was very simple and such indeed was the whole appearance of the place. The only light that illuminated this curious improvised chapel came from a kitchen lamp which was standing on the table near the preacher's Bible. Nor was any more light required, for Bibles were scarce in those days, and hymn-books could not be used, as singing was dangerous. So the audience had nothing to do but to listen. And this they did with heart and soul. What the preacher said, it is true, was nothing extraordinary as to language, style or eloquence; neither did it contain anything beyond the old fundamental truths of the Gospel. But these old truths were new to them, and the earnest belief with which the preacher proclaimed these truths made him more eloquent in the estimation of his hearers than the greatest orator was held to be by his audience in Athens or Rome.

"Mind, beloved," he said, among other things, "a great mercy is bestowed upon us, that we are deemed worthy to suffer for the name of our blessed Lord and Saviour. You know that He did not refuse to give His blood for us to save us from the wrath to come. So we ought to be ready to give our blood for Him to show that we count Him worth more than life itself. You also know that it has pleased God, in His boundless mercy, to permit me to bear in my body a few scars as a witness of His truth. I am outlawed by the priests, though I was a priest myself, and my relatives have cast me out, and I am hunted from place to place, being every day in danger of life, and in fear of death. But I thank my God that He gives me grace to rejoice with St. Paul at the prospect of being offered upon the sacrifice and service of your faith if God should will it so.

"Only, my beloved, let me have this great consolation, that I may be assured that the word which I have preached to you, and which I am willing to confirm by my blood, has not been in vain, but powerful in the strength of God to pluck you out of the power of darkness, out of the errors of Antichrist, and to lead you to the only Mediator, even Jesus Christ, the Son of the living God. For to know Him is life, and there is no salvation without Him ; but any other mediator, whether Pope, prelate, or priest, that places himself by His side or between Him and us, is a curse, and damned and destined to everlasting destruction. For our God is a jealous God and a consuming fire who does not give His honour to another. But He is plenteous in mercy to those who with broken hearts and contrite spirits, as poor lost sinners, come to Him through the only way, the new and living way which He has appointed, even the Son of His love. So then, my beloved, I beseech you——"

Here, suddenly, a soft rap was heard upon the back-door of the barn, and a voice whispered "Alarm, the soldiers are coming."

Every one started to his feet, and looked at the others with suspended breath. Then the low and clear voice of Van Alphen was heard distinctly.

"My friends, listen one moment. Fly through this door, which will bring you into the yard. A little gate to the right of it will bring you to a garden belonging to one of us. Through that garden you can get into another, and thus on to the Quay. I shall help Master Barends. Let the men help the women, and God help us all."

"Amen," said Barends. The light was turned out and the door opposite to that at which the warning cry had been given was opened. There was a little moonlight, and it enabled the reformers to see, although indistinctly, what they were doing. The seats were thrown down or put hurriedly aside and every body crowded to the door. At that moment voices were heard at the back door and a command was given. Immediately the noise of wheels followed, a heavy blow sounded on the door and a voice cried "Open this door." The trick of the servant in putting three large carts before the door had helped them but little for they had already been removed.

"They are coming, Agnes!" whispered Maria, as they had just disentangled themselves from their seat which was nearest the door, at which another blow and a louder injunction to open was just being given. Many of the people had by this time reached the yard, and fled into the adjoining garden ; but not so Agnes and Maria. Having ventured to come without a protector they were now left alone, and as they had but little experience of personal danger they scarcely knew what to do, when a blow with the butt of a matchlock made the doors fly open, and some twenty soldiers entered the barn, headed by a priest who held a torch. The persons inside uttered a stifled shriek and pressed into the yard, but the soldiers perceived them and rushed off in pursuit.

Before long they returned with some dozen men

and women. I shall not attempt to describe the scene that now ensued, illuminated as it was in a ghastly fantastic way by the red glare of the torch which the priest held in his hand.

The soldiers with ferocious-looking faces and in their frightful attire, seemed to represent a pandemonium. The men and women whom they surrounded could be likened to sheep which are being led to the slaughter. Some of the weakest wrung their hands in terror and seemed ready to swoon away. Some, still under the impression of the word which they had just heard, seemed to prepare with determined resignation for the hardships which they were expecting. Some of the more courageous joyfully and enthusiastically exhorted their fellow-sufferers to rejoice in God, and to continue steadfast in the faith. Among the latter was Agnes. Like a true heroine she stood in the midst of the dreadful confusion, beseeching Maria who was ready to swoon away by her side, now to show her strength in Jesus.

"The Lord is with us," she cried, "keep up courage dear; with Him we are more than conquerors. He will not forsake us."

Her words were not in vain. Suddenly, as if grasped by an invisible hand Maria raised herself up by Agnes's side and said:

"You are right. He who is with us is mightier than they who are against us," and looking Agnes in the face, she added with a smile; "if we die we shall die together, shall we not; but thank God that Wouter Barends is saved."

The two girls, whose appearance singled them out

from the rest of the prisoners, immediately drew the attention of the priest.

"Are you Agnes Vlossert?" he asked.

"I am," was the answer.

"And is that girl by your side, Maria Galama?"

The priest's look made poor Maria shudder. Her voice seemed choking in her throat.

"With what right do you put these questions?" asked Agnes, in a dignified tone.

Her boldness so surprised the priest that he felt for a moment disarmed. Indeed, it seemed to inspire one of the male prisoners, for stepping forward, he said:

"And what is the reason why you have disturbed our harmless meeting?"

"Harmless meeting!" repeated the priest, who had meanwhile resumed his insolence, "full well you know, you cursed heretics, that your gathering is an abomination in the sight of God and all His holy angels."

"Why?" asked the prisoner.

"Because—because—why?" said the priest working himself into a passion. "I have not come here to argue with such cursed dogs, like you, you shall soon know it when you are on the rack."

"We have done nothing against God, nor yet against the King of Spain," answered the prisoner, "we are as loyal as we are good Christians."

"Hold your tongue, you accursed heretic," cried the priest, and turning towards a troop of soldiers, who had just entered the barn he asked:

"Have you found the preacher?"

"The bird is flown," answered the sergeant, "we have

searched the house from top to bottom, but we have seen
no living creature except an old grandmother and a
baby."

"Well then, let us go," said the priest; "do your duty,"
he added to the sergeant.

Chains and cords were produced, and the men were
fettered with the former, the women bound with the latter.
Only Agnes and Maria were excepted.

"These are Sextus's two little doves," the priest said to
himself, and turning to the sergeant he said; "I'll take
charge of these two ladies."

A moment later the barn was empty and nobody knew
whither the prisoners were conveyed.

Chapter Twenty-First.

JUST MISSED.

WE shall not venture to describe the consternation of
the Baroness when on that evening the two girls did not
return.   On reaching home, after vespers, she had been
informed by the old, half-deaf servant that the two
young ladies had gone out and would be back in little
more than an hour.   She had then felt a sensation of
fear, but resolved to wait calmly until they should return.
But one hour elapsed, another passed, a third was sounded
on the bell of the cathedral, and the girls came not.
With a beating heart the poor woman then crept upstairs
and knocked at the door of the room where her son and
Block were sleeping.   It was opened by the latter who
was still dressed.   Complying with her half-choked wish
to come downstairs, he followed her and calmly listened
to the poor woman as she told him her fears and terrors,
and asked him for advice.

What ? the two young ladies not come home yet ?
when had they gone out ? Three hours ago.   They could
have had no intention to elope or anything of the sort ?
No, none whatever.   Did the Baroness think, had she
any suspicion that they were at all heretical ? The Baron-

ess grew pale, and said she had. Perhaps they had gone
to some meeting which had been discovered! The
Baroness covered her face with her hands and burst into
a fit of weeping. Block, as a sympathizing friend, tried
to console her. It might be nothing, after all. They
might have escaped and be at some friend's house. Or
they might not have been at a meeting, and perhaps they
were all safe at some friend's. What was the use of sorrowing before there was any reason for it? He would go
out and find out all he could; he would be sure to hear
of something. Oh, no, he must not leave her. He was
at present her only help and protector and her son would
not be able to do without him. But at last he prevailed
upon the Baroness to allow him to put on his mantle
and creep out in the darkness.

He was absent for about an hour, during which time
the Baroness poured out her heart before her little crucifix and soaked her kerchief with tears. When at Agnes's
pressing invitation she had allowed Maria to go to Brussels
she had done so with a heavy heart. She knew that her
daughter was timid and inexperienced, and though Karel
after his first term at Louvain was in raptures about his
cousin, she could hardly be prevailed upon to allow Maria
to go thither alone. She deemed it necessary, however,
that her daughter should see something of the world, but
as she once for all had made up her mind never again to
visit the capital, as long as it was the seat of the tyrant's
government, she gave her consent reluctantly. Since
then she had spent her days in loneliness, hoping for her
child's return, watching with eagerness the movements
going on in the country, and dividing her time between

religion, charity and her friends. Now however she began
to reproach herself for her carelessness in not sufficiently
guarding her children against the dangers of heresy.
She saw the evil, she felt already the approach of its
dreadful consequences, she shuddered as she thought of
what might yet become of them all, and she implored
the holy Virgin to protect them.

When Block came back, he confirmed all her fears.
He had spoken with five or six watchmen and one
soldier, who had nearly discovered him, and from them
he had learned that there had been a heretical meeting
somewhere on the Quay and that soldiers had come and
taken everybody off. Whether Agnes and Maria had
been there and whether they had escaped or not, he
had not been able to find out, but he would go out again
the next evening and get more information.

Very little did the Baroness sleep that night and when
Galama saw her pale face and swollen eyes the next
morning, it was but a few moments until he knew all.
He became half mad. He leaped up in bed and but for
Block would have leaped out of it. He insisted upon
dressing and going to the magistrates; he would give
himself up instead of the girls; he would promise to
tell them the most important things; he would force
them, threaten them; he would———. And he buried his
head in his pillow and wept.

The Baroness prayed him to be calm and wait. The
fate of Agnes and Maria was not certain as yet and at
any rate rashness would do no good. And Block, when
Karel had become somewhat calmed, put the case clearly
before him, railed against the priests, insinuated some-

thing as if Hans had a hand in it, praised the two noble girls, grew intensely patriotic, but advised him to be quiet and get well as soon as possible. He would in the meantime try and find out where the girls were; at any rate, find out something about them, and perhaps they might yet be able to get them back without imparting to the magistrates any secrets. Nor had he any difficulty in finding out plenty about the whole affair. The quiet little town of Brill had not had such a stir and excitement since the image of the Virgin in the cathedral fell upon one of the bishops and killed him on the spot. Every one spoke about it, every one pointed out who had been taken, every one wondered where the preacher and Van Alphen could have gone, and most people lamented the prospect of having to witness the execution of some of their fellow-citizens. They were spared the spectacle; for two days after all the victims were taken away to Brussels, but, as Block who told all this to the Baroness and her son, asserted, Agnes and Maria were not amongst them. From that moment a gloom setled upon Karel's face, and he set himself with a determination, so to say, to get well.

He often jumped out of bed and walked round the room as if nothing had ever been the matter with him. He caught up a sword and began fencing with Block, and though he was soon disarmed, it was a warning to the Jesuit not to delay the execution of his plan much longer. Nor did he. In the long hours that the two were necessarily alone together, Block crept deeper and deeper into the unfortunate Yonker's confidence. He had already obtained some very valuable information, and he reasonably hoped to get all he wanted. But he was resolved to proceed cautiously, and not lose his game a third time. Nor were caution and care at all out of place.

It is true, in a moment, perhaps of boasting pride, certainly of irritation, Galama had told Hans that he had no secrets for Block. But when the heat of his emotions had vanished and he was again the calm, thinking Frisian, he acknowledged to himself that it would be as well not to tell his friend everything at once, but to wait till further events should make further disclosures desirable or necessary. Thus, as the Jesuit had rightly conjectured, where torture or the threat of death would produce nothing but scorn with the high-minded Dutchman, it was possible, nay likely, that in moments of confidence and of mutual sympathy the youth might be made to hand the priest the key to that important secret correspondence, in which he had played such an active part, and which was doing so much damage to the cause of tyranny and Popery in Holland.

As the sources of the Jesuit's information were naturally very extensive, and the secret sign of his order procured for him a general assistance and obedience, he was able to use all the weapons which his craft and his system, put into his hands. By degrees, as the Yonker's strength became greater, and his energy and courage required food, the Jesuit gave him the detailed news of everything that happened in the country. He wept with him over the account of the execution of his own uncles and the two Counts. He stormed and raged over the terrible defeat which the Duke of Alva had given to

S

Count Louis' troops. He bitterly cursed the same Duke who had imposed another tax upon the already so heavily burdened inhabitants ; and he exulted whenever news came to Brill that one of the ships belonging to the Sea Beggars had seized a Spanish trader or damaged a Spanish troopship.

Thus, by degrees, did he spin his web around his victim. Thus, inch by inch, did he draw into the snare the unsuspecting patriot who was already rejoicing in the glorious deeds which Block never intended that he should do. Thus each day the Frisian's heart became more and more entwined in the coils of his fascinating, but venomous friend.

One evening, the Baroness, after having performed her duties in the household with a heavy heart, went up to her little bedroom, which communicated by a door with the room in which her son and Block were sitting. The disappearance of the two girls affected her more deeply than she would acknowledge to herself. When she thought of them, her meek, her silent, her loving daughter, and her frank and noble-minded niece, she felt inclined to lie down and die. She went into her little closet, and throwing herself down before the image of the Virgin, passed her time in weeping and in fervent prayer.

Meanwhile, Karel and Block had a conversation in the next room. The Yonker who was almost as strong now as before, was sitting on a low chair near the window ; Block a little way from him and nearer the door which communicated with the Baroness's room. An oil lamp on the table threw an insufficient light upon the two men.

Their tone was earnest, and on Karel's side, somewhat passionate.

"And do you not think it a glorious thing to be fight_ ing in behalf of our dear country, and of the Church?" asked Block.

"Not I, Gerard. My great aim, henceforth, will be twofold : to free our country from the tyranny of Alva and from that of the Pope. Which of the two is most hateful, I know not, but both must be abolished," answered Galama.

"I acknowledge that there are fearful defects in our Church," resumed Block, "but still we must remember that notwithstanding these, it is the only saving Church. You must be aware that even Count Egmont died in this belief, and that the Prince of Orange upholds it."

Block was right so far. Count Egmont had died a Roman Catholic, though Count Horn had refused the aid of the priest, and had died a Protestant. The Prince of Orange, though he, too, had become a Protestant, had not yet publicly intimated this great change in his religious views.

"Supposing your assertion to be true, my dear Gerard," said Karel, "I shall not attain to salvation by following the examples of all the counts and princes of the world. My only guide is God's Word, and when that tells me that all ideas about priests and a saving Church are wrong, what more do I want ? But I deny that the Prince thinks about these matters as you suppose. I have heard him say myself that real liberty and Popery cannot go together. Have you ever considered that question ? "

"I have ; but I never came to that conclusion."

"And I know," continued Galama, "that the Prince did not say that upon the spur of the moment, but that, with him, it was the result of deep thought, and of careful observation, and could any one call him a Papist when he believes, that the very principle of Popery is slavery itself ? "

"Ah, Karel," sighed Block, "when you come into contact with such reasoners, and hear the arguments of such great men as the Prince, it is no wonder, that you become convinced, and enthusiastic. I envy you in having been chosen for so honourable a post. Many a time, I have lain awake of a night, thinking how I would employ every particle of my energy in doing the work that you have been doing. I would consider it the object of my highest ambition."

"If it is honourable it is perilous also," said Galama, not a little elated by his companion's adroit flattery ; "every hour you run a thousand risks, every man you approach has to be looked upon with suspicion" (Galama might have reproached himself here), "your sword, your dagger, your pistols have to be ready at a moment's notice, and not once must your heart give way before the stupendous task you undertake."

"I do not know," said Block, "whether your words imply a reproach or even a hint. I think I have given you sufficient proof that both my courage and my skill in weapons are sufficient for anything that may befall me."

"Nay, Gerard, you entirely mistake the meaning of my words," said the Yonker, "I would be the last person in this world to accuse you of anything like cowardice or incapacity, having had so evident a proof of the contrary in Brussels. But you forget that you know nothing of the dangers of which I speak, and that not knowing them, you cannot tell whether you would be equal to the emergencies."

"You are mistaken, Yonker, when you imagine that I know nothing of them," said Block. "Have I not crossed the whole breadth of the land after I separated from Peter Blink to find you? And more than that, I am intimately acquainted with Herman de Ruyter, the *Emissario*, as he is called by the Spaniards, and he has told me many things, which even you know little of."

"The Emissario?" cried Galama, in a voice of pleased surprise, "do you indeed know him? You never mentioned his name before. What like is he? I have heard much of him, but I never saw him."

"I did not mention his name, because I thought you knew him," answered Block, "but to tell you what he is like is more than I can do. He is tall and broad-shouldered, with an immense muscular power and a clever head, that is all I can say. For the rest he is like everybody and like nobody—a cattle-drover, a hawker, a beggar, a soldier, a priest, a farmer, even a woman he acts with an accuracy as astonishing as his courage is remarkable. At the same time he is wonderfully good-natured and kind-hearted, and many a time has he risked himself in protecting a poor man or woman against oppression and cruelty."

"Ah, he has the privilege of holding direct communication with the Prince," said Galama, with a little sigh, "which I only had so long as he and his brother were in France with the Admiral de Coligny."

"But you had surely to employ many arts before you could see the Prince?" said the Jesuit, who felt himself coming nearer the mark, "for I have heard that even he is surrounded by spies, employed by the Spanish Court and the Jesuits."

"Yes," answered the Frisian, "that was sometimes the most dangerous part of all. For it was possible that his nearest friend was his enemy, and no letter was ever delivered into any other hands but his own and those of Count Louis."

"Even his very secretary that wrote the answer might be a secret traitor, and paid by Spain," said the Jesuit, musingly.

"He had none," answered the Yonker. "It was beautiful to see his decision. He read the letters as soon as he could decipher them, and immediately sat down and wrote the answer himself, sealing it with his own ring."

"And did you always know the contents of these letters?" asked Block.

"Not I. And it was far better, too, for had I been seized, no information of any kind could have escaped me had I been tortured."

"But the letters would have been seized," the priest said, inquiringly.

"What of it. Firstly, they were written in cipher, then every town had a different name————"

"And men have different names, too, sometimes," sounded a deep voice behind them. Both looked up.

The door was open and about a yard within the room stood the figure of a man wrapped in a large cloak and with a felt hat on.

The rays of the lamp, faint as they were, failed to make his features distinguishable at the distance at which he stood.

"What means this intrusion," said the Yonker, frowning, as he rose from the arm-chair in which he sat.

"No intrusion, I hope, Yonker," said the stranger, making a few steps forward and taking off his hat. Both at once recognized Hans. "I have only come to pay you a friendly visit," he continued. "I could not so soon forget the old connection between us, and I have come to beg your pardon for all the wrong that I may have done you, and you too, sir," he said, turning to Block, "and," he continued in a slow and significant tone, "I hope to make amends for what I have done."

There was a mixture of hatred and playfulness in the look which he cast at the Jesuit. The latter sat immoveable with one hand resting upon the table, while the other played with the hilt of his dagger; his face was cold, and he returned Hans's look with one of haughty defiance and disdain. Galama, on the other hand, sat in his chair restless, and like a young horse chafing under the harness. He opened his mouth once or twice to interrupt Hans, frowned, looked calm again, and apparently was at a loss how to treat the new comer. Hans soon helped him out of his dilemma.

"In the few weeks that I have been away, Yonker," he said, "I have got hold of some very important information. I have heard that neither my Lord de

Treslong nor your great uncle, Igo, died in the battle of Jemmingen. So far, therefore, we may rejoice. But excuse me, Yonker, will you allow me to bring in a fellow Beggar that I have brought with me. He is a friend, at least an *acquaintance* of both of you I think————"

"Ay, Ay! Hans, don't call it friend," said a voice which came from the door.

"Here he is," said Hans, "he has not waited for your consent, apparently, Yonker. But I suppose you will have no objection. Come in Peter. It's only Peter Blink, gentlemen."

Both men turned their eyes a second time from Hans to the door, and beheld a figure, which at other times would have evoked general laughter. It certainly was the figure of a man, but its proportions were somewhat out of the common. A little fat body supported and flanked by a magnificent pair of legs and arms which threw and flung themselves in all directions, and would have been long enough for a man of twice his size, short thick neck and a round head, the hair, the beard, and the chubby cheeks partaking largely of the fiery hue, presented a man whose appearance was sufficiently peculiar to be remembered when once seen. The general impression which he made was one of good-natured stupidity, but those little grey eyes of his which darted all round the room, and had taken in everything at a glance ere he had reached Hans' side, spoke a direct contradiction to this first impression. Four words will suffice to give the readers a proper idea of what he really was. He was very cunning, very quiet, very strong, and very brave ; thus, though nobody suspected the fat-cheeked farmer, who sat in a corner dozing or quaffing his beer, and many amused themselves at the expense of the dwarf who sung old ballads for a few groats, yet many a one felt the strength of his arm when at the head of a select band he acted promptly and cleverly upon the information which he thus picked up. Swinging his long arms and taking immense strides he stood in a moment by the side of Hans, and made a bow to the Yonker.

When the Jesuit perceived the figure of Blink in the door he turned ashy pale. A look of ferocity and hatred came over his face, and his hand spasmodically grasped the cup of wine on the little table. Hans, who had eyed him attentively, smiled slightly when he saw this, and looked at his former master, who did not seem to notice it. When he looked back the priest had composed himself. He lay back in his chair and eyed the new addition to their company with perfect calmness.

"There must be some mistake here," he said, slowly. "If this man's name is Peter Blink, it certainly is not the Peter Blink who recommended *me*."

"Ah, but it's the Peter Blink who wrote the letter," said Hans, "eh, Yonker?"

"Certainly," said Karel, jumping up from his chair, and grasping the dwarf's hand. How do you do, Peter, my old friend? As brave and as stout as ever?"

"Blooming, Yonker, thank you," said Peter, with a gasp.

"And do you really not know this gentleman?" he asked, at the same time turning to the Jesuit.

"Well enough, well enough," said Peter, and added with a chuckle, "too well!"

"Perhaps the gentlemen would like to sit down, so that, at any rate now, we can make acquaintance," said Block, half rising, and at the same time moving his chair a little nearer the door.

"Thank you," said Hans placing a chair for Peter, "now that you mention it, and the Yonker has no objections; take a chair, Peter, I prefer standing, that will help us quicker through the business." And he placed himself in such a position that he could prevent any movement the Jesuit might make upon his master.

"Have you no brother or relation who bears the same name as you do, Master Blink?" said Block, in a tone, as if he desired to begin a friendly and interesting conversation about common topics.

"No," said Blink. "Only one Peter," and stretching forth his hand, he seized the can of wine and took a vigorous draught of its contents.

"Suppose we refresh your memory a little, Master, h'm, Block is it not?" said Hans, "perhaps you do not remember seeing this gentleman in the city of Amsterdam, where he pulled you out of the canal into which you had been thrown by some of your enemies, of which, now that I come to think of it, you must have a good many. Was not that the case, Peter?"

"Right, Hans. Out of the Spuy, near St. Clovis's bridge," answered Blink, taking another refresher.

"And perhaps you do not remember how he carried you, wet as you were, to his own house, and nursed you there; and perhaps you do not remember, either, how one day when you were nearly better, you heard this gentleman here and a friend of his, Gerard *Bock*, talk about Yonker Galama. Eh, Peter?"

" All right, Hans ! Go on," encouraged the dwarf.

" And of course you forget how, when you saw Peter write the letter of recommendation, you got out of the house at night and had both him and Gerard imprisoned in the morning, while you walked off to the Yonker with the scrap of paper. Is not that correct, Peter ?"

" Beautiful," answered Peter, wiping his mouth with the back of his hand, but whether this referred to Hans' tale, or to the contents of the can, which he had by this time removed we cannot say.

The Yonker, in the meanwhile, had watched and listened to the dialogue in silence. He breathed heavily. His eyes stared now at one of the speakers, then at the other, then at the Jesuit, while his colour came and went alternately, as the gravest suspicions, the darkest forebodings or the slightest hope that he was dreaming or that it was a mere trick, were uppermost in his mind. When Hans had done speaking, he looked at Block, who lay in his chair eyeing the two men with calm indifference.

"I do not know," said Block, "what object you may have in passing off a damnable imposture upon me, but this I will swear that the Peter Blink from whom I received my recommendation was a different personage from this miserable, wine drinking, fat-faced dwarf who looks as if he could not count three. I hope the Yonker does not suspect me of such ingratitude ; but to give him better proof of my innocence, let me get the letter which is in my cloak on the door."

He rose. But Hans stepped between him and the door and extending his arm he said :

" Do not trouble yourself. You cannot get out that way.

There is one of the Sea-Beggars at the top and another at the bottom of the stairs, and both would run you through the body if you attempted to pass them. I have been cautious this time. But we will dismiss this little business of Master Blink's for the moment, and suppose that you have been noble and grateful towards him. You can not get away yet, so have patience."

"That's right, Hans, my boy. There's more coming," said Peter with a look at the empty can.

"Unfortunately," continued Hans, "your plans with both of us failed. You did not know that Peter has as many friends in Amsterdam as you have in Rome, and that his jailer happened to be his own cousin. No more did you know that I have got friends here in Brill who would help me against all the soldiers and spies which you had put out to catch me when I was sent away. So though you had not bargained for it, I got out of Brill, and Peter out of prison. And we two set to work to find you out."

"And we have done it too, Hans, my boy," chuckled Blink, rubbing his hands.

"Now, Yonker," continued Hans, changing his tone from one of bitter mockery to one of earnestness and energy, "just listen to what we have discovered, and after that keep him as your friend and dismiss me if you like. I have discovered that this holy man, after Mistress Agnes and I were caught in the Broodhuys, had a long conversation with the *visitor* of the Inquisition, for both of them belong to the well known order of Jesus, or, as it should be called, of the devil. Gritta, who is by no means such a fool when she talks to *me*, saw both of them through the keyhole of the kitchen door."

Galama gave a start, when looking up he saw the Jesuit turn pale once more, and cast an anxious look about him. He endeavoured to speak, but emotions choked his throat, and the only thing he could do was to feel for his sword that stood against the wall.

"Sit down, Yonker," growled Peter Blink, pressing him into his chair, "there's more coming yet. Bless ye, we have only begun."

"Then we have found out that this reverend gentleman, whose name, by the bye, is Father Sextus," continued Hans, keeping his eyes fixed upon the Jesuit who evidently had great difficulty in keeping calm under thes low and measured tones of Hans's accusation, "had the best reasons for thinking that there was *no cavalry coming*, inasmuch as he mounted a horse and returned home with the officer when all the fallen Beggars had been despatched. That is the man, Yonker, who lingered and dawdled and prolonged every action until we should all be caught in the trap. When I heard the cavalry coming on, I watched him, and I heard him say 'At last!' Do you remember *that*, Father?" And Hans stretched forth his neck and peered at the Jesuit.

"I deny your accusations," said the latter with a voice trembling with rage. "They are base, lying calumnies, and were I master here instead of guest I would bury this dagger in your lying throat."

"Oh, we'll have a turn at that presently," said Hans with a sneer. "Only you will have many things to atone for; such as the skipper, who risked his life for the Yonker, and poor Gritta herself, who, I suppose, will be hanged by this time, too."

The Yonker flew up with every passion expressed

upon his face. But happily for the Jesuit, Blink once more pressed him down.

"Do not spoil the game, Yonker," he said, "there is plenty more coming."

"Well, Hans, for God's sake, make it short!" gasped Karel "If all you say be true, he is already guilty enough. Take him away, and do with him what you think proper. And may God have mercy upon him."

"Ah, but hear the rest first, Yonker," said Hans, " I have found out that he had a hand in the disappearance of Mistress——."

"What?" gasped Galama, nearly choking and struggling under the grasp of Peter Blink, who held him in his chair. "He——"

He fell back overpowered by his passion and looked tremblingly and with flaming eyes at the Jesuit, on whose face the scowl of defiance and the look of guilt were enough to confirm what Hans had said.

"That is the holy father," cries Hans "that is the follower of Jesus who brought Mistress Maria hither to suit his purpose and who, when he saw that she was likely to be troublesome, removed her and sweet Mistress Agnes God knows where. Say, villain, if you do yet hope for a morsel of grace from my hands, the hands of Hans, who never spared an enemy yet, say, speak! where are they? I know they were taken away by your orders. Where—— ?"

A roar rang through the room. Karel bursting his bonds flew out of his chair when the whole truth stood before him. He seemed to crouch so as to take a better leap upon his enemy. But the Jesuit was before him.

While he sat there he had calmly calculated his chances. Quick as lightning he put his foot between Hans's leg and made him tumble on the floor. Then seizing the light, and dashing it in the Yonker's face, he turned round :

" They are out of your power at any rate," he cried. All was darkness and confusion in the room.

· Hans scrambled to the door and roared out, " Seize him !" He was met by the Beggar who had kept watch outside the door with drawn sword and who swore that no one had passed him.

At that moment a faint cry was heard. Then a window was opened and a sound as if some one jumped from a height on the earth fell upon their ears.

" He's in the next room !" " He's gone." " Seize him below !" " Break open the door !" were the first ejaculations heard.

" Silence ! I have the lamp. Light it," sounded Blink's monosyllables through them all. All were silent till the lamp was lighted and showed the state of the apartment. Hans was standing near the door at which they had entered, Peter Blink stood near the table and Karel was lying under it on the ground. In a moment he was on his feet and cried, " where is he ?"

" He's gone into this room and shut both doors," said Hans, pointing to the door which communicated with the Baroness's bedroom.

" My mother," shrieked Karel, putting his hand to his forehead. He rushed to the door and tried to open it. But the firm bolt withstood his effort and he wrung his hands in despair.

"Get out," said Blink pushing him away. He lifted his leg, gave the door a tremendous kick near the bolt and made it fly open. All entered the apartment and Karel rushing forward threw himself impetuously upon the form of his mother which lay in a half kneeling position before the little crucifix.

"Mother! mother! he has killed her! Great God, mother," he moaned.

"Karel, my son!" lisped the Baroness, opening her eyes feebly, "He has fled through the window! what is it."

"Yonker," said Peter Blink tapping him on the shoulder. "Must fly at once. Take your leave. Hans, let us prepare things."

They withdrew and left the all but unconscious widow alone with her son. To describe the scene which took place between them, when in short words he told her what had happened and that he must go, is altogether out of my power. Nor was it much of a scene so far as action and outward appearance go. For the most part, Galama remained clasped to that faithful breast which had nourished and sheltered him so often while he was young, and which he must leave for ever. When in short accents he told her of Block's treachery, and that it was he who had taken the two girls away, she was overcome by grief. She had confided in him so thoroughly, and he had made himself so agreeable and so meritorious that she felt his treachery all the deeper. She said not a word. Her tears refused to flow, and she stared at the floor as if she had lost all thought, all power of action. Karel witnessed her condition'; his heart was well-nigh breaking. He knelt down before her and taking her hands in his, breathed a fervent prayer to Him who alone was able to comfort her. Then, realizing all the danger of his position and knowing that he could do no good by staying, he tore himself away.

Hans and Peter had meanwhile been occupied with the preparations.

"You had better go down stairs, Peter, and catch up whatever arms you think the Yonker can use," said Hans. "His pistols are in the kitchen above the chimney. That is where I hung them ; I shall get his things here."

Blink went downstairs, and Hans, going to the large cabinet, began to lay out a few articles of clothing, and all the money and valuables he could find.

"Are you ready, Hans?" said the voice of Galama, behind him, "at least, that is, if you will forgive me for the injury I have done you, and follow me once more through the wide, wide world. I shall be quite alone now, you know."

Hans turned round, and flinging himself on his knees before his master, he seized his hand and kissed it. Big tears rolled down his cheeks, and pointing to the door of the little room he sobbed: "I promised her to take care of you, twenty years ago, Yonker,and God knows that I have tried to do it. But I have been the cause of all this."

"Get up, old friend," said Galama, with a tremble in his voice. "We shall not part again ; but let us fly from here, and consider in a safer place what's to be done ! *You are* not guilty, at any rate."

In a moment they had taken up what was worth

T

taking, and descended the stairs.   At the foot they were
met by Blink, who carried a couple of pistols, a large
battle-axe, and an immense two-handed sword, both of
which had belonged to Galama's ancestors, and were
kept in the family as relics.   Galama smiled when he
saw the armament, but Blink said,

"Never mind, Yonker. You take pistols, Hans sword.
I'll keep th' axe," and with these monosyllables he dis-
tributed the articles.

"Which way best?" he then asked, looking at both
men.

"The Water Gate is worst," said Hans, "Sextus has
warned them there, and he has probably gone along to the
Long Gate next. So for the Quay Gate, I think. They'll
be here presently."

This counsel was generally admitted to be the best,
and presently the men issued from the house each with
a pistol in one hand and his sword in the other, Peter
Blink shouldering the axe with perfect grace.

As has been said before, the house of the Baroness
stood on the canal called the Maerlandt, at an angle of
fifty degrees from which another canal, called the Quay,
ran round the east side of the town, and flowed into the
fosse around the bastions and fortifications close to the
south gate.   From the middle of the Quay a path
through some out-gardens led straight on to the Quay
Gate, which was seldom used, and except in time of war
slenderly watched.   To this gate the five Beggars ran.

It seemed, however, as if their presence in the city
had become known.   From the neighbouring watch-
house of the Water Gate, a shout went up when they

were seen to cross the narrow wooden bridge which led
to the other side of the canal. Some shots fell, but fell
harmlessly, and then half-a-dozen soldiers set off in pursuit

"They shall not catch us this way," said Hans, who
closed up the rear, and setting his sword into the wood,
he gave a vigorous push and sent the bridge, which
turned upon a pivot at the other end, almost over to the
other side.

" Come on," he said, " Koppestock is waiting for us
with his boat. We shall have the whole town behind us
presently."

On they flew, up the ramparts, their feet crushing the
grit beneath them. In a few moments they had reached
the Quay Gate, the guard of which, consisting of about
half-a-dozen men, alarmed by the noise of their steps,
had come out of the house not knowing what was coming. The gate itself was built on the bastion, which lay
like a little three-cornered island in the fosse ; a wooden
bridge connected it with the city on the one side, and
the country round about on the other. Before they knew
by whom they were attacked, the Beggars were upon
them, Blink in advance. With a desperate flourish of
his axe he broke the line of the enemy, and sent one of
them to the ground. Without pausing to renew his
attack he flew to the gate which was left unattended,
and the tremendous blows of his axe fell like
hail upon the iron lock. It soon gave way and he
stepped outside. But there a second work awaited him.
The drawbridge was pulled up, and the chains were
fastened by another lock. A shout arose behind him.
He looked round and saw the four Beggars running to-

wards the open gate, while at the bridge-head there appeared the numerous helmets of their pursuers.

" Here, Hans, cut down these two locks, and leave the rest to me," he said. Hans flew through the little door, and the axe was soon heard upon the locks.

"I'll get them," chuckled Blink to himself, "pepper and salt, that's the thing for them." He quietly allowed the three other Beggars to go through the door in the gate. Then opening the little square hole, which was cut out in it for the sentry to speak through, he stepped outside, too, and closed the door behind him. Then, seizing his pistol he held it through the hole, and throwing some powder on the pan, he aimed and fired.

The foremost amongst the soldiers who had just come to the end of the bridge, staggered and fell. His comrades gave a yell and fell back, not having expected such a reception.

"Come on, ye cowards," cried the voice of the Jesuit, " seize these men and your reward shall be heaven."

Hardly had he said these words, when a second shot sent him on his back. At the same moment the bridge fell down with a crash, the chains ringing and clanking heavily.

" *Vivent les Gueux !* " shouted Blink, and firing a third pistol into the midst of them without aiming, he followed his comrades over the bridge.

The soldiers ran outside the ramparts, but in vain. In the deep darkness nothing could be descried, and even the most experienced ear could not distinguish a sound.

About half-an-hour afterwards a boat with six men was rowing across the Meuse.

"You and the axe did for the officer," said Hans to Peter, "but I think I must have killed all the rest, for that immense sword gives one the swing of half-a-dozen others. Are you not afraid to row us across, John?" he continued, addressing the ferryman.

"I row everybody, Hans, and I'll row old Nick when he comes," answered the oarsman, "only do not talk so loud or they might hear us. Not that I am afraid, but may be you are."

"Well Yonker, I do not suppose you have any objections to becoming a sailor for some time," said Hans turning to the unfortunate nobleman who sat by his side, silent and in deep thought. "You are nowhere so free as on the sea, and as long as that Jesuit is alive you will have no rest."

"Whose ship is it to which you intend to take me?" asked Galama curtly.

"Sonoy's, if you like, until you have taken one for yourself," answered Hans. Galama nodded assent.

"Take me anywhere," he said, in a listless tone. "I say farewell to my native land, for I have lost every-thing—everything." And he bowed his head upon his chest.

"I say, Hans, you are coming back some day are you not?" said the rower to his friend.

"O yes," said Hans, "we shall come back soon and take the town."

"Right," said the other, pulling at his oars, "then I shall help you."

But neither of them, as both smiled at the boast knew how soon it was to be fulfilled.

Chapter Twenty-Second.

BEGGARS' ETHICS.

THREE and a half years had elapsed since the above events took place, when a small frigate was making her way under full canvas towards the southern coast of Britain, apparently coming from the coast of Holland. It was towards the close of March, 1572. The sharp and cold north-wind, carrying along with it an occasional shower of sleet, swelled the sails to their full extent, and made the vessel shoot through the water. It was a fine though not a very large ship, carrying some twenty guns, and, to judge by the rigging and accoutrement, one was the privateers of which in those days every sea was full. The biting cold and the hard work which they had undergone, had sent the crew below, for with the exception of the man at the helm and the necessary hands, the deck was clear. A young man, some five-and-twenty years old, whose dress half soldier, half sailor, revealed the rank of officer, was pacing up and down, his hands hid in the pockets of his cloak, and his felt hat pulled over his eyes. He cast an occasional glance at the sails and at the course of the vessel, and giving a few directions to the man at the helm pursued his walk.

It would be difficult to recognise in the stout and robust frame, the long beard and the browned features of

the officer, the lithe figure, and the youthful appearance
of our hero, Karel Galama. But three and a half years
of seafaring life had strengthened his already powerful
limbs, and the influence of weather and sun had tanned
the almost womanish fairness of his skin. Not to his
disadvantage, however, for if formerly he looked an
enthusiastic youth, he now appeared as the calm, considerate and thinking man. His features had lost none
of their commanding expression, his eyes none of their
haughtiness, but a deep sorrow, a hidden pain was silently
gnawing at the soul of which that face and those eyes
were but the mirrors. It was afternoon, and the sun,
which through the day had appeared by fits and starts,
prepared to take his leave, with all the beauty over
which he had command.

The Yonker looked at the beautiful spectacle in silence,
and with his arms folded on his chest, he muttered :

"How many times shall I see this sun rise and set
again before I go to that place of rest, where there shall
be no weeping and no sorrow."

"It will not last much longer, Yonker," said a voice beside him, which we recognise as belonging to Hans, "if
this kind of life is to keep on. For upon my Beggar's
oath we have not provision for more than two days, and
what even that is, you may judge by this specimen."

And Hans who was sitting astride a gun, with one
hand held up the half of a raw herring of a very small
kind. He had a piece of dry bread in the other.

"It is your own fault, Hans," answered the Yonker,
"why did you not bring back some more provisions from
the people at Wieringen ? You might have filled half

the ship, had you not shown the white feather to a parcel of boors."

"Boors!" cried Hans, "May-be they are, but they have their own way of fighting which is certainly not a bad one. For you know as well as I do, that eighteen of us were killed in the last scramble, and I was as near being one of them as anything. For Tom, poor fellow, and I were both lugging away at an immense pig. It was a tremendous beast, and it kicked at such a rate that I who unfortunately had hold of the hind legs, was all of a sudden thrown on my back. 'Hold on Tom!' cry I. But poor Tom was worse off than I, for at that moment the owner of the animal had come up with a tremendous pitchfork and was just going to let me feel its teeth when I fell, and crash went the fork, right into the pig's hams. The animal gave one squeak, and down went Tom under the pig, and before I could get up, the farmer had despatched him. That cured me, I can assure you, and I made myself scarce, for I saw ever so many pitchforks coming along, and I could not very well guard myself against them."

"I hope some of the other ships at Dover will be able to give us something," said Galama, who had not listened to Hans's story, "else I really do not know what to do. What do the men below say?"

"They do not care as long as they have something to eat, and plenty to drink; but when that is done they'll turn upon us," answered Hans. "They are in a rage, already, because we did not take some of the fishing-smacks that passed us."

"Fools," said Galama. "A house divided against

itself cannot stand. They would have us war against the whole world, and make our friends as much afraid of us as our bitterest enemies. How little do they understand what they are fighting for!"

"And how little do they follow that religion which they profess to defend!" said a voice behind him.

"Ay, Master Barends," said Galama, turning round to the speaker with cordiality, "it is perhaps for that very reason that our cause prospers so little."

It was indeed the preacher whom we last saw in van Alphen's barn at Brill. He had fallen in with Galama, in a rather peculiar and certainly providential manner. When Galama fled out of Brill with Hans, Blink and the other Beggars, he had taken himself to Diedrich Sonoy, who was at that time the admiral of the Beggars of the Sea. After having been on his ship for some time, he found an opportunity at last of rigging out one of the captured ships for his own use, and having found a good crew, he commenced life as commander of a little privateer carrying six guns. His spirit at that time, being still agitated by what had happened, he could not bear the slow routine of cruising about in the rear of the fleet, and obtained leave to cruise on his own account. And now he began a life of audacity, such as he could only have consented to lead in his present state of mind. It seemed as if all the good impressions of Agnes's conversation had left him ; as if, driven to despair by the calamities which overtook him, (for on a foray to Brill he learned that half a year after he fled out of it, his mother died of a broken heart), he had cast away all those good intentions which he had made upon his

sick-bed, and which he had often repeated in his prayers.
A day seldom went by without some fierce fighting.
Either he crept at night into a harbour and suddenly
attacked the unconscious Spanish merchantman that
happened to have cast her anchor there, or landing his men near some small town, which was known to
be wholly Spanish and making a sudden foray,
leave the people terrified, and astonished at his boldness.

Upon one of these expeditions, as he was one evening
marching at the head of his men along a dyke, he became aware of the form of a man lying across it. A
light having been produced, it appeared to be that of a
middle-aged man, who was bleeding from a wound in
the head, and who probably in consequence of it, had
lost his consciousness. Karel dimly recollected the face,
as that of a preacher in Brussels, and commanded his
men to lift the wounded man and carry him back to
the ship. By a great deal of attention the preacher
was at last restored to life and to health, and it gradually
came out in his conversations with Galama, that he knew
the two girls, and could give the anxious youth more information about their imprisonment than any one else.
And gradually as the pious man spoke words of comfort and of divine love to the Yonker, all the afflicted
youth's old feelings revived, his former intentions came
back to him with renewed strength, and he now resolved
not to let them depart again.

It is true, he remained in his ship, and he prayed
Barends to remain also, which the latter gladly consented
to, first, because he saw that he could do a great

deal of good among the crew, and, secondly, because at
that time the Netherlands were getting too hot for him,
he having three times escaped death by a hair's-breadth.
Consequently both remained, but Galama stopped his
career of plunder, and once more attached himself to the
fleet. Shortly afterwards, Treslong begged him and
Barends to come over to his ship, he having lost his lieutenant, and thus we find them here together. They were
both liked by the crew; Galama for his skill and his
bravery, without which they would never have listened
to the words of reproof which he sometimes gave them ;
and Barends for his warm-heartedness, his readiness to
help, and above all for his skill in medicine, which he
had picked up in his eventful life and by means of
which he often gained access to an otherwise hard-
ened heart.

"I cannot but deplore the fact," continued Barends,
"that with all their courage and bravery, they are little
if at all better than those against whom they fight.
Almost the only difference lies in the name."

"Well, Master Barends," said Hans, respectfully, looking at his little fish, "you see many of us have gone
through what others have not, and I know there is not
one on board this vessel who has not a clear understanding that he is fighting against those who ignore our
liberties, who rob us of our hard-earned money, and all
that kind of thing. But then, you see, most of us have
had some hard injustice, some fearful wrong, which has
been done to us by the Spaniards, or the priests, and you
cannot be astonished if we become half mad when we have
them in our clutches. Who cut off Gerrit's nose and

ears, and who tore out the boatswain's tongue, so that
whistling is the only thing he can do now? These are
no trifles!"

"Ah, Hans," said Walter Barends, "I should like to
hear you once speak of them with compassion, and as
erring sheep."

"Erring sheep!" answered Hans with a fierce expression
on his face. "They are tigers, Master Barends, blood-
thirsty tigers. I do not know what you have experienced,
but I can say nothing less of them."

"And still they are more to be pitied than hated, Hans,"
said the preacher. "You know I was a priest myself
once, and the wife and child which I had after I left them
have been killed, and I myself have suffered from them
severely."

"I have been one, too," said Hans, his face darkening
as he spoke. The two men started and looked incredu-
lous. "I dare say you do not know it," continued he "and
I do not like speaking about it, because whenever I think
of that time, my blood begins to boil, though it is twenty
years ago now. I was about eighteen then, Yonker, I
was a novice in Brussels, when one day my mother, my
sister, and my elder brother were seized. The two
women were put in prison, but my brother, the finest
fellow that ever lived, was first tortured on the rack, and
then drowned in a water-butt because he could not
stand on his legs, and what had they done? Nothing but
give Evert Hagel, the preacher, a week's shelter on
their farm."

"Evert Hagel!" cried Barends, joyously, "he was my
teacher. I have often heard him say that he met with

some truly kind people on his tours, who gave him shelter whatever the danger might be. Pray, was your brother's name Jakob Everink.

"It was," said Hans looking up in astonishment. "Why how do you know it ?"

"Because Hagel often told me about it," answered Barends. "Your brother must have been a very godly man, for Hagel always spoke with affection of him."

"So he was," said Hans gloomily. "He was a good deal better than I am ; what did Hagel say about him?"

Barends told what he recollected, and found both in Hans and his master, profound listeners.

"Ah," said Hans, when there was a pause, "it made me so desperate that I fled from the priests, and your father, the Baron, gave me money to go to Germany, and took me afterwards into his service. And what can I do now but avenge on these priests, these blood-hounds, my brother's, my mother's death ?"

"Hans!" said Barends, earnestly, laying his hand on the fellow's shoulder. "Do you know what your brother's last words were ?—'Father forgive them, for they know not what they do.'"

At this moment a lad acquainted Galama that Treslong desired to see him, and judging it wisest to leave Hans alone with Barends, he slowly directed his steps to the cabin.

He descended the steps and entered the cabin. It was a small apartment, and a table, a few chairs, a, stove and two or three chests were the only furniture, beside the hammock in which, with one leg trailing on the floor, lay the Captain of the vessel, the Lord Blois de Tres-

long.   He had apparently gone to sleep without taking
the trouble to undress, for he had a cuirass on, a sword,
a helmet, and a pair of pistols lay on the table as if
they had been thrown there hastily and carelessly.

"How is the wind, Yonker?" asked Treslong lifting up
his head, and greeting Galama.

"North, North-East, and plenty of it," was the answer.

"Do you think we shall reach the fleet to-morrow
morning?" inquired the captain.

"We'll be off Margate Sands some time to-night if
all goes as it does now," said Galama. "But are you sure
they have not sailed?"

"If they have, we shall be in a nice pickle," said Treslong, sitting upright in his hammock, "for where are we to
get ammunition and victuals?   But I see no reason why
they should have sailed unless a whole Spanish squadron
came upon them, and then they would not have made off
without giving battle."

"It is not so unlikely as you think, my Lord," answered
Galama, "for you know that lately Queen Elizabeth has
turned rather crusty toward us Beggars.   I fancy that she
sees she can get more benefit out of the Duke and
the King, than out of the Prince and his allies, and
judging from a purely political point of view only, there
is little doubt that she can gain but little by protecting
the despised Sea Beggars with their twenty or thirty ships
against the whole of the Spanish nation and navy, which
would give her trouble enough."

"Trouble be hanged," said Treslong, jumping from his
hammock and undoing his cuirass, "what harm does it
do Queen Elizabeth to have our little fleet lying off

Dover or running into the Thames? We surely do not harm any of her vessels, and we pay for what we get like honest men, and I do not know that Sir William Cecil is in any way against us. Moreover, at the end of last month, Alva and the Queen were at loggerheads, but this confounded ice has kept us so out of all news, that they may be friends now for all I know."

"But even if they were no friends," answered Galama, "I am very much afraid that the latent protection which she has given us as yet will not be of very long duration. Think you, my Lord, King Philip will allow her to give shelter to his most desperate enemies without remonstrating with her and it may-be threatening her? We do her no harm, it is true, but Queen Bess is by far too acute to risk a war with mighty Spain, for the sake of us, who are Beggars indeed, and yield her not a farthing of profit."

"And do not *we* risk a war with that mighty Spain?" said Treslong, beating on a silver bell on the table. "Are we then for ever to be everybody's enemy? What a noble thing it would be for the great Queen of England, to take our part. She is Protestant, and she herself has suffered from persecution, as I have been told. But I daresay she is no better than that filthy Count of Embden, who though he is a Protestant maltreated me nevertheless."

"Well, you paid *him* out with his own coin, my Lord," said the Yonker, smiling. "So you have nothing to complain of there."

"Ay," said Treslong smiling over the cup of wine which his page had brought him, "I never received his sum mons yet, but some day methinks I shall go and ask for it, through my metal mouths. But no," he added, emptying the cup and handing it filled, over to Galama, " he may be what he likes, but he treated me hospitably, and but for that fool of a Roobol, we might be friends yet."

After some talk about matters which will not interest our readers, he continued :

"I have had enough rest now, so you can turn in, and I shall wake you when we get in sight of the fleet or the clear coast. No objections, Yonker. Orders must be obeyed. You look weary and troubled. Oh, I know you will deny that, but I can judge of your looks better than you can. Turn in, sir, and be neat and trim by the time we get to Lumei's, and do not let us look like starved sheep."

The Yonker knew that it was of little use resisting his captain, so he went to his own cabin and fell into his hammock, where, despite his assertion to the effect that he was not in the least fatigued, he was soon in a sound sleep. Treslong put the pistols in his belt, and the sword with its beautifully embroidered leathern scabbard and scarf over his shoulder, and stepped on deck where the grey evening was well-nigh changed into a clear and starry night.

To explain to the reader the allusion which Galama and Treslong made about the Count of Embden, we will shortly relate the curious change of fortunes which Treslong had undergone since we left him after the unsuccessful affair in the forest of Brussels.

He reached Count Louis' army in safety, where he was heartily welcome ; for his skill and his courage were

alike highly valued. After the terrible defeat of
Jemmingen he succeeded with Count Louis and a few
others in swimming across the Ems ; but on reaching the
own of Embden, he became, severely ill in consequence
of the very dangerous wounds which he received in the
battle, while fighting at the head of a company of horse.
His strong constitution, however, enabled him to recover
and he was preparing to take the field again, when his
lieutenant and confident, Roobol, had the stupidity to
levy black-mail from a citizen of Amsterdam, who was
staying in the town. Such things, it is true, were not
of rare occurrence ; but the Count of Embden, wishing to
remain on good terms with the opulent city, caused both
Treslong and his lieutenant to be imprisoned. For
two long years did the impatient noble pass his time
in the small town, begging that his case might be
heard and judgment delivered. Probably, as the Count
was in secret understanding with Alva, he had determined to keep him a prisoner till he could con-
veniently hand him over to the Duke. They were at last,
however, allowed to go at large upon promising not to
leave the territory and to appear whenever they were
summoned.

Of this Treslong took advantage. He procured from
the Prince, letters of marque, as captain of a privateer for
two vessels, manned them secretly, and sailed away one
bright evening, maintaining, that he was still on the
Count's territory, by which he meant, the water, and leaving
behind a promise that he would appear whenever he was
called upon. On the cruises which he now undertook he
fell in with Galama, who knew more about seafaring, and

U

was very glad to share with his friend and former guardian the command of one of the largest, if not the largest, ship of the little fleet. In the beginning of the year they were compelled by frost to take shelter under the island of Wieringen at the mouth of the Zuyder-zee ; but were soon prevented from moving by being frozen in. Making the best of his situation, Treslong sent detachments of his men out on foraging expeditions, which however proved fatal at times, especially the last one, upon which eighteen men lost their lives, and Treslong was made to promise on oath to stop his crew from plundering the neighbourhood.

As if his position were not awkward enough, the Spaniards hearing of his presence sent a troop of soldiers over the ice to capture him. His broadsides, however, answered the Spaniards so well that they were beaten back, and before the attack could be renewed the united efforts of the whole crew succeeded in getting the ship out of the ice, when, having received intelligence, that the fleet of the Beggars was lying off Dover, he sailed thither, as we find him now. His lieutenant, Roobol, had, in the meantime sailed away with the other ship, and thus badly manned, with little provision, and less ammunition, they were glad to steer for a place where they could supply their wants and meet with a friendly reception.

Chapter Twenty-Third.

A HOPELESS PROSPECT.

THE grey light in the east had scarcely announced the break of day, and the fresh morning breeze was still dispersing the mist which hung over the water, when the Yonker refreshed by his sleep of which he had lately enjoyed but little, turned out of his cabin and stepped upon deck. He paused for a moment at the sight which met his eyes. The rays of the rising sun, playing upon the water, which was now almost perfectly calm, revealed at some distance, the white cliffs of the English coast. A few small fisher-boats were rowing towards or away from the land, and the fishers called to each other in hearty accents. To the right of him, the water stretched away glittering in the sun, and heaving under the broad swell of the Atlantic. To the left, and as far as his eye could reach, he saw a fleet, of some twenty vessels, most of them of a small size and, none larger than the ship on board which he was. It was the fleet of the Beggars of the Sea, the terror of Spanish merchantmen, and the continual object of suspicion and anxiety to both France and England. Turning his eyes to his own ship, he discovered that she was riding at her anchor with all sails reefed. A part of the crew was busy in preparing the long-boat, and it was evident that some one was leaving the ship.

At this moment Treslong came up to him, and said, in a tone of astonishment—"What, Yonker, not ready yet? Make haste. We are going to the Admiral."

"I would rather be excused," said Galama. "I can do no good there. You know very well, that upon almost all points, my opinions run exactly contrary to those of Count Lumei de la Marck, and, consequently, there is, not much love lost between us."

"Well," said Treslong, "that may be, but that is no reason why you should not go and pay him your respects. My opinion is, in many cases, directly opposite, to his; but still he is a daring and clever admiral, and I shall always admire him."

"His courage springs from a wrong source, my lord," said Karel, "you see these men that are working yonder; anyone of them, if he had been born a count and educated, could do what he does. He fights not to liberate our countrymen from the galling yoke of popish tyranny, but solely and alone for the sake of plunder, excitement, and revenge. I detest alike his principles and his bloody practices, and if you insist upon my accompanying you, I promise you beforehand that I shall raise my voice decidedly and loudly against your plan, for if the poor inhabitants of Enkhuizen are left to his mercy, they will henceforth detest and hate the Sea Beggars and the Prince of Orange, under whose banner they commit their deeds."

"You look at things in too dark a light, Yonker," answered Treslong. "It is possible that de la Marck is

too much of a freebooter and too little of a patriot for
our taste. But there is no doubt about it that he has
done a good deal of damage to our enemies. And he is,
surely, not the only man of influence in the fleet. There
is de Ryk, and Brandt, and van Haren, and if they
support me in remonstrating with him on his ferocity, he
will not dare to persist. He knows me, and fears me, for
I could deprive him of his command by one word to
the Prince. Come along, Yonker. We shall be able to do
something for the liberty of our country yet," and he
slapped him confidentially on the shoulder.

But Galama's gloomy ideas were not so easily dis-
pelled. He shook his head and said :

"Not unless you command me, my lord. I am
almost afraid that the time has hopelessly gone by when
anything short of a miracle can do aught for our
country. The state of affairs has grown worse and
worse, and the people have no spirit left in them to
resist even the most dastardly deeds of Alva."

Treslong turned away. He seemed to be desirous of
shaking off that same feeling which possessed Galama,
and which he felt creeping over him. He stepped
towards the middle of the ship, saying in a light tone,
as if he treated the other's words as mere fancies:—

"Well, just as you like, Yonker. I shall not command
you, but at any rate I shall take Hans with me. He is
an intelligent fellow, and can come back with orders and
ammunition. So farewell for the present," and in a few
minutes the long-boat conveyed him and Hans to the
admiral's ship which could be distinguished in the
distance.

There was reason for the gloomy view which Galama
took of the state of affairs in the provinces. In the
years in which he had been engaged in cruising and
capturing ships, the state of the country had become
worse and worse, and even the most sanguine were
beginning to lose all hope of an eventual change. It was
not long after the defeat of Count Louis, that the Prince of
Orange determined to take the field himself. His brother
had offered battle to Alva in direct opposition to his
wishes, his position being at that time anything but hopeful ; but far from being discouraged by the disaster, it
seemed to give him new energy. His estates and revenues
in Holland had been confiscated. His German property
and his household plate and valuables were all he possessed. Living in a foreign country and compelled to be
a guest of one or another of the German sovereigns,
his endeavours were put forth under their tolerance. The
heavier the yoke of tyranny began to rest on his countrymen, the more zealous did the Prince become in agitating
in favour of them, but the less became also the
sympathy he met with. Almost every one advised him
to sit still, some forbade him their territory, many refused
him a loan of money, and all condemned his patriotic
endeavours, as foolish and Quixotic.

" But, with God's help," said the Prince, I can do without them. He pawned his plate and valuables, his very
clothes. He collected money from far and near. He
issued, as sovereign of the provinces, letters of marque to
the Beggars of the Sea who brought him many a good
prize. Meanwhile the Emperor of Germany openly forbade
him to levy troops in his dominions. The Prince answered

as openly in a " Justification," in which he told the whole
world his principles and the reasons of his actions, at the
same time declaring war against Alva as an enemy to
the liberties and the people of Holland, and a traitor to
their lawful governor the King of Spain. Within
three months of his brother's defeat he crossed the
Rhine in a masterly manner at the head of thirty thousand troops.

The whole country was then on its knees praying
weeping, trembling with anxiety. Should the Prince
succeed in defeating Alva's troops, the people were
ready to rise and throw off the hated yoke for ever. But it
was not to be ; Alva, imitating the example of the
Roman General Fabius, followed the Prince like a
phantom, skirmishing, dodging, robbing his provisions,
retreating as soon as a battle was likely to come on, and
leaving his enemy frantic with rage and impotence. The
Prince's general, Count Hoogstraten, and his whole rear-
guard consisting of three thousand men were butchered.
At the end of little more than a month, the Prince had
to disband his troops without being able to give them
as much as a month's pay. He and his brothers fled to
France, the Duke of Alva made a triumphant march
back to the capital, and in remembrance of his bloodless
victory erected a famous statue in honour of himself
in the citadel of Antwerp.

Another faint streak of hope appeared on the horizon, but died gradually away. Alva involved himself
in a scheme to murder Queen Elizabeth and to put
Mary Stuart on the throne of England. Elizabeth
threatened, Alva recedes and by degrees the matter was

settled. Meanwhile Alva resolved upon a new measure wherewith to extinguish the last spark of resistance that might have been left in the hearts of the Dutch people. He convoked the States-General and coolly informed them that he had resolved to impose three taxes upon the provinces. The first was a tax of one per cent. upon all property whatsoever, to be paid once for all. The second one of five per cent. was imposed upon every transfer of real estate such as landed property, &c. And, thirdly, a tax of ten per cent. was laid upon every single article of merchandise ; or anything that was sold, to be paid *as often as it was sold*. In other words, an article being sold ten times would have to pay its whole price in taxes.

The States-General who saw that these taxes, and especially the two last, would do away with all trade, immediately and firmly refused at the risk of their heads. To make the discussion shorter they granted the tax of one per cent., and then settled themselves with a resolute air to resistance. Even Viglius, the Duke's greatest helper, denounced it in open words and voted against it. The Duke was mad. He raged, he stormed ; he swore that he would hang every man, that he would sell the whole country, he threatened, he begged. Overcome by his terrible threats, the States without army, and without defence, one by one reluctantly delivered their last bulwark against tyranny into his hands, upon one condition, that all the provinces should agree to pay the tax. All did, except one. The province of Utrecht held out, and it was heavily visited. One of the most mutinous, brutal and ill-paid regiments of the

Duke's army were quartered in the capital. Violence of every imaginable kind was of daily occurrence, but still the city would not give in. It was then summoned before the Blood-Council, and after some delay judgment was pronounced. Every law, charter, privilege, freedom, and custom of which it had become possessed during many ages was declared null and void. Every pennyworth of property of any kind was confiscated and seized. All tolls, rents, taxes, imports were appropriated. Thousands were ruined and brought to beggary, and the whole province looked as if it had been visited by the plague. A deputation to the King returned from Spain with no result, and its members were glad that they had at least returned alive.

The other States, trembling at this example were glad to make a compromise by which the levying of the tax was to be deferred for two years. There was a little relief, but it did not last long. An amnesty had long been promised. At last it arrived, and proved to be a complete mockery. No one who had ever done anything contrary to Alva's orders was included, and even those suspected were not to be forgiven. The Inquisition and the Blood-Council set to work with renewed vigour, and the amnesty was ushered in with a fresh onslaught of burning, hanging, and beheading.

At the same time a fearful inundation swept over Holland, by which thousands of people found their death in a watery grave. It was as if everything combined to make the descendants of the old Batavians upon their little streak of marsh, as miserable as possible. In 1571, the year in which the taxes were to be collected, the controversy became as hot as ever, and the resistance almost as determined. Both parties were furious, the more so because it was now not merely a matter of religion. Everybody felt himself directly attacked ; everybody, whether Roman Catholic, Calvinist, Ana-Baptist, or Lutheran joined in opposing what was threatened. But the Duke of Alva was exactly the man to persist where such resistance was made. He protested that he had collected heavier taxes than these from his own people in Spain, and he swore that he would deal harder with them yet, if the rich burghers of the provinces refused to do what the poor people in Spain had done. The rich people were silent. The shops were shut. The bakers, the butchers, the coal-merchants declined to do business. The ships rotted in the havens ; the cattle could hardly be sold. The people passed each other in silence and wondered how long this was to last.

The Prince of Orange, never despairing, was in France with his brother. He had succeeded in at last paying the claims of his former army, and was collecting money for a new one. But it seemed that there was now but little courage left in the country. The year had gone by, and the new one entered with the same gloomy death-like silence reigning over the provinces. Alva himself felt the effect of this total stagnation of business, and resolved to put an end to it. He ordered the tenth-penny to be collected in Brabant and really succeeded by violence in gathering part of it. But he could not open the shops and force the people to buy and sell. He could not dispel from their faces that fixed look of sorrow and gloom as if the whole country had been stricken with a terrible plague.

According to his usual practice, he determined to make an example. He commanded the shops in Brussels to be opened, or he would hang every shop-keeper on the post of his own door, as an example to be followed throughout the whole country. The shops remained shut, and the whole country looked and waited with suspended breath what would be the the result.

Such was the condition of the Netherlands when Treslong's ship arrived off the coast of Dover. Galama who had lost almost everything which tied him to the land, but whose patriotic disposition made him feel the state of his country very deeply, resolved to remain on board rather than mix with the captains of the fleet, most of whom, though they belonged to good families, were somewhat dissipated and appeared in a mood of joviality and carelessness which he knew would grate upon his own feelings. Again, he knew that Treslong was going to advise the admiral to undertake an expedition to *Enkhuizen*, a wealthy town on the west coast of the Zuyder-zee, where there was at the time but a small garrison and many adherents of the Prince. Galama, however, feared that the expedition would do their cause more harm than good, as the ferocity and piratical disposition of Lumei would not stop short at taking possession of the town, but would pillage friend and foe alike.

He was nowise sorry, therefore, when the day went by without receiving a visit from any of the captains, though he was rather astonished that Hans did not re-

turn. The weather was chilly and wet, the wind
shifting almost every moment. As he sat in the cabin
by the stove, he already congratulated himself upon the
failure of Treslong's plan, when towards the evening
the door of his cabin opened and Hans appeared as
usual, grinning from ear to ear.

" Here is a nice kettle of fish on for us, Yonker," he
said, shaking his head," just you read this, and I will tell
you all about it, afterwards."

And Hans handed his master a paper sealed with
wax. Galama hastily broke the seal. It was in Treslong's
handwriting and ran thus :

" Admiral's ship."

" The Thirtieth of Spring month, 1572.

"We are to sail immediately for Enkhuizen. You and
Roobol, who is here with his ship, are to lead the van.
We have had a sharp discussion, de la Marck has promised to commit no outrages. Make everything ready,
and if I am not with you within two hours' start. Make
sure to let no vessel pass either way without taking it
or warning us. If I am not with you, after you have
doubled the Helder, wait for me or orders.

" WILLIAM BLOIS DE TRESLONG."

A shade of deep displeasure passed over Galama's
face as he read the order. " Have you brought plenty
of ammunition and provision?" he said turning to Hans.

" Not a morsel of either," was the answer. " You
never saw such a mess as there is in the fleet. Nobody
has got anything to eat or drink, and the best of it is
that Queen Elizabeth has sent the admiral a notice, that

he must forthwith leave her coasts or remain at his peril, while she has forbidden any of her subjects to sell us a groat's-worth of provision or amunition. Here are real Beggars for you. I hope we may get something nice and hot at Enkhuizen, or else I shall stew my little dog and eat him."

" But have not the other captains—has not Roobol something he can give or lend us till we get what we want?" asked the Yonker.

" I asked Roobol, and he said he had been feeding that day upon nothing but raw herring and biscuit," answered Hans, " and you may judge of the scarcity amongst them, when I tell you that the officers who were holding a council of war in Count Lumei's cabin were drinking gin-and-water instead of wine."

Galama smiled, for it was a ludicrous idea that such men should ever come to what was then reckoned a great extremity. He poured out a cup of wine, and gave it to Hans, who tossed it off with apparent pleasure.

" But how could you see that?" asked Galama. " You were not in the council."

" Of course I was, Yonker, what do you think?" answered Hans, as if his dignity had been offended. " And I made a speech, too. There was a very sharp discussion about plundering and sacking, and the Count swore he'd rob all the churches in the town, but my Lord Treslong and I settled him, I can tell you." And he stroked his beard with an air of superiority.

" Curious thing," said Galama as he mounted the deck, " the Count is so very particular about grades and rank, that I do not believe he would have allowed you to sit at the council table. All hands on deck! What did he say?"

" Well, " said Hans, " you know, Yonker, I did not exactly *sit* at the table, but I was in the cabin, you know, for giving advice and that kind of thing. And as I knew what my Lord's opinion was, I expressed the same thing, you know, and gave the Count a hint about his swearing."

"Oh !" said Galama, who knew how much to believe, " I see what it was. You were called in to give evidence. Here are the men. Clear the deck !"

The whole crew of the ship, not more than thirty men altogether, were by this time assembled on the deck of the vessel which was in some confusion owing to the slackness of work Quickly the order to clear the deck was executed, and when they had all again assembled round Galama, he said :—

" I thought my men that we might have been able to give you provisions to-day, but it seems that the whole fleet is in the same condition as we are, and does not possess enough of its own. We have enough yet for some days, and as we are now starting altogether for Enkhuizen to make a foray, I hope you will do your several duties quickly and well. We must start in two hours."

There was deep disappointment in the men's faces as they heard that there was no chance of a present supply of provisions ; but when they learned where they were bound for, they gave a cheer, for the town was well known as rich and opulent, and even in these times something could be had there. During two hours the crew were busy in preparing again for the voyage. The guns were cleaned and sails got ready, swords and daggers, pistols and carbines were furbished and sharpened.

"I say, Yonker," said Hans, who had been looking at the ammunition, "suppose we fall in with a Spanish man-of-war, what then? We have no more than three balls for each cannon, and precious little powder."

"Well, Hans," answered Galama, complacently, "we must let her come up and board her, if nothing else can be done. Our time is up. My Lord de Treslong I suppose will not come. Now for it. Weigh the anchor!"

In a few minutes the monotonous clack of the windlass was heard. The wind which had settled into the west gently filled the sails, and Galama against his will set out on that memorable journey of which he knew not the end.

"Send two men up aloft, Willem! and let them keep a good look out for any vessel," commanded Galama and went downstairs to take some refreshment.

Chapter Twenty-Fourth.

SHIP AHEAD.

"Ship ahead, Yonker," was the intelligence with which Hans entered Galama's cabin next morning.

"What is she?" inquired Karel, jumping out of bed and hurrying on a few clothes.

"A Spaniard, as far as I can see, and she has perceived us, too, for she is making all sail. She seems to be frightened," was the answer.

Galama flew on deck. It appeared to be as Hans had said, a Spanish trader.

"All hands make sail," rang his command, and in a few moments every stitch of canvas having been put on, the quick-built vessel flew before the wind.

The crew were eagerly watching what was to follow. They were a singular-looking lot. There was hardly one amongst them who had not some mark in his body or in his face of the cruel treatment which he had undergone at the hands of the Inquisition. Some were without ears, others without noses, others again had lost their teeth or a hand, or their faces were cut, or burned, or their bodies frightfully mangled. They were fantastically dressed, without regard to uniform or order, and presented altogether a ferocious and unsightly spectacle. They were armed to the teeth with formidable axes and swords, with pistols and daggers stuck in their girdles, and they were evidently excited at the idea of a capture.

All of a sudden Hans felt himself pulled by the sleeve.

"Another to port, Hans," said the gruff voice of our old acquaintance, Peter Blink, while he pointed towards a speck on the horizon. Hans looked for some time

"Is that Roobol's ship close behind us?" asked Galama, looking back and pointing to a third ship behind them.

"Yes. Can we signal?"

Galama was for some moments dubious which ship to prefer, but when he saw Roobol's vessel steering in pursuit of the second trader, he directed all his attention to he one before him. It was clear that they were gaining upon her every moment. She was under a heavy press of canvas, but being heavily laden, and not built for fast sailing, she could not keep ahead of the privateer.

"She is altering her course, Yonker," remarked Hans, "suppose you run right into her. Would not that be a scene. Let them all go to the fishes."

"Suppose you hold your tongue," said Galama, sternly, directing the course of the ship to be altered so as to follow the trader.

But it seemed that she intended to show fight. Suddenly changing her course again she was put about and ran back upon her track, passing the privateer at some distance. A flash issued from her deck, a shot fell and a ball came whizzing through the rigging. The Beggars

x

gave a loud cheer and flew to the guns, when another ball followed the first and passed right before her bow.

"Silence," shouted Galama, stamping on deck, "every one at his post and not a word. These fellows do not know how to shoot, at any rate," he continued, "so I shall give them a lesson."

And stepping to a long gun he pointed it with some care and fired. The shot told, for the Spaniard's bowsprit was smashed to atoms.

"Take her mizzen mast, Yonker," prayed Hans who was all in fervour.

"Better take rudder," growled Blink, who belonged to the gun.

"I think so," said Galama, and aiming again he saw with evident satisfaction that the ball passed just above the rudder and smashed the gallery of the cabin.

"A little lower this time," muttered Karel to himself, while he saw that the Spaniard was putting on every inch of canvas she could carry.

"They are throwing the cargo overboard," cried Hans, as bale after bale, and barrel after barrel, was thrown out of the trader and floated on the sea.

"We'll stop that soon enough," said Karel, and fired another gun. The ball struck the rudder just below the water, and the foam splashed up into the cabin-window. A cheer went up from the Beggar-crew, and the effect of the shot became immediately apparent. The merchant-man veered before the wind, and staggered like a drunkard.

"Had not Master Barends better go below?" said Hans to his master, as he noticed the figure of the

preacher near the cabin-door. The sea air had undoubtedly done him good, for his erect frame and healthy
colour contrasted strongly with his appearance at Van
Alphen's in Brill. Just as Karel (who did not like to
expose the preacher to the dangers of the fight which
must ensue) was going to ask him to step into the cabin,
Barends anticipated him by walking up and saying:

"Do you not think, Yonker, it would be a good thing
just to tell the men that they can do no good by murdering, but should take prisoners all who do not resist?
As little blood as possible will make victory all the
greater."

"You are right, Master Barends; but had you not
better go downstairs, for you may be killed," answered
Galama.

"I am not afraid," said Barends, smiling, "and I can
shelter myself." The fact was that the preacher loved
Galama deeply, and had resolved to remain on deck,
that he might see how it should fare with his frin
Little did he know that his help would be wanted so
signally.

With evident satisfaction he saw that Karel called
the men around him, and told them in short and
energetic words that all unnecessary bloodshed must be
avoided; that their object was to prevent the vessel from
reaching the Zuyder-zee before them, for by giving that
warning that they were coming she would defeat their
whole expedition. He saw how the men looked up to
their young and handsome chief with pride, and in many
a face he could read the determination that his words
should be followed. Galama then sent them to their

several posts, and turned all his attention to the ship, which they were now fast approaching.

"Boat-hooks ready and down with the gunwale," sounded the command, and in a few moments long poles with tremendous iron hooks at the end, were thrown out at the Spaniard. She was a large three-masted vessel, expensively fitted up, but apparently badly manned, for but few heads could be distinguished on deck. As she was heavily laden, she lay level in the water with the privateer, and as if to add to the confusion, the whole deck was covered with bales and barrels, the crew having apparently been stopped in the attempt to throw them overboard. Galama stood in front of his men with his cutlass drawn, waiting till she could be boarded.

Down came the hooks with a crash, tearing down the Spaniard's gunwales in several places. Some of the crew made a faint attempt to cut them, but soon stopped when they heard the bullets whistle past their heads.

"Over," shouted Galama, and taking a tremendous leap, he led his men sword in hand to the enemy's ship. But they met with a warmer reception than they had bargained for. It appeared that the Spaniards had made a bulwark of the bales and barrels, right along the middle of their deck, from stem to stern, from behind which they now fired, and fought with desperate courage. For a moment the Beggars fell back. Then Galama's voice was again heard, cheering them on, and his form was seen on the top of the bulwark. Suddenly a tall, thin man rose up from behind it, and lifted a terrible iron-club, with which he dealt him a dull-sounding blow on the helmet. The Yonker staggered and fell back upon the deck.

No sooner did Barends, who had remained on the privateer, see this, than, heedless of any danger for himself he rushed to where he saw the Yonker fall. A terrible struggle had at that moment commenced over his body. The Spaniards rushed upon their bulwark, and the Beggars, maddened at the loss of their captain, flew against them. With an almost superhuman effort, the preacher succeeded in dragging the senseless body of Galama out of the *melée*, and with every nerve and sinew strained, he lifted him in his arms and carried him back into his cabin. There he laid him upon his bed, unfastened his helmet, which had a tremendous dint in it, and began to bathe the pale face with water, moistening the lips at times with drops of wine.

The noise overhead became terrible. The sharp report of the pistol, the clash of the sword, the groans, shrieks, curses of the wounded and dying, sounded horrible through each other. All at once, there was a lull. What could it mean? Were they defeated or victorious? Suddenly, the report of a cannon shook the ship, and made its beams creak and tremble. A deafening cheer followed, and the noise became more fearful than ever. Each time as by the action of the waves, the two ships, which were fastened together, struck their hulls against each other, a dull heavy sound went through the ship as if it were beating a sombre time to the horrible and death-like music overhead. By little and little, the pistol-shots stopped, the clash of the swords became less frequent, and at last nothing was heard but footsteps hurrying over the deck.

"Where am I?" said Galama, feebly opening his eyes

"God be praised, you are alive again," said Barends

joyfully reaching the Yonker a goblet of wine, "drink some of that. Does your head ache?"

"Yes, my head," said Galama, dreamily, "what have I been doing?"

"You were attempting to board a Spanish merchantman," answered Barends.

"Oh, I remember," said Galama, quickly, as he glanced round his cabin, and the whole scene again stood before his mind." I hear no noise. Are they fighting? Have they won, or what?" and he endeavoured to rise.

But Barends pressed him down softly, saying:

"Do not rise, Yonker, you have been unconscious. The fighting has only just ceased, but I shall go and see what is the result."

As he rose to go to the door, some one was heard coming down the ladder. Galama seized his pistols expecting it to be an enemy. But it was only Peter Blink, who tore open the door, and thrusting his head in asked :

"Yonker here?"

"Yes, Peter. Come in and tell me what is the result of our fight," said Galama.

"Oh, Yonker, I am so terribly glad to see your honour alive again," said Peter, with a burst of genuine joy, for once relinquishing his shortness. "We've taken them. Smashed 'em. Gold, silver, wine, bread, meat and prisoners."

Galama and Barends smiled, at this account of the capture, when the mate Willem entered the cabin, and likewise showed his joy at finding the Yonker alive. In answer to Galama's questions he said—

"We have captured the ship, Yonker. She has a

valuable cargo of silk, and wine, and there is a large sum
of money. She carried fifteen men all told, and seven
passengers, all of which have been made prisoners,
besides ten of the crew. Five have been killed. The
admiral has signalled to cast her adrift. We have only
lost three men, but some are badly wounded."

" Where is Hans ? " asked Galama, with some concern.

" He is looking after some of the prisoners. But for
him we might not be so fortunate as we are. The bulwark was not to be taken till he aimed one of the long
guns at it, and shot a gap in it. From that moment we
had won. There was one priest amongst the passengers
who fought like a very devil."

" I shall go and see the wounded and the dying," said
Barends, rising. " You must take some rest now, and not
attempt to rise for some hours. Willem will arrange all
matters for you, and have the deck cleared and cast the
prize adrift. I daresay you feel well enough, but no in-
subordination. I am your doctor now, so obedience! "
And he tenderly pressed the youth down on the bed.

As the Yonker did not feel well enough and could
trust Willem perfectly, he took the advice. The evening
came on, and he awoke out of a refreshing sleep and
going on deck, sent the other away to take some rest.

The night air became cold, and the sea which was
running high was at times sweeping over the ship ; but
the Yonker, whose inward emotions were somewhat
in harmony with the elements, found a positive pleasure
in thus battling with a more powerful foe than the
Spaniards. As he stood at the helm, giving his directions, his mind ran upon the events of his past life, when

suddenly he saw Hans before him, faintly illuminated by the light of the compass. The whole of his body was hidden in the darkness, but his face as it stood out with the greater clearness, had a strange expression upon it such as Galama had never seen there before.

"I want you to come down to the cabin, Yonker," he said curtly and with a little tremble in his voice.

"Why?" asked the Frisian. He could not explain, Hans' manner, and thought some mutiny had broken out.

"I've got a prisoner down below, that you would like to see," answered Hans pointing to the cabin.

"Who is it? Here take the helm and keep her head North North East," he said, giving the helm to one of the Beggars and following Hans to the cabin. The door opened and as his eyes became accustomed to the dim light, he saw upon the same chair which he had occupied, no other person than Gerard Block *alias* Father Sextus, his hands tied behind him and two men by his side, guarding him with drawn cutlasses.

Galama started and grasped Hans's arm. He felt giddy, and it seemed for a moment as if the passions which were evoked by the sight of the prisoner were too strong to be mastered. But he calmed down, and when he had looked at the Jesuit for some moments, he laid his pistols upon the table, and said to the two men. "You can go, but one must watch before my door."

The men departed and the trio were once more left lone.

Chapter Twenty-Fifth.

THREE MEET AGAIN.

"At last then we meet again," said Galama in a calm voice, stepping towards the Jesuit, who sat on the chair with an air of dogged indifference on his face.

For some moments the two men looked at each other in silence, Galama with a touch of pity in his eyes, and Sextus with an undaunted, if not triumphant look of defiance.

"Unfasten the ropes with which he is bound, Hans;" commanded Galama, "and leave only his hands tied. If you make no attempt to move or liberate yourself," he continued, addressing the priest, "I shall speak to you without hurting even your body. But know you that at the least attempt, your death will be inevitable."

"You do not mean to say that you want me to let this fiend loose again, Yonker?" asked Hans, in astonishment. "Why it took me and three or four others to bind him. He fought like a tiger; besides hasn't he deserved it?"

"Never mind. Give him no more pain than we can help. He knows what he has to expect now. Cut the strings and stand behind him."

Hans slowly cut the strings, and, taking a chair, sat down beside the priest, who seemed greatly relieved.

"The thing that astonishes me most in you," said Galama after having looked at him in silence for some moments, "is that you can bear meeting me, and can look me in the face again without flinching. You must be singularly destitute of feeling not to experience at least part of the pain that you have caused me."

"Had you listened to my advice, and had I been allowed to work out my plan, Yonker, I assure you, you would be better off than you are now," said the Jesuit in an earnest tone.

"That's a good one," said Hans, and putting his mouth close to the priest's ear he said: "How about the cavalry, old father, eh?"

A shade of anger passed over the priest's face, and after a moment he said:

"Of course, being in hostile hands and bound, I must submit to insults, which otherwise no one would have dared to have offered me. But you, Yonker, who at one time seemed to feel some affection for me, suffer at least that I be not degraded by the poisonous breath of this boor."

"That boor gave you a good knock on the head one day, ha, ha!" said Hans.

Karel gave his servant a look to silence him, and again addressed the Jesuit.

"I suppose you know that you are in the hands of the Sea-Beggars, and in the midst of their fleet, so that escape is this time impossible. I have seen enough of your duplicity to make me distrust every word you say, but I would warn you to answer my questions straightforwardly and without any attempt at prevarication.

You have everything to lose and nothing to gain by not complying with my wishes. I will not use violence with you, but you must answer me."

"I know that I am in the midst of a small fleet of vessels owned by men who style themselves Beggars of the Sea, and who pretend to wage war against Spain. But I would warn you, Yonker, because I have a great regard for you still, not to hurt a hair on my head. The ship in which I was this morning, belongs to a fleet of merchantmen, the convoy of which is following closely and may be upon you this night. I am a more important person than you think, and my death would be signally revenged upon every one of you, were it to happen."

"Talking about Beggars," said Hans, "I think you are the coolest of us all. What do you mean, sir, in threatening me and my master on board our own ship with the result of our acts? We'll see your fleet coming and pull their ears for them when they come," and he proceeded to perform that operation upon the priest.

"Let him alone, Hans," said Galama sternly.

"He's only a lying hound of a Jesuit," grumbled Hans falling back in his chair, "I would not make so much palaver with him, if I were you."

"Where's Agnes? Where's my sister?" said the youth stepping in front of the priest and contracting his brow. His lip trembled with emotion.

"She's lost to you for ever!" said the undaunted priest in a sombre tone.

Galama's cheeks became ashy pale. He pressed his lips firmly together and his eyes seemed to shoot flames. But he remained calm.

"I did not ask you that," he said. "Where are they ?"

"They are lost to you for ever!" was the answer again, given in the same tone.

"That's not the way to talk to him," muttered Hans, and looking fiercely at the priest, he growled, "I'll drive my dagger into your ribs presently. brother, if you do not answer properly. Speak out."

"Silence, Hans," commanded Karel. "Sextus, or Block, or whatever your name may be, I warn you that your fate lies in your own hands. It is my strict duty to give you over to the admiral, and you know enough of Count Lumei's character to expect but little grace from him. But I can also hand you over to the commander of this vessel, my Lord de Treslong, and I can use my influence in averting your fate as much as possible. Which of these two do you choose ? You must and shall answer my questions, or I will have you conveyed to the admiral to morrow, and God have mercy on you then."

"I do not expect mercy from anyone," answered the priest. "Think you, I am terrified by your threats, Yonker. I thought you had seen enough of me to know that I do not flinch before the drawn sword, and that death to me would be as sweet as life. My death would but be an entrance to a blessed heaven, and rather than evade it by a disgraceful act, I would run to meet it, if it had been decreed in the counsels of the Almighty. I scorn your mercy."

"Oh, you hypocrite, you lying cur," cried Hans, flying up and catching the Jesuit by the throat. "Do you remember this grip? Do you remember how I throttled you till your face was black, and then you cried for mercy and promised to tell all? Out with it, you hound, or I'll squeeze you to rights this time."

"Leave off, Hans. Quit the room. Do you hear me!" commanded the Frisian in an imperious voice, releasing the priest whose face had become purple.

"And why, Yonker, should this fellow be treated as if he were a baby?" asked Hans looking very fierce. "He's my prize, and if I had known that you were going to treat him in this manner, I would have cut him to pieces first. Don't you see that he is playing with you, and that he thinks you very soft. He's a kind of dog that should not be fed with pastry. Your nobleness and your Christian principles will not have the least effect upon him."

But his master pointed silently to the door, and, muttering a curse between his teeth at the foolishness of some persons, Hans took his station before it.

"Is there nothing, nothing that will make you tell me?" the Yonker said in a tone of agony, stopping before the Jesuit. The latter was silent.

"You have done me a great deal of harm, Sextus," continued the Frisian, "but I forgive you that. Without having ever seen you before, and for some object which is up to this moment a mystery to me, you have crept into my friendship, and cruelly and cold-bloodedly maltreated whatever was dearest to me. Through you Count Egmont was sacrificed, and but for you my unhappy country might have been as free as the fishes beneath us. You have no reason for keeping Agnes and

Maria confined. Tell me what I can do to learn their prison and if mortal man can get them out of it I will."

He looked in anxious suspense at the prisoner who hesitated a moment.

"First of all, my liberty," he said in a clear voice.

The Yonker frowned, and for an instant a heavy battle seemed to be going on within him. At last, he spurned the thought from him.

"That I cannot give you, but I will plead for you."

"Plead!" repeated the Jesuit scornfully. "I ask you for my liberty. You will not?"

"I cannot," said Galama, haughtily.

"It would not be of very much use were I to tell you," said the priest. "I've told you before, they were out of your power."

Something in his tone seemed to imply what the Frisian hardly dare to think of.

"What?" he gasped. "Are they indeed out of my power? Are they dead?"

"They are dead," repeated the priest.

Galama sank down on a chair. His head fell upon his arms and rested upon the table. There was a dead silence in the cabin for some moments.

"*I* know she's not," said Hans to himself, and going up to his master he touched him on the arm. The Yonker looker up, and even the priest seemed to shrink back from a sight so full of intense suffering.

"This will never do," said Hans. "He's not made of the same stuff that you are made of. I am sure a little torture will bring it out of him. Do just let me heat this dagger and burn his lips. It is a splendid prompter."

The reader will perhaps shudder at the ferocity of Hans, but he must recollect that torturing in that age was held legitimate by most persons, and that Hans spoke the language of nine out of every ten men in power.

Galama gave no heed to his servant's offer, and remained for some time in the position which we have described.

"Let him be taken to my cabin," he said, rising. He was calm but pale as death. "Two men outside must keep strict watch, and allow no one to pass either way. Not even you, Hans. Wait, I'll lock the door and take the key. He must go before his judges. I have not the power to punish him."

And having locked the priest in his own cabin, he went on deck.

When next morning the faint glimmer in the east again heralded the coming of day, the Frisian was still on deck. The sea ran mountains high, the wind shifted from one quarter to another, and blew from all alike, with great force. All hands were constantly at work shifting the sails, and flying about to execute the commands of the Yonker, which followed each other in quick succession. The whole night they had been endeavouring to double the Helder, but owing to the foulness of the weather, they were obliged to give up the plan and wait for daylight.

"I don't think we'll be able to do it, Yonker," said Hans, who was assisting Willem at the helm. "Do you see yonder vessels? I'm sure the whole fleet is lying here in the same position in which we are. You had better go down below, and take some rest. We will drop the anchor, and I shall call you in a few hours."

"Yonker looks very bad," said Peter Blink, who was limping about.

And so he was. His face was pale, his eyes swollen, and his hair and beard wet with the salt water, were hanging in wild disorder.

"I shall go and wash myself, at any rate," said he, handing his speaking-trumpet to the mate, and, descending the stair, he unlocked the door of his cabin softly and opened it without making the least noise. It was a small compartment, and was flanked on one side by Treslong's cabin, and on the other side by the store-room where the ammunition was generally kept. The partition between the two latter compartments was, as is usually the case, not very thick.

As he entered his cabin he paused. There was a faint glimmering of light inside, and yet he was certain that the priest had been put on his own bed, well secured, and no light or anything inflammable was to his knowledge to be found in his room. Holding himself on by the door he stepped inside, for the ship was rocking dreadfully. A few seconds afterwards, he flew back out of the cabin and on to the deck, while at the same time a fearful explosion shook the whole ship, and clouds of smoke and flame filled the cabin.

"All hands at the pumps and fire hose!" shouted out Galama, and flew down the stairs again followed by Hans and Peter, who was run over by a half-a-dozen of his companions. Immediately, the whole crew without know-ing what was going on flew to their posts, and seeing smoke issuing from the direction of the store-room a line was soon formed and the buckets flew from hand to hand.

In the meanwhile Galama had reached the bottom of the stairs. The first thing he did was to shut his own cabin door, and then running to the door of the store-room he gave it a tremendous kick. It flew open and a burst of smoke and flames met him. Heedless of the danger, and shaking off Hans like a feather he dashed through the flames. A moment afterwards he emerged, carrying a black mass in his arms, and making his way through the crew, who were in the meantime busy carry-ing water under the directions of Hans and Willem, he laid his load on the ground of Treslong's cabin, and re-turned to the crew.

"The fire is in the left-hand corner of the store-room, and in my cabin, my lads," he cried to the men, "keep everything wet. There's no fear of an explosion. Here, give me this bucket," and taking a bucket from one of the men, he hastened back to the cabin.

"Here! out of the way! this is better than all your water," cried out the voice of Peter Blink, as he pushed the men away and stumbled downstairs laden with the weight of an immense sail, which was dripping wet.

"Well done, small one; good idea!" cried the men as they made way for the dwarf, who seemed to have forgotten his sprained ancle. With the help of two or three others the dripping sail was carried into the store-room, and thrown over the flames. The remedy proved

Y

effectual. In a few moments the flames were subdued, and soon there was nothing left of the fire but the smoke and the smell.

"How did it come on?" cried several voices as the men assembled round Hans and Peter, who was now the hero of the hour.

"First thank me and Peter for having saved you all from death," said Hans, "and then I'll tell you." But the men would give only honour to whom honour was due, and as Hans had to acknowledge that he knew no more about it than they did, they were all in the dark and gave themselves to guessing.

Leaving them to guess, we shall explain the cause to our readers. When Galama had entered his little cabin he became aware that the light did not shine in the apartment, but came through a hole in the wooden partition. Looking closer he saw that a plank had been torn away, and through the opening which was hardly large enough for him to pass through, he saw the light shining. A thought flashed across his mind. Could the priest have got loose and made this opening? Could he be in the ammunition room preparing mischief? He pressed himself before the opening and looked.

True enough, there was the priest with a taper in one hand, and a match in the other. By the dim light of the taper, Galama could see that one end of the match was attached to a keg of gunpowder, which, with three others, lay in the farthest off corner of the room. This, however, did not frighten him, for he knew that all the barrels were empty, the powder having been given out by himself in the late fight. But behind him, and close to the door and to Galama, stood a little square box filled with gunpowder, which had also been used in the engagement of that day. Attracted by the noise which Galama made, the priest turned round. He uttered a cry of surprise when he saw the Frisian's face, and not knowing the contents of the box, dropped the taper in his consternation; Galama flew back, and a second later the afore-mentioned explosion took place.

Let us now follow Galama to the cabin, where he had carried the body of the priest. Upon the floor, his head resting upon a pillow, lay the form of the Jesuit. It presented a horrible spectacle. His clothes were for the most part, scorched and burned to ashes, showing in some places the raw flesh underneath. His face was coal-black, his hair singed, and his red lips as they parted in apparent agony, displayed his scorched tongue. He breathed with difficulty, and but for the long gasps which he gave at intervals, one might have supposed that nought but a heap of cinders was lying there. Galama lay beside him on his knees, occasionally wetting his lips with some water.

At last Sextus opened his eyes, and for a moment they rested on the anxious face that hung over him, with a vague and meaningless expression. But perhaps the movement of the ship, or the expression in Galama's face, restored him for a moment to his full consciousness. He cast at the Yonker a look of triumph, and something like a smile, something fearfully in contrast with his disfigured face, passed over his lips as they tried to mutter some words. Galama bent down and caught the faint-whispering—" Going down together."

He shuddered. The rocking of the ship, the confused noises of the men who were still engaged in putting out the fire, the splashing of the water, these might indeed be taken for the sounds that are heard in a sinking vessel; and the idea that the man who had done him so much harm, and whom he had newly dragged out of the flames, should triumph in their dying together, was almost too much for him. He had no conception of a spirit so relentless, so defiant.

But, as he rose to leave the miserable man to himself, for he saw that the Jesuit had but a few moments to live, the recollection that he knew the secret of Agnes's fate, came upon him, and without further thought he resolved to make one more attempt to find out whether she was really no longer among the living. He flung himself on his knees before Sextus, whose breathing was becoming more and more difficult, and putting his lips close to his ear he said—

"Sextus, remember that within a few moments you shall stand before your Judge; I beseech you in His name and upon your eternal salvation, to tell me where Agnes and Maria are. I forgive you all you have done me, but in the name of that merciful Jesus whom you profess to follow, tell me."

He paused, and with every pulse within him throbbing, he put his ear to the dying man's mouth to catch the faintest accents. For some moments nothing but the priest's breath fell upon it, but suddenly, as if with the last flickering of the candle, he made a movement with his hand, and said in scarcely more than a whisper—

"Blessed Mother of God! They are dead, dea—d."

A slight quiver passed through his frame, and the Jesuit was a corpse.

For some time the unfortunate Yonker remained in the same position on his knees beside the body. He had not the strength to rise, far less to go on deck, and possibly he would at that moment have been thankful to die too. There was now no more hope. During all these years that he had been at sea, there had been within him a faint glimmering of hope, at one time weaker than at another, but never entirely extinguished, that Agnes was still alive, and the very idea that such was possible, inspired him with new energy and courage. Even that night, when the priest had told him that they were out of his power and dead, he could not bring himself to believe it. But now the only being that could give him the answer to his question had passed away, and had passed away with the answer on his lips.

There lay Galama, with his head against the table, his arms by his side and his eyes shut, almost as motionless as the body at his feet. Softly he repeated Agnes's name to himself, and every time he repeated it he felt as if, by some giant's hand, the foundations of his castles in the air were struck away. And from the bottom of his heart he sent up a prayer for strength.

"Come, Yonker, this will never do," said Hans who had noiselessly entered the cabin and looked at the scene for some moments. He saw what had happened and he knew what to do. He induced the Yonker to lie down in Treslong's hammock, and then calling Peter Blink, they took up the Jesuit's body between them and carried it to Galama's cabin, where he had formerly been confined.

"I say, Peter," said Hans, "I think he is done with once for all, eh? But do not let us make another mistake. This fellow was so awfully clever that you do not know but what it may be all feigning now, and he may be as sound as we are. Tell you what. We shall pitch him into the sea. No cavalry there, eh?"

"Right," said Peter, "wrap him in his mantle," and having fetched the Jesuit's mantle, which had been left in the other cabin, proceeded to wrap it round the body.

"Stop! what is this? There is something in these pockets," said Hans, as his hand met a stout object in the folds of the cloth. He soon found the pocket and drew out a little pocket-book, and four or five letters.

"To the Vicar-General of the Holy Inquisition, Brussels," said Hans reading the inscription. "To his Excellency, the Duke of Alva." "To the Reverend Father Hubert, Brussels." Ah, what is this? Father Hubert! That's the little fellow. There may be something in this. Let's see," and he opened the letter hastily and began to read it, "what, Brother Sextus? 'Agnes Vlossert remains heretic! Maria Galama died in the'——I say, Peter old fellow, pitch this carrion away by yourself, and look out for more letters. I've got something here that will freshen the Yonker up."

And Hans ran into the adjacent cabin and awoke Galama out of his stupor, and talked such a great deal about letters, and Jesuits, and nunnery, and Father

Hubert and Agnes, that his master became quite bewildered and snatched the letters out of his hands.

They were despatches written by the abbess of the nunnery of St. Clara, in Brill, by the burgomaster of the same town, and by the abbot of a convent in Flushing. The first addressed to Father Hubert informed him that since her last communications Maria Galama had died, but Agnes Vlossert remained a heretic, and was suffering the penalties of her conduct. The two others, amongst other matters, complained to the Duke of Alva and to the Vicar-general, that both towns were entirely without garrison, and that there were not enough soldiers to keep the peace. After careful examination the entries in the little pocket book convinced the trembling Yonker that after all his hopes were not extinguished.

Chapter Twenty-sixth.

MAN PROPOSES, GOD DISPOSES.

"MAN the long-boat, quick! Cast the anchor!" shouted Galama leaping on deck. "Come along there; what are you about? Down with the long-boat!" and in his impatience he seized a boat-hook and stamped with it on the deck. In a trice the men were on deck busy lowering the boat, which however was not easy as the sea ran very high. At last, however, it was got clear off the ship and then the desperate work began. Up one wave, down another, tossed this way and that way, all but buried under the billows one moment, and almost thrown into the air the next, it seemed impossible for the boat to make its way to the admiral's ship, which was still tossing about with half-reefed sails. The men, however, were experienced, and had had many a hard pull upon the water. Silently did they bend at their oars, and notwithstanding the continual breaking of the waves over them they advanced slowly towards their object. And the Yonker sat at the stern, looking only at that one object. His eyes glistened, his cheeks glowed, he recked not of the waves that drenched him, nor the gusts of wind which carried away his hat and floated it far behind him on the water. He continually cheered and encouraged his men, and offered to take one of the oars himself, which however they would not allow ; he seemed a changed man. The old fire had returned in his eye, and upon his parted lips there played ever so little of a smile.

At last ! The boat has reached the admiral's ship, and ere the crew can catch the ropes which are thrown out to them, Galama has seized the rope-ladder and swung himself on deck.

" Where is my Lord de Treslong ? I must see him at once, immediately ! Tell him it is his lieutenant, Yonker Galama," said he to one of the men who were standing round, and who seemed to be in authority.

The man turned round, and hastened to the cabin from whence he presently returned with Treslong, whose astonishment at seeing our hero may be imagined.

" What is wrong, Yonker, that you come here, and in such a sea ? But, no, there cannot be much wrong, for I have never seen you look so well in your life," said the astonished nobleman.

" On the contrary, my lord," said Karel, " glad tidings. Tell the admiral to signal the fleet to turn round. We must all go to Brill. We shall capture it to-day if we get there in time. There is not a man of garrison inside. We must go !"

" Eh ! what ! Brill ! No garrison in Brill ! Nonsense ! Come upon the quarter deck and tell me all about it," and Treslong hurried his visitor to the quarter deck.

" Do you see the whole fleet lying before you, my lord ? " said Karel pointing to the vessels which were by this time all lying before the entrance of the Zuyder-zee, battling with the wind that blew from the coast with great briskness. "We shall not be able to double the Helder; not one of us. Yesterday I captured that priest—the Jesuit—of whom I told you. Through him I know that if we sail to Brill or Flushing, neither of which had any garrison in them, when he left two days ago, we may easily master the town and do with it what we like. If we could get possession of either of these places we should achieve a greater victory than the Prince has yet done.

"If we could! indeed," answered Treslong, "think you Alva is such a fool as to allow either Brill or Flushing to be without garrison? When you have had my experience, Yonker, you will think otherwise. That Jesuit of yours has played you another trick, or perhaps he has said it to escape the torture with which you have threatened him."

"He is dead," said Galama spreading rapidly. "In an attempt to blow us up he hurt himself so severely that he died, but after his death there were found upon him papers and a pocket-book which told me that he had just come from Flushing to go to Spain, and intended to run into Ostend and deliver despatches from his order in Brill and Flushing to the governor in Brussels. And here is one of the letters, read it and see whether it does not corroborate my statements."

Treslong read the letter quickly. A smile came over his face and before he had finished it he waved it in his hand, and cried out "Magnificent! You have made a prize indeed, Yonker."

"I wish he would give me some of it if it's eatable at all," said a voice behind them. They turned round and cordially greeted the speaker. It was Adam van Haren, one of the cleverest seamen of the whole fleet, as he was one of the bravest soldiers.

"How do you come upon us so suddenly, captain?" asked Treslong.

"I suppose in the same manner in which you came, at least to judge by your boat," answered van Haren. "I cannot get into that confounded Zuyder-zee and I won't. I propose that we sail to the Channel. There are always Spaniards about there. But look there is Simon de Ryk's boat coming hither too. See what haste he makes, he must like me have come off with very little breakfast. Confound this east wind, I was just rejoicing in the idea of a fine ham or cheese in Enkhuizen."

"I do not know whether it is such a bad wind after all," said Treslong, "what say you if we sailed to the Meure and dropped anchor at Brill? There is not much of a garrison there, and I do not suppose there are ten fighting men in the town that would not join our sides were we to turn up."

"Whew!" whistled van Haren; "Brill! Strong place that. Do you really mean it, my lord?" and he looked at Treslong as if he had some doubts whether he was not mad.

"Mean it?" cried Galama "of course we do, and so will you if you read this letter which I intercepted on its way to Brussels."

"So that was your prize, Yonker," said van Haren, returning the letter, which, owing to his indifferent education in that respect, he had rather spelled than read. "I could not fancy what was the reason, when I saw you actually smiling, a thing that I have not seen you do for years. I hardly know what to say to this. If its true it is simply magnificent. If it is false, why then of course we shall be beaten tremendously. I for one mean to try it. Here comes de Ryk. Let us hear what he says."

The new comer, a short stoutish man of martial appearance, was heartily welcomed by all three. He had formerly been a wealthy merchant of Amsterdam, but having been banished in consequence of the operations of the Blood Council, he equipped at his own cost a ship of war. He was prudent, intelligent and brave, and his love of country was equalled by his ardent affection and admiration for the Prince. He listened to the news with a slight frown, and having heard all the *pros* and *cons* he stood for some moments in silence.

" There is a great likelihood," he said "that the letter is a hoax, and I do not attach much importance to it. But let us risk it. Surely we can fight on land as well as on sea, and though we are but few we can make away with twice our number, I know. *Vivent les gueux !* say I, and let us talk to the admiral at once."

There was something noble in the manner in which these men grasped at the idea, and were willing to risk their lives in the execution of a plan the boldness of which verged upon desperation. For some time our heroes stood discussing the matter. At last van Haren said—

" My Lord de Treslong, go you and acquaint the admiral of our plan."

" On the contrary, go you two," said Treslong, " the Count is in bad temper with me and the Yonker."

De Ryk and van Haren went away to find the admiral, while Treslong and Galama stood with their faces
towards the helm eying the fleet as it lay riding at anchor.

"Here's the admiral, what do you want with me, eh?"
said a voice behind them. Both turned round. Before
them stood an immense man with a mass of thick black
waving hair hanging down on his shoulders and mingling
with his equally long beard of the same colour. He
had a high and perfectly white forehead, grey cat-like
eyes, and a well-shaped nose. The lower part of his
face was hid by his beard. But the sound of his voice
was harsh and unpleasant, and the fire seemed to dance
and flicker in his eyes, like those short and intense flashes
of lightning which we see in the dark and gloomy cloud
that threatens us with destruction. Although in his
morning attire, he was dressed with great richness, and
his well-fitting garb showed the magnificent proportions of his body to great advantage. He held
one hand on the splendidly ornmented hilt of his sword,
n his equally splendid belt were two pistols, the butts of
which were made so as to represent the head of a wild
boar, and his other hand, which grasped the baton, his
badge of office, swung by his side. His whole appearance was that of a tyrant with a will as despotic as it
was changeable; clever, haughty, and cruel; dreaded
and abhorred by his foes, and by his friends feared,
admired and despised. It was William de la Marck,
Count de Lumei.

No sooner did he see Galama's face, than he started
back a step, and frowning terribly at the young man,
he said in a harsh and imperious voice:—

"Sanglier! Lieutenant Galama! Why the ——, sir, are

you not on your ship? What the —— are you doing here? I wonder you did not bring your whole crew with you! Go back at once, sir, or I shall have you sent back in my own way. I thought you were ordered to lead the van and double the Helder by sunrise this morning?"

"Which, as you see, is a physical impossibility, Count," said Galama, quite coolly. He knew the admiral and was prepared to receive his language quite calmly. "I do not know," he continued, " whether, you have discovered any power to move our ships independently of the wind, for otherwise I know not how to execute your order this morning. We have been trying to do it the whole night, and I do not suppose we have come an inch nearer Enkhuizen than we were. We must alter our plan, Count."

"Alter our plan," broke in Lumei with a tremendous oath. "You shall, and must go back to your ship, and you too, my lord, and if you cannot sail round the point, you must row it in boats, sir. By my father's soul! we'll make these —— Enkhuizers pay for it. If I get near them I shall hang every mother's son of them, and fire the city," and the admiral was just going to indulge in another volley of oaths, of which he seemed to have an unlimited supply, when a new comer joined in.

"Not thus, not thus, my Lord de la Marck. These poor Enkhuizers have done us no harm, nor have their houses; and thou knowest our good Prince is dead against violence."

"You too, de Ryk, and you van Haren!" exclaimed the admiral, turning round fiercely upon the two captains, who had returned to the quarter deck. "Is this a concerted plan, and are you four the leaders of a mutiny on the fleet? If so, by the spirit of the Wild Boar of Ardennes, my ancestor, I shall arrest you all," and he stamped fiercely with his foot on the deck. "Speak, my Lord de Treslong, do you perhaps intend to change places with me? Think you, your talents or your blood befit you more to be the leader of this fleet than me? If so, why are you silent?"

"Because, Count, the moments are too precious to be wasted in a dispute about the nobility of our races, even though that dispute take place betwixt the descendants of the Wild Boar of Ardennes, and of the Duke of Gelre," replied Treslong, with dignity. "I knew not of the arrival of any of these gentlemen, but, now that they are here, I beg to greet them, for I have important news to communicate. Our Yonker here, as you well know, captured a Spanish merchant-ship yesterday, in which there was a priest, the carrier of despatches between Flushing and Brussels, which despatches have come into our hands. They tell us that both Flushing and Brill are without garrison, and may be had for the asking. What say you, sir Count? Shall we steer thither, seeing that we cannot enter the Zuyder-zee to-day."

"I am sure there is no garrison in Brill," cried de Ryk. "The wind is changed, Count, and your own vessel has cast her anchor. Brill is not very populous, nor large, and our fleet would strike a terror in the hearts of the poor burghers. Let us put about and steer for the Meuse."

"Are you the admiral appointed over this fleet, or am I?" thundered De Lumei, who had been chafing

under the speches of both Treslong and de Ryk. "We
have resolved in full council to go to Enkhuizen, and
before the capture of a miserable hound of a priest or a
little adverse wind shall make me change my plan, I shall
run my vessel on to yonder downs, and march my men
straight through the country to the town. I have never
been crossed in my plans yet by God or devil, and all
the winds that ever blew will not induce me to prefer a
wretched parcel of hovels like Brill, to the wealthy and
large city of Enkhuizen."

"You are entirely mistaken, Count, in thinking that
Brill is so poor," said Treslong, gravely, and the manner
in which he spoke, forced even de la Marck to listen to
him. "You know my father was governor there, and I
know the town better perhaps than anyone in the fleet.
There is a magnificent cathedral, two monasteries and
one nunnery, and there are far fewer partizans of the
Prince, and consequently more plunder than in Enkhuizen.
Such as we are now, we can do nothing. What we can
do there, we know not, at any rate not less than we
do here, where we are in danger of being thrown on
the coast in a gale."

"Our brave admiral is afraid!" said van Haren with
a sneer, "we are but five hundred strong and what can
we do? I fear that we shall get bloody heads, and I
advise all of you to sell your ships and go and live in
Germany or England."

"No, mine friend," said de Ryk, slapping him on the
shoulder, "we two shall sail to Amsterdam first, and
cannonade the town. I told the burgomaster there that
I would come back some day and wring his ears for him.

Come along, since we are going to lie here and do nothing."

"I wish I had been with Herman de Ruyter," said Galama, passionately, "when he took the Castle of Louvesteen with twelve men. Courage seems to have died with him."

The poor admiral found himself in a cross-fire. Naturally impulsive and passionate, he was as obstinate as he was changeable and arbitrary. He would not give in to the four captains, though he acknowledged that to follow their advice was the best thing. But, at last, after half an hour's vehement discussion, van Haren's irony, de Ryk's sarcasm, but above all the earnest reasoning of Galama and Treslong changed his convictions, though to the last moment he kept up an appearance as if he would never consent to the plan.

"Farewell, Count," said Treslong and Galama as bitterly disappointed they turned to leave, "we thought you had sworn to leave your hair and beard unshaven until you had revenged Count Egmont's death. If you go on in this manner, your hair will soon grow too long, and like Absolom's it may become the cause of your death."

"D——n," roared out the admiral, stamping with his foot, and swinging round; he caught up a speaking-trumpet.

"All hands on deck." Then turning to the captain who came rushing up, he commanded with a running commentary of oaths. "Fire the signal gun and hoist up the signal to put the fleet to the wind, and tell them that if the order is not executed within half-an hour's time, I shall sink every ship that has not weighed anchor. Quick

z

about there. My Lord de Treslong, you shall lead the van, for you know Brill well. Good day," and as if to escape either their taunts or their thanks, he hurried down below.

"Thank God," cried Galama, as he grasped Treslong's hand in feverish excitement, "now for it, my lord. Captain van Haren, allow me to thank you personally as having done me a great favour, and you too, de Ryk."

"We've tamed the wild boar," said de Ryk, as in high spirits, each prepared to join his own ship. "The whole country will ring with our exploit in a week."

"Hem! I wish I could get hold of some bread and cheese for my men," said van Haren, "for I'm sure I do not know how to feed them for another day."

All the captains laughed at this prosaic turn of the conversation.

"We shall have a splendid turn out in Brill," said de Ryk, at the expense of the Duke and his tenth penny. *Au revoir*," and his head disappeared down the ladder.

"There must have been something beside this letter, which you got from that Jesuit," said Treslong after they had gained the deck of their own ship, and their orders to weigh anchor and trim the sails having been executed, they were shooting through the waves toward the mouth f the Meuse, "for I have never seen Yonker Galama so excited and feverish before. Not even on the eve of the execution of the two Counts."

"The horrible end of that poor Jesuit has worked upon my nerves, I daresay," said Galama "and you must recollect that this is indeed a stupendous undertaking."

"No doubt of it, Yonker. We must now show the

Spaniards what we can do," answered Treslong, gravely. " Of course we must keep very good watch lest any of the real partizans of the Prince in Brill be in any way discomfited. But at the same time I think we must show that we have an abhorrence of everything that smacks of Popery, and I therefore think of proposing a new plan to punish all the monks and nuns in the town. We have so long played martyr, I wish to give them a turn."

Galama was silent and looked down. Had he looked Treslong in the face he might have noticed ever so little of a twinkle in his eyes.

" What I propose doing is this," continued Treslong, " after we are masters of the town, a party of soldiers must encircle the two monasteries and the nunnery of St. Clara, so that no one can escapes, and then set fire to them. Then we shall see the bees swarming out of their nests. Just as the Spaniards did with our people at the Geta, when Count Hoogstraten and two or three hundred poor devils had fled to a church, they stood round it, set fire to the church, and saw every man-jack die before their eyes. Would you not like to see some of the little nuns jumping about in the fire ? "

" Never !" exclaimed Galama, colouring.

" Well," said Treslong, " I was only in fun about the burning, But I am determined upon one thing. I shall break open the doors of the convents and tell my men to play old Harry with the tiny creatures. They can marry them if they like, and I daresay they will find a handsome dowry within."

" My lord," said Galama eagerly, his cheeks flushing and his eyes brightening as he spoke, " I know not whether you are in earnest, but I charge you on your honour to forbid your men from doing any such thing, as you have just said."

"Chivalrous youth," sneered Treslong. "Has not Popery done enough with you yet?"

"It has, my lord, but I shall never consent to this. Most of these creatures are innocent of all the crimes imputed to them, and how do you know but that amongst them—there may-be——a—— ;" he stopped and blushed at his own eagerness. He was trembling at the very idea which Treslong had broached.

Treslong looked at him for a moment with a smile upon his lips, and then bursting into a hearty laugh he said:

"When another time you tell me your secrets, Yonker, do not forget afterwards that you *have* told them. I saw you turning red when I mentioned the nunnery on the admiral's ship, and there is not much sagacity required to make me suppose that one dweller within its sombre walls, is at least the cause of one half of your ardour."

Galama blushed and was silent. Treslong continued, kindly:

"I hope you have seen enough of me to know that I would never dream of committing such cruelty as I proposed. I feel for you, and if there is anything I can do for you, in helping you to recover your betrothed, Agnes Vlossert, you have but to mention it, and you may depend upon me."

He gave the Yonker his hand, which was cordially accepted.

And thus that little fleet of twenty, or twenty-two

vessels, of which the two largest, those of Treslong and de la Marck, were both smaller than a frigate of the present day, set out upon that famed expedition which was destined to open that memorable struggle, at the end of which Spain with her immense wealth, power and influence, was to succumb to the determination and courage of a people, not one fourth her equal in number.

But noble as was the enterprise, it was not at first conceived in the manner in which it was afterwards executed. De la Marck, the ferocious corsair, consented to it solely because he had nothing else to do, and preferred a little plunder to none. Van Haren was willing to risk his life in it, because he wanted to provide his men with victuals, for, as he sagely said, "if we are to die, it is better to die in storming a city, than by starvation, which is a meagre glory indeed." And such was the feelings of almost the whole fleet. Desperate almost to madness, the men were ready to do anything, if there was the least chance of success, and as Brill was known to contain a good deal of wealth and provision, the men were eager to come to action, though they should be opposed by twenty times their number. Even Galama, we must confess, did not act from purely patriotic motives. One of his chief reasons was if possible to liberate Agnes, and after having taken Brill, to stock their fleet well, both with provisions, men and money, to spike the cannon, to destroy the defences and to leave the town, thereby as he hoped to inspire his countrymen with some courage, and to let them know that there were still men to be found who would be able to fight, and to fight well, whenever the time came. That was the idea which Galama had at first pictured to himself.

It was only the clear head of Treslong and, be it said, of Simon de Ryk, who looked farther. They saw that instead of spiking the guns, and destroying the fortifications, instead of leaving the town to fall once more into Spanish hands, instead of reviving the courage of his countrymen by an idle show of bravado, they could with the same trouble, and with infinitely more advantage make Brill the first stone of the bulwark of independence, and turn those cannon, and those fortifications into instruments in their own hands for the destruction of their oppressors. While he and the Frisian sit discussing the scheme in their cabin, and all the important consequences rise up before their eyes, we must for a moment leave them, and lead our readers to the nunnery of St. Clara.

Chapter Twenty-Seventh.

REST AT LAST.

IN a small cell, sparingly furnished with two beds, and such articles of furniture as are indispensable in sleeping apartments, we find two women dressed in the unvarying grey woollen garments of the convent of St. Clara. One of them reposes in a low wooden chair, and turns her eyes with an expression of great anxiety to one of the beds where the thin and worn face of Maria Galama rests upon the pillow. It is Maria, but ah ! how changed. The straggling mass of naked boughs and withering branches can offer no greater contrast to the once blooming forest with its varied splendour of foliage and all its grand effects of light and shade, than did Maria, as we see her now to the once blooming and buoyant maiden. There was beauty still in her face. The gripe of | death, though merciless, could not altogether dim the lustre of her eyes, or disturb the soft and delicate outline of her rounded chin. But the eyes were sunken, the cheeks were wasted, and the lips only parted to give passage to a short cough, or a hard and difficult breathing.

During the years which the two girls had spent in the convent, the disease from which Maria had long been a sufferer had advanced more rapidly every day. She felt that she was approaching her end, and she rejoiced in the prospect. As we have already seen on the eve of their imprisonment, Agnes's example and influence had not been without effect upon her. And after they had been removed to the nunnery, and its doors had closed upon them, she had made the firm resolution never again to recede. She felt her faith strengthened, and she was now even willing to undergo persecution if it should be God's will to bring it upon her.

The reason why Sextus had conveyed them to the nunnery instead of sending them with all the other prisoners to Brussels was very simple. He considered his plan this time so perfect, and was so confident of its success, that he foresaw the possibility of making a great use of these girls after he had obtained as much information from the Yonker as he could, and most of all, that he might get a great deal out of them, should he again happen to be unsuccesful. The abbess of the nunnery was his aunt, and he respected and admired her as a clever and strong-willed woman. She had, in the opinion of many people, a special gift of conversion, and her nunnery was always full of girls of all ranks, who were either afraid of coming in contact with the many heresies which were abroad, or who, having been already to some degree tainted by them, were confided to her care in order that she might bring them again into the right way, and shelter them at the same time from the hands of the Inquisitor. To this woman Sextus confided his prisoners, and to her he applied after he had been frustrated in his treacherous designs by our friend

Hans who he knew had escaped the trap that had been set for him, though he did not expect him once more to venture in the lion's den merely to save his master.

But if he hoped to get possession of the two girls again he reckoned without his host. The abbess flatly refused to give them up, nay, she would not permit him to see them or to employ any means whatever in forcing them to confess. His promises and his threats were alike met with indifference. The abbess pointed to her charters from the Pope, and from Charles V., protested that she was neither afraid nor ambitious, that she had never allowed any nun to leave the convent, and that she had resolved not to give two such pupils for heaven out of her hands. Very much disappointed, but disinclined to vex his aunt, who had been of great use to him in his ambitious career, he allowed her to have her own way, and left the two girls to be prepared for heaven in the abbess's best style.

At first Agnes and Maria occupied the same cell and received their daily training side by side. But ere long the abbess found out that she had to deal with harder metal than usual, and must employ other arguments than finery, music and ceremony to produce the desired effect. For, what she taught them in the daytime, was discussed and refuted by the two girls when they were alone in their cell, and, like the Donäids, the abbess perceived that she made no progress whatever. They were separated, and only allowed to visit each other in the presence of one of the sisters who shared their respective cells. And now there began a trying time for the two girls, but especially for Maria. They had daily to listen to what they knew to be utterly false, without being able to console and strengthen each other. They were frequently punished for not complying with the orders of the convent; they were moreover entirely in uncertainty as to what had become of the Baroness, and of Karel. Day by day Maria faded under the blast of this north wind, and day by day as Agnes saw her lovely cheeks grow thinner, and her body waste away under a dress so sombre, so expressive of eternal sameness without hope of escape, a deep sigh escaped her breast, and she turned herself with more intense love towards that Saviour for whom they were thus suffering.

And the bitterest part of Agnes's agony was her fear that the continual dripping might wear out the stone, and that Maria unsupported by her, and without even so much as a Bible, might again be brought to hesitate. When she saw her, she had but little opportunity to speak with her, and never could she speak about those matters which were dearest to both. Thus three years passed slowly and tamely; every day exactly like the preceding and the following, and every day diminishing the dormant hope that they would regain their liberty.

But one day even the abbess was pleased to become anxious about Maria's condition. There could be no doubt about it that the poor girl was dying fast, and in the opinion of the abbess, the meek, and silent patient had a strong claim upon as much attendance and skill as could be had. Instead of the old woman, who used to share her cell, she received permission to have beside her a younger sister, Anne, who, next to Agnes, seemed to be her best friend, and who became her careful and tender nurse from that moment. The abbess also allowed Agnes to visit her cousin, such not having been the case for more than a year. The two girls, once more together, sobbed on each other's breasts, and could hardly be separated, though, but for the evidently good effect which her visit produced upon Maria, Agnes, the obstinate, the fearless, the heretical Agnes would have been condemned to remain in her narrow and lonely cell, while she knew that her cousin was gently passing through the borderland between life and death.

The second time that Agnes visited her cousin, they found out to their intense joy that sister Anne, instead of being, as the abbess thought, the most bigoted of all her flock, was deeply tainted with heresy herself. After having assured herself that no one could witness or hear what passed between them, this good nun requested Agnes to speak to her of Jesus and the Bible, nay, produced a copy of the New Testament which she kept carefully hidden in the folds of her dress. The joy of the two girls may be imagined. They hung over the precious book, and many a time the walls of the little cell were the silent witnesses of their devotion as they kneeled before their invisible and adored Saviour.

It was necessary to observe great care, however. Sister Anne could not always watch by Maria's bedside, and she had to share her post with another sister who was in reality as bigoted and devoted a Catholic as Ignatius Loyola himself.

It was sister Anne whom we now find resting in a

low chair by the side, of Maria's bed. She was a woman, of some thirty years, not handsome, nor with anything about her that might be called striking or even impressive. But she looked the very picture of honesty and fidelity, and it could be foretold that she would be the last person to betray her friend. She watched the sleeping Maria, with a grave look on her face. At last she said to herself, as she rose :—

"I do not know, but I feel as if Maria will not live much longer. Agnes has not seen her for a week now, and I think it would do them good to see each other. The abbess forbade me, but perhaps they may never see each other again. I will go and fetch her."

And softly opening the door of her cell, she stepped out of the room. The convent consisted of a square court enclosed by three galleries, and an abbey, or church, the latter being situated on the side of the square, opposite to the iron gate. The galleries or oblong buildings which formed the three other sides, had on the ground floor the apartments used as dining-halls, infirmaries, libraries, working rooms, etc., while the second floor consisted of the dormitories. The room of Agnes lay at the other end of the northern gallery, and walking softly in order not to disturb the sleepers or the occupiers of the other cells, she went to Agnes's cell and fetched her. It was not long before the two women were sitting at Maria's bedside, and watching her, as her bosom rose and fell under her irregular breathing. There was a great contrast between the two cousins as their faces were brought so close to each other. All the persecution, punishment, and suffering which Agnes had endured had

not been effectual in robbing her of her health nor
her cheeks of their roses. Her carriage was as elastic
and erect as ever, and her eye shone with its wonted
clearness. She, too, remarked the great difference which
the last week had made upon Maria, and as she pressed
a soft kiss upon the cheek, that was coloured with a little
burning spot a tear fell upon it, Maria opened her eyes,
and when they met those of her cousin she smiled
happily, and tried to rise and embrace her. But her
strength failed her, and she sank down again coughing
painfully. Agnes knelt down at the bedside, and encircled
Maria with her arms, who seemed perfectly at rest within them, and laid her head with a beautiful look of peace,
upon her shoulder.

"Do you know that I was dreaming Agnes, dear?" said
Maria in a soft voice, "and I dreamed that I saw you
dressed in gay clothes, and by your side walked Karel."

Agnes blushed, and pressed Maria closer to her with a
sort of spasm. She had been trying to forget Karel, for
she thought that it was God's will that they should meet
no more on earth, and if that were true, to think of him
would only be to nurse within herself an incurable
disease. She might have known that the disease was
incurable already, for fight and pray as she might, his
image was before her for ever, and every mention of his
name filled her with a longing which she could not bring
herself to acknowledge as anything wrong. She pressed
another kiss upon Maria's forehead and said :—

"If it be God's will, Maria, I shall see Karel again.
But I am afraid that He has determined it otherwise. It
seems so perfectly hopeless to think ever to escape out

of these sombre walls. And even then, I would not know whither to turn."

"We are in God's hand, sister Agnes," said Anne, "and He can work wonders."

"But I dreamed more than that, Agnes," said Maria. "I dreamed that I saw my dear mother, bright as an angel, beckoning me to come, and I think I am going home, Agnes. I am tired of lying here at the gate of heaven, and of hearing heavenly music mingle with the dying sounds of the tide of worldly thoughts as its waves still play around me, and try in vain to bear me away from that happy shore which God has pur- chased bought for me."

Agnes said nothing. It was a hard struggle for her thus to part with the only being she now had on earth whom she could speak with and trust. It was a hard strugle for her to acquiesce in God's will, when it bereaved her of the only joy in her present life. And yet she was glad, for she knew that it was best for her cousin, whom she was now fully assured, no human power could tear out of His hands.

There was a moment's silence which was interrupted by the dying girl's cough which seemed to give her great pain, though through all her illness not a single complaint had escaped her lips.

"Have you much pain, Maria?" asked Agnes, softly.

"I have not so much now as I have had, Agnes dear,' answered Maria, "but my only fear is that I have not had enough of it. When I think of the sufferings of Jesus, and of those of the martyrs who die every day for Him, I am ashamed that I have shrunk from it, and have preferred this miserable life to the crown of everlasting glory. I sometimes fear that I have incurred God's irrevocable anger already." And tears stifled her voice.

"If we confess our sins, He is faithful and just to forgive us our sins, and to cleanse us from all unrighteousness," said sister Anne, reading out of the little Testament before her.

"And I have sinned greatly," said Maria, and her face showed that she felt deeply what she said, "but the Lord will not deal with me according to my transgression; I have never been happy since that evening at Brussels, Agnes. There was ever a voice within me, reminding me that I had denied Jesus, and at one time it almost drove me to despair I had grown almost well again, and I was rejoicing in the prospect of going back with you to Brill, when that fearful night intervened. From that moment, it was as if all hope, all joy was past for me, and the very idea of heaven and of God filled me with despair. Oh, Agnes, I *have* suffered. It is a fearful thing to deny Him, when we come to look at the object for which we do it, for the paltry things which we preferred to His heavenly peace. He is surely very gracious to forgive so great a sinner."

"And I, too, have denied him before men," sobbed Anne, who lay on her knees, with her head bent over the little volume which rested on the bed, "I have been afraid, I have thought it better and wiser to make the abbess believe that I was a Catholic, though I hate and abhor it. From this time, I shall do so no more Agnes. We shall praise Him and suffer for Him together. I can bear this no longer."

"Read the fifth chapter of Matthew to us, Anne," said Maria.

Anne turned to the chapter, where Jesus proclaims to the multitude those wonderful doctrines. There was but a little lamp burning in the room, and the whole convent, as they thought, had gone to rest. With a soft and tremulous voice, the nun began—

"'Blessed are the poor in spirit, for theirs is the kingdom of heaven.'" Her voice gained strength, and firmness as she proceeded, and in a low and yet clear tone, she read out the following verses. She came to the tenth verse,

"'Blessed are they which are persecuted for righteousness' sake; for theirs is the kingdom of heaven,'"—when a shriek startled them in their pious reverence.

"Holy Virgin! Blessed Mother of God! What is this! Sister Anne say what is this!"

With these words the stately and bewildered form of the abbess, who had heard the reading as she passed the door, rushed in amongst the three girls.

For a moment both Agnes and Anne were too frightened to speak. The abbess caught up the little book which lay on the bed, and which they had not endeavoured to conceal.

"The holy Evangel of Saint Matthew!" she cried out, "dare you read such heretical books in this convent? You, sister Anne, who have professed to me over and over again that you were a pious Catholic."

"But who shall do so no more," answered Anne calmly rising, "I am no longer a Roman Catholic, so help me God, if it is sin for a Catholic to read these words to a dying girl who thirsts after something better than mere Latin masses."

" Dying? Who is dying? Is it——?" she looked at Maria, and her face told her that Anne spoke the truth. The mere thought that a soul should thus pass away from earth in the midst of heresy made her almost frantic. She seized the dying girl by the shoulder and said,

" Maria! Maria! would you die and be eternally lost! Would you die without having received absolution and extreme unction, and having partaken of the most holy Sacrament? Jesus! Maria! child, awake, listen, not to these foul-mouthed advocates of Satan, but pray the saints that they give you an hour in which to prepare yourself for entering purgatory!"

The abbess was in a fearful excitement. She trembled in every limb and her voice shook with emotion. She watched the face of the sick girl with breathless attention as did also the two.

A beautiful smile lit up the face of Maria, and with her eyes looking up to heaven she said, or almost breathed, " Jesus." There was a pause, and then fixing her eyes upon the abbess, she said, " No one cometh unto the Father but by me."

The abbess stood terrified, and ere she could recover breath to answer, Maria again spoke,

" Agnes," she said, pressing her cousin's hand," I am going—my sufferings are over—I have at least been allowed once to proclaim—Jesus," and with these words on her lips her spirit passed away into fellowship with Him.

" This is your work," said the Abbess, turning to Agnes," who lay kneeling before the bed, whilst she sobbed and prayed for strength. She felt entirely prostrated, and could almost have asked God to let her pass away too.

" You two shall suffer fearfully for that you have allowed this spirit to pass away without invoking the aid of the Church," said the abbess, in a low and trembling tone, in which there lay a whole wealth of anger, and snatching up the little book she went out of the cell and locked the two girls in with the corpse.

They passed the night beside it in with prayer, repeating such passages of the Bible as they could remember. The next morning they were both seized, bound, and conveyed to separate cells under the Church. The abbess had spoken the truth when she said that they should suffer. It was no acute pain that was inflicted on them. It was diabolical, slow torturing, with hunger and thirst, relieved at times that they might afterwards feel the want all the more. Thus Agnes lingered on in darkness at times, in dusk always, singing psalms and praying, and often an involuntary listener to the mass which was chanted above her, and which she accompanied with her own words of unshaken faith.

One day about a fortnight after she had been brought thither, she lay feverish and hungry on her little bed of straw. She had just had a visit from the Abbess and it needed all her strength to withstand the priestess who now by entreaties and promises, now by threatenings and inflictions endeavoured to induce her to change her faith. She was fervently praying God that He might take her away, or send help, for she felt that she could not much longer have the strength to withstand the temptation. Suddenly the door of her cell opened and the abbess again stood before her.

" Rise," she said in a harsh tone, " you at least shall suffer as much as any of us ; you who are such a martyr."

Agnes rose and followed the abbess through the halls. The whole convent seemed to be in commotion. Vans full of valuable tapestries and robes were standing in the garden, and many of the nuns were running hither and thither as if in great alarm. At a loss what to think she followed the Abbess and a few other nuns through the streets of Brill, which she had not trodden now for four years. But all her recollections, every sensation was drowned in curiosity, for wherever she looked she saw scared faces, or tears, or people loading their valuables on vans and carts. She was all wonder, " Could the town be besieged by the Prince ? " she dismissed the suggestion as ridiculous and asked the nuns, but was answered with silence.

At last they arrived at the monastery of St. Peter, which was far stronger than the nunnery, and here in a small room with other nuns, she heard that the Sea Beggars had come with their fleet and were going to storm the town in an hour and murder everybody. The reader can judge of her joy at this intelligence. She counted the minutes and grew impatient when the clock struck the hour, nay two hours, and darkness fell over the city but no Beggars came.

But hark! do you hear that shout! There they are, God be thanked ! They are coming. No, it is only boys and apprentices. But no, the noise increases. Blows are heard on the door of the monastery. The nuns grow frightened and shriek. The blows are redoubled, the nuns fall into each other's arms and weep, only Agnes and Anne sat there trembling with impatience, whispering hopeful words into each other's ears. At last the door gives way, and with a shout of victory the men run in the direction of the shrieks, with which their laughter mingles. The door flies open and a motley crew apparently half men, half devils, burst in upon them.

Agnes is seized by a tall man without nose or ears, who curses and swears he will have some good spoils out of priestcraft, at any rate. Agnes cries out that she is a patriot. But the fellow snatches her in his arms and carries her out of the convent into the street. She struggles, but in vain ; she is almost swooning.

Gathering her last strength she cries, "Karel, Karel, Galama !"

" Hallo," shouts a gruff voice before them, " Galama ! what's this ! By all the powers it must be Mistress Agnes."

And a little fellow jumps like a cat at her assailant's throat. A terrible combat ensues and Agnes swoons away.

But we have anticipated the course of events and we must now resume the thread of our narrative.

Chapter Twenty-Eighth.

THE FIRST OF APRIL.

" COME, ferryman, give me and my two friends here a speedy pull across, and I will give silver for thy trouble which I warrant thou seest not every day."

So saying, a little man, whose dress nothwithstanding a long sword at his side made him known as a clerk or student, followed by two others of a more martial appearance, stepped into the ferry-boat, where Peter Koppestock, the ferryman, was ready to do his duty by conveying them across the Meuse to the town of Brill. It was a bright morning, or rather noon, on the first day of April, 1572, and the sun danced merrily upon the rapid stream.

" May-be I have had more silver to handle than you wot of, master," answered Koppestock, as he seized his oar and pushed off. " But to be sure," he continued, there's no one now will be inclined to boast of great possessions, since he has to give it all away in pennies. I for one do not covet them, for he who has nought has nought to lose."

" What sayest thou about these pennies, friend?" inquired the little man nervously. " I would not say that they were bad, and yet they seem to me to press heavily upon thee."

" Not upon, me, master," answered the ferryman, rowing lustily," for I have nought to pay them with, and as I said to my wife, a tenthpenny of nought is nought. But even although I had it, I would assuredly pay nothing of it to the Duke."

"Heigho, my man, thou speakest boldly of the Duke," said the other with a tone of authority. " Thou knowest perhaps not who we are else thou wouldst curb thy tongue somewhat! We are officers in the army of his most Catholic Majesty the King of Spain, and were we not of very good humour we might make thee repent thy rashness."

" I thank thee, sir officer,"replied Koppestock, putting a stress upon the title, for he saw the two passengers smile when they heard the revelation of their dignity, " but I am none the less inclined to repeat my words. Surely a man may be a good and pious Catholic and as good a subject of the Count of the Netherlands, for kings we have never known in these parts, without con- senting to be utterly ruined for the sake of a parcel of pot-bellied monks and priests, and an army that has no right to be here. The most devoted of subjects if he does not belong to the army objects to become a beggar."

" Well, by our good lady of St. Clara," ejaculated one of the other two men, " I never dreamt that Peter would beat thee in thy tongue so well, Ralph."

" Thou hast good laughing," replied the little man, " but I swear ere this sun has set upon us sinful mortals, I shall make this rebellious fellow rue that he has used such untoward language. Knowest thou not, fellow, that there be vessels unto honour, and vessels unto dishonour, and that the latter should never think of pronouncing judgment, or putting themselves on a level with their higher brethren. Thou shalt rue it, I tell thee."

"Then I would say," responded the ferryman, not heeding the threat of the manikin, though he sat boldly and puffing with wrath in the boat, "then I would say that *those* are the most honourable vessels that are the most useful. For she who carries nought but ornament has little on her."

"I know not what ye talk of honourable or dishonourable vessels," said the other companion, who had been looking attentively towards the mouth of the river, "but methinks yonder I can see some vessels coming hither that are likely to be neither. They seem too numerous and out of shape for merchantmen. What may they be?"

All turned their eyes in the direction in which the speaker pointed, and saw a crowd of white sails glittering and shining in the sunshine, and advancing up the river. They were as yet too far to be clearly distinguishable, though red banners and streamers were seen flapping in the wind. For some moments all were intently occupied in gazing.

"It is a peculiar flag, anyhow," said Koppestock, resuming his oars, which for a moment he had dropped, "and all of the same kind too. I have my suspicions."

"Tell us what they are, my man," said the little fellow, "since thou art better acquainted with all manner of ships than we are."

"You seemed to be excellently acquainted with all

kinds of vessels, master," replied Koppestock, "but since those threats which you have held out to me, I dare not breathe the name of an enemy within your loyal ears for fear of losing mine."

"Thine are *not* loyal," said the other, "but I command thee in the King's name to tell me."

"In what King's name?" asked the undaunted ferry-man, pulling slowly.

"Well, in the Duke's then, if thou fearest him more, or thou shalt rue it."

" Again?" cried Koppestock. " But since you have commanded me I must tell. Yon fleet there, is to my best knowledge, the Sea Beggars' fleet."

"Eh! What? Sea Beggars!" cried the three men, starting up together and gazing at the sails. The ferry-man bent over his oars and chuckled.

" There are at least fifty ships," said the little man, "and they are approaching quickly. Here, my good man take this and row us quickly to the shore, for they might come upon us and do harm. What say you."

" They'd certainly murder you if they caught you, sir officer. So I shall row," and taking the large piece of silver that was offered to him, the ferryman pulled for his life. It was hardly necessary to pull at all, however, for in two strokes the boat lay alongside the shore. The three men jumped out, and discussing the matter in evident astonishment, they left the ferryman with his quickly earned silver to himself.

"Ha, ha, I never saw so great a fool! He was not ten yards from the shore, and grew afraid. The Sea Beggars too! I wonder what they want here. They are a queer set. But, never mind, there's no one to row across, so I'll just go and meet them." And turning his boat, he rowed in the direction of the fleet which came up in full sail.

He had not rowed for more than ten minutes when he stopped, for he thought he heard his name called, and turning himself in his boat, he looked at the first ship which was now close to him.

"Ha! what do I hear? Hans? and Treslong's arms in the flag! Am I dreaming or——no——yes, by the holy Virgin, they *are* the Sea Beggars."

"Peter, Peter!" at this moment cried Hans, leaning over the bow of his ship, which was foremost, "do you hear, Peter! Come here."

"What d'ye want?" growled Peter Blink, limping up behind him.

"Get out of the way, you fellow," said Hans, "do you see I am calling Koppestock. Peter!"

"Hullo!" answered the ferryman, shooting up to the bow of the ship, "who is calling me? Is that you, Hans? Is this Lord de Treslong's ship?"

"One of them," said Hans, with an air of importance. "Come up! I want you."

"I am coming fast enough," said the ferryman, and seizing a rope that was thrown out to him, he dexterously swung himself up and stood beside Hans on deck.

"So you have come at last," he said, shaking his friend's hand cordially. "You have been long enough about it. What are you going to do with all these ships? Are you the captain of this one. It is a fine one and no mistake."

"The Yonker and I we take it between us," said Hans

gravely. "We are coming to cannonade the whole town. Come along to my Lord de Treslong. He's on board."

Treslong, Galama, Barends and Willem, were standing near the stern of the ship, apparently engaged in a deep discussion. They were looking at the town which could be distinctly seen about a mile off the shore. A crowd of people were on the walls gazing at the ships.

"My Lord," said Barends, " God has given us this fine opportunity. Let us not spoil it by being rash, and turn His first blessing into a curse. Let us send a parley, and demand surrender first, before we take other steps."

"Your suggestion is not bad," said Treslong, "the Yonker is somewhat too impatient. But is it not likely they will hang the messenger, and shut the gates? But who is coming here? Hans and—what Koppestock? The ferryman! he's exactly the man we want. Hail my friend."

"My Lord, may the holy Virgin bless you for ever, and prosper your race," said the ferryman, sinking on one knee, and seizing Treslong's hand with a passionate and yet respectful gesture. " I have not seen your face since you saved me and mine from starvation, nor could I ever express my thanks to you. Receive them now."

"Oh, I forgot that circumstance," said Treslong, good-humouredly. "But it was more my father than I who did it. But rise, my friend, and tell me is there any garrison in Brill. You see our fleet here takes a bold position. What know you of the state of the town ?"

"I know that there are scarcely half-a-dozen soldiers, within the walls, my Lord," answered Koppestock, "and were you now to march your soldiers to them, you would easily get in. There has just been high mass and the churches are full of silver and gold vessels of all sorts, which alone, to be sure, would pay you your expenses."

A short consultation between the four men took place. Then Treslong turning round said

"Come along with us to the admiral. I suppose you fear not for yourself to carry to the town a message from the Count?"

"Not I, my Lord, not I," cheerfully answered the ferryman, "all that I have is thine, and since thou art a Beggar, so am I. Command me, and I'll do it."

Treslong, Galama, Koppestock and Hans, now went to the ladder, where the long boat lay ready to receive them. Treslong had gone down, and Galama was just following, when he saw Hans standing beside him, ready to follow him. He stopped and said : "Remain here, Hans! You know for what!"

"Not if you hang me! Why should I stop?" asked Hans.

"I told you. Pick out a dozen hearty men. We have yet to enter the convent of St. Clara!"

"Ah!" said Hans, putting his finger to his nose. "I forgot that." Then turning to Koppestock, he said in a confidential whisper,

"I cannot go with you to the admiral, but the Yonker will. Don't mention my name to the Count, because he and I are at loggerheads. I'll see you back presently."

The ferryman who rejoiced to find that Hans had become such a great personage, thanked him for his instructions, and descended the ladder. A few strokes of the six men who rowed the boat, brought it alongside the admiral's ship, where great preparations for landing the men, were evidently being made. Count de la Marck stood on deck, dressed in a magnificent breastplate, and equally costly Beggar's hat, made of the skin of a wild boar, the plume and diamond buckle of which alone, were worth a little fortune. When he saw Treslong he exclaimed:

"Ha! my lord, I was going to send for you. How shall we do, think you? Storm the town at once, or ask them to buy us off? They will give a handsome sum."

"I would advise neither, cousin," said Treslong, coolly. "I have brought you a ferryman, who is well known in the town, and has known me for years. He says there is no garrison in the town, and there will hardly be any resistance. Let us demand a surrender."

"Ha," said Lumei, pouncing upon the ferryman, "is that God-forgotten Papist of a Meertinck, still burgomaster of Brill?"

"Ay, ay, my lord, and frightened he will be at this moment," answered Koppestock.

"Go and tell him that, I William Count de la Marck, Baron of Lumei, Admiral of the fleet of his Highness the Prince of Orange, the lawful Governor of these provinces, demand the instant and unconditional surrender of the city of Brill. And tell the scoundrel in my name, by way of confidential advice, that if he is not here in half-an-hour with the keys, that I will cannonade the town, and hang every mother's son that's worth a groat, on his own doorpost. Go and tell him that."

"Stay," said Treslong, retaining the ferryman, "half an hour is too little——"

"No, not a moment," roared the admiral. "Half-an-hour, I say."

"I can scarcely reach the city in that time," said the man, "and then who will believe me, when I bring your message. Have you no token?"

"Here," said Treslong, giving his signet ring, "they know *that*, at any rate. Tell them that we are landing, and shall wait one hour from this moment. Go now."

The next moment the ferryman who could hardly retain his pleasure within bounds, was in the boat, rowing towards his own. At the foot of the ladder, stood Hans, evidently waiting for him. He had no sooner reached his own boat, when Hans, leaning over to him, said,

"I say, Peter, what are you going to do?"

"Going to demand the surrender of the city," laughed Peter.

"Tell them there are *five thousand* of us," said Hans gravely, "and two hundred and fifty cannons, and that there are as many more coming."

Koppestock nodded his head laughing, and pulled for his life a second time.

The stipulated hour had nearly elapsed, and the boats were busy conveying the men from the ships to the shore, where, nothing loath to have a change, they squatted down in companies and regaled themselves with the little beer or wine, which they had been able to scrape together.

In the meantime the admiral and such of the officers as were not employed in superintending the landing, had betaken themselves to a house not far from the shore, the inhabitants of which, probably frightened at behold-

so unexpected and warlike a scene, had fled to the city in terror, and caused the alarm of its citizens to reach its highest pitch. The whole town was in commotion. High and low, young and old, rich and poor, were standing in groups on the canals, in the streets, or on the walls, discussing the event, and the best steps to take, with eager gestures and faces upon which anxiety, dismay, or even terror were readable. For the Beggars of the Sea, thanks to the ferocity of their admirals and captains, had earned for themselves a name synonymous with desperate courage, great obstinacy, and unbounded cruelty. Many of the women were in tears, many of the men were desponding, and stood with their hands in their pockets, or assembled on the market-place, in front of the town-hall, in which the magistrates were assembled, gravely discussing the best means that could be adopted to meet the emergency. Many, too, closed their doors, and shut themselves with their families in the back apartments, where upon their knees, they implored God that the hope, now being kindled might not be extinguished.

While these opposite feelings of consternation and joy, of terror and hope, were being aroused in the city, there was another scene enacted in the house which we have mentioned above. In the largest room sat de la Marck—at the head of a square deal table, his portly form resting in a clumsy chair, and a can of wine standing before him. Around the table we find the leading captains of the fleet standing or sitting in different positions, all armed, and mostly dressed in a picturesque and fantastic style

"As a worthy relation of him who presented the Request," said Lancelot de Brederode, a magnificent-looking young man, and a brother of the "madman," "I heartily applaud your proposal, Sir Count. Let us give no quarter to those that gave us none."

"How then," cried Adam van Haren, "would you despoil our cause for ever, by letting us commit those deeds which we pretend to abhor?"

"Abhor?" said another captain, Gillis Steltman, speaking vehemently. "Have we not sworn that we would revenge the insults done to our countrymen, and that we would wash the stains on our banners in the blood of our tyrants? Have we then forsaken our goods, have we risked our lives, have we abandoned all hope for grace, and made our name a terror on the seas, that we should show ourselves a parcel of old women the moment we intend to do ought else but plunder a merchantman. Have ye forgotten the deeds *they* have done, the blood *they* have spilled. Have ye forgotten the fate of Utrecht, the fate of Ghent. Do ye not see the streams of blood flowing at Jemmingen and at Heiliger Lee. I, for one, I have sworn never to rest till every Spaniard I could lay hold off was bled to death, since I stood not a dozen yards away from the scaffold where the Counts of Egmont and Horn were executed. And if nothing else should remind me of my oath, I would still have this———"

And with a vehement and passionate gesture, he dashed upon the table a cambric handkerchief, upon which large stains of a deep-red colour as of blood were visible. A cry of sympathy went up from amongst the

captains. It was a handkerchief dipped in the blood of
he two nobles Egmont and Horn, as three years ago
.t flowed warm and reeking out of the headless trunks.

Treslong frowned and was going to speak, when an
officer named Herlijn, whose face without nose and ears
presented a horrible spectacle, drove his dagger into
the table and said with a tremendous oath—

" I will stop my practice for no one. If there are
priests in the city they shall know me."

His practice consisted in seizing all priests and burning them alive, after having deprived them of their nose
and ears, the same having been done some four years
ago to his father, his brother, and himself, though he
had escaped the burning.

" And I declare that I shall not allow such beastly
cruelties to be perpetrated as long as I have a pistol
with which to shoot the perpetrator," cried out Entes de
Mentheda, a resolute warrior who looked at Herlijn
with flashing eyes. He was vice-admiral of the fleet
and was much respected.

" Away with the priests! kill the tyrants! shoot the
dogs!" cried three or four captains of Herlijn's stamp
together.

" Shame! We are Protestants! We serve a noble
cause! No cruelty," cried others, who were of opposite tendency.

" Silence, gentlemen!" said de la Marck, who knew at
times how to preserve his dignity, " let us consider
what we have to do and not bring our passions to our
aid."

" It is not long since I had a note from the

prince, Count ! " said Ruikhaver," and he entreats us to use no cruelty, and not to disgrace our name."

" I would for one moment beg your attention, gentlemen," said Treslong, seizing the opportunity and speaking calmly. " We have heard many opinions ; we have listened to threats, to invectives, to passionate rehearsals of wrongs, but we have had but little advice Gentlemen, let us remember that the eyes of our countrymen are upon us. Let us remember that we are the only persons to whom they, to whom the Prince now looks for assistance. Our countrymen are weary of cruelty, they are sick of bloodshed, they abbor plunder. If our tyrants had come to us without swords, if they had executed their designs without spilling so fearful an amount of our blood, and let it be said of our noblest blood, I ask, is it not probable that not half the repulsion which is now experienced, would then be felt? I ask, is it not probable that without the Inquisition, without the Blood-Council, the name of Spaniards would not be half so horrible in our ears as it is. Our countrymen look around for help, they look around for those who can defend them without committing these cruelties, they acknowledge that defence, that attack is necessary, nay laudable, but they acknowledge too that revenge is unjustifiable and disgraceful. I ask you, Herlijn, how did Count Egmont win his laurels ? Was it by cruelty ? His name is unstained by a single drop of blood unnecessarily spilt. The Prince's strict command too is that we should do nought but what is *laudable*, *honourable* and *fair*. When the citizens of other towns hear that we can hold a town for the Prince without

B B

carnage, they will follow our example within four-and-twenty hours, but when the way we take is marked everywhere by burning houses, by mutiltated corpses, and by violated women, I say, that, instead of doing good, we shall alike disgrace our cause and ourselves, and have no more right to pray for assistance from God, than our bitterest enemies the Spaniards."

These noble words, spoken in an impressive and earnest manner, had a great effect. Even de la Marck was affected by their truth, and allowed a discussion to take place, as to the best way to make use of the occasion. In the midst of the discussion it was announced that two deputies from the town had arrived. De la Marck who had forgotten the stipulation he had made, bade them come in. They were the two men whom we have seen in the ferry-boat, and who were important citizens of Brill. Their companion, the clerk, a compound between a schoolmaster and a priest, had already found an opportunity to make off with himself.

It was to be expected that the deputies should address the admiral with due respect. The warlike preparations going on between the shore and the house, as well as the appearance of the assembly in which they now found themselves heightened their respect for the Beggars, and not being able to count the forces, they fully believed the enormous exaggerations made by Koppestock. They presented to the admiral the respectful regards of the Burgomaster and city of Brill, and requested that a further grace of two hours might be granted them in order to come to a unanimous conclusion how to answer the summons which had been received. That the city was by no means so defenceless as not to be able to sustain a siege of at least twenty-four hours with some chance of success; that it was a matter of grave consideration, forasmuch as Alva had once already threatened the city with punishment, and that the fame of the Sea Beggars being well known, the citizens would far rather remain in Spanish hands, than endure all the horrors and cruelties which were said to have been perpetrated by them.

After the message had been delivered, and the deputies had gone outside a violent discussion once more took place. But the effect of Treslong's speech remained, and those who were for hanging the parleys and rushing upon the town were overruled, the more because the landing had not yet been effected. The deputies were recalled and informed that another two hours would be granted. That no violence of any kind would be perpetrated inside the city, and that the only object of their summons was to take the city out of Alva's hands, and place it in those of the Prince of Orange. The deputies departed astonished at the moderation and leniency of the far-famed Count de la Marck, and the captains went to superintend the finish of the landing and to get their men in readiness.

Glad that his words had had such good effects, Treslong stepped outside the house, where he was joined by de Ryk, van Haren, de Mentheda, and others, who thanked him for his timely speech. While they were winding their way through the groups of soldiers, who were standing in the fields, or amusing themselves by skirmishing together, Treslong looked round and said,

" But where is my brave lieutenant, Yonker Galama ? He has taken no part in the discussion, and I do not remember having seen him in the house."

" Nor have I, my Lord," said de Ryk, " and if I am not mistaken he is yonder with the soldiers of your ship, and that of the admiral."

Galama approached them at that moment. His face was pale and, though calm, Treslong saw that he was inwardly excited.

" Well," he said, "are we to march at once. I have hurried all the men, but they are such lazy brutes and talk of hunger, that I do not think they are ready yet."

" Nor need they be, Yonker," answered Treslong, " for we have two hours yet before we can do anything. So you must be patient and wait."

The Frisian frowned and stamped angrily with his foot. The time however flew by more quickly than he had thought. After all the men had been landed, they were reviewed by the admiral, de Mentheda and Treslong. It was but a small party to take a town, and there was many a heart there wondering whether they would really succeed in executing their design. The two hours had not yet elapsed when some men who had been sent out to reconnoitre, came running back and announced that all the gates had been shut, and that most of the wealthy inhabitants were making their escape by the south gate.

" Ha ! " said the admiral with an oath," the traitors ! Now they fly because having spared their lives they

do not think us worth their hospitality. My Lord de
Treslong take half these men and enter the south gate.
I shall enter the north gate. We shall meet on the
market-place. Forward!"

" Forward!" was the cry re-echoed by the Beggars as
they followed their leader. The first two ranks of Treslong's men were those selected by Galama who headed
them, all impatience to get inside the town.

" I say, Hans," said Peter Blink, walking beside his
friend with the tremendous sword on his shoulder,
" we are going to look for Mistress Agnes, are we not?
What like is she?

" Beautiful," answered Hans, seizing his axe, " that is
all I can say. "And mind when you find her do not touch
her, but watch over her till either I or the Yonker
come up."

" Close up, close up," here commanded Treslong, as
a troop of armed men appeared outside the gate and
seemed inclined to dispute the passage. Treslong
halted for a moment, and then seeing that the party
was not large, commanded an attack. The whole body
flew forward, Hans and Peter first of all. But without cannon, and but few fire-arms a bridge is not so
easily taken, and this was found out by the Beggars.

Though there were some two hundred of them, their
foremost ranks, consisting of some twenty men had all
the fighting to do. They were at first kept at a distance by
the very effective fire of the three of four dozen men
on the bridge. Peter Blink brandishing his sword and
laying all around him in the dust happened to stand on
the edge of the bridge which, as we have said in a

former chapter, connected the island on which the gate stood with the ramparts. Missing his footing, he stumbled, and would have fallen into the water had he not caught at the wood. Now Peter was very strong, and, taking advantage of his position, he swung himself along the bridge, his feet touching the water, and by the side of the fighting men who in their heat did not discover him. His stratagem succeeded. He reached the island, and suddenly raising a cry of " *Vivent les Gueux*," began to attack the Spaniards, for such they were, in the rear. In a moment all was confusion. The Spaniards, thinking they were in reality attacked behind, turned to fly. Some jumped into the fosse, some begged for quarter, some rushed upon the enemy's swords and died, and in the space of ten minutes the gate was taken.

"Now for the nunnery," cried Galama, as he waved his sword, which was dyed red with blood.

"Now for the abbess, Hans," said Peter, giving Hans a dig in the side as if nothing had happened, and wiping his dripping weapon upon the body of a Spaniard who lay with his helmet, head and neck split. "It's the finest piece of work I have ever done," he continued, pointing to the body. "In one blow, too. The fellow never said a word." And they ran after Galama admiring their work. Such is the excitement of war. In a quieter moment, they would both have shuddered to have spilt that blood, or thus to mutilate a fellow-being. And Cain, too, who gave the example; will often have wondered, when in after times stung with remorse he sought in vain for a place to hide in, how he could ever have done so horrible a deed.

It was not long before the ten men were at the gate of the nunnery, and made the halls resound with the heavy blows of their axes. But the door gave no signs of opening, and save the echo of the blows no no sound was heard within. The men redoubled their blows, but the door remained as firm as ever. Peter Blink, in the meanwhile, who had seen in the beginning that the door could not thus be opened, and shrewd as he was, knew at once what was wanting, soon came back with a kind of petard he had obtained from the ammunition stores which he knew were close by. Galama thanked him eagerly and fixed it to the door with trembling hands.

"Now then, out of the way, anybody on the other side," said Hans and set fire to the match. In a few seconds the wall shook with the report of the instrument, and rattling the doors flew out of their casement and into the gateway. The men gave a shout and rushed inside headed by Galama and Hans. Through the galleries, in the garden, in the cellars, in the church, everywhere did they fly, shouting and calling out Agnes! Maria! and knocking the walls to see whether there might be any hidden stairs, but not a soul, not a single person answered their calls. The convent was regularly cleared out. No silver, gold or any valuables whatever were to be found.

Galama leaned against the gate, after he had completed his search, as pale as death, his lips compressed and his breath coming and going heavily.

"Come, Yonker," said Hans encouragingly, though he felt but little hope himself, "all is not lost. They may be in the town yet, for all we know."

"A poor booty we have had," said Peter Blink, coming back with a gold chain in his hand. Galama saw it, and snatched it away. It was the chain he had first given to Gerard Block. He remembered that Maria had taken it again. He pressed it to his lips, and gave a deep sob, as a hot tear fell on his hand.

"Come, my men," he said dashing it away, and hiding the chain in his bosom. "Follow me to the market-place. There I will reward you for your trouble."

And striding at the head of his men, and battling with his deep and bitter disappointment, he left the convent

Chapter Twenty-Ninth.

FOUND AGAIN.

WITH a feeling as if the whole world had lost its interest for him, the Frisian stepped along the street at the head of his men in the direction of the large square where stood the cathedral. The night was falling, and had already wrapped the city in a veil of dusk which hid all but the nearest objects from view. But the city was very lively for all that. Sounds of gaiety, of revelry, proceeded from many houses, the windows of which were thrown open and displayed a heap of the invaders helping themselves to such of the good things of this earth as had been left by the many citizens who had employed the grant of two hours in packing all that was packable, and flying. Everywhere laughter and song, sometimes the clash of weapons, or the sound of a quarrel were heard, and it could be seen that the Beggars were indemnifying themselves for their late starvation.

Suddenly both Galama and Hans started. They had come in the vicinity of the town-hall when the screams of two or more women fell upon their ears. Both of them recognized or thought they recognized Agnes's voice, and forgetting everything else they started off in pursuit. A few moments brought them in front of the town-hall, where an extraordinary scene awaited them. It was a large and antique building, forming one side of a square, which was used as market-place. The square was full of Beggars, some armed with lances, others with swords and daggers, some with sticks. They seemed to enjoy themselves immensely, for every moment some burst of laughter broke out from one side of the square or another. Pushing his way through, Karel looked on and almost laughed himself. In a space encircled by Beggars, five or six stout priests, with their shaven heads and magnificent dresses were being hustled and chased and pulled about by the men, who considered it excellent fun, the more so that the well-sized fathers were blowing and perspiring under the weight of clothes which they had been forced to put on.

Karel saw at a glance that most of them were van Haren's men, and inquiring from one of them where he was, he was answered that Captain van Haren and Treslong had broken into the monastery of St. Peter on the Maerlandt Square. Now the Maerlandt Square, though it lay some distance from the town-hall, was not far from the place where they fancied they had heard the screams, and it flashed in his mind that they had just run in the wrong direction. He looked round for Hans and discovering him nowhere, he flew alone in the direction of the square. On the square stood the Maerlandt church, the second Catholic church in Brill, which though it was small and less handsome externally than the cathedral, possessed far more valuables than the other, being situated in the neighbourhood of the wealthy monastery of St. Peter. When the Yonker arrived in the square he was for a moment puzzled what to do. By the red and flaring light of torches he saw his own men busy in making the best of the inside of the church. Some had smashed the manificently painted windows and were standing on the sills throwing to their companions whatever they could manage to seize. Others were running away, their arms full of silver vessels or candlesticks. One man was ludicrously arrayed in a long robe of light-velvet with golden stars sewn over it, and a bright crown of gold on his head. It had belonged to the image of the Virgin over the altar, which costly work of art lay now in the dust, broken into a hundred pieces.

Suddenly it occurred to the Frisian that Treslong's house, or rather that of his late father, stood on the square, and directing his steps hither, he was soon able to recognize ħt. A flood of light came through a parting in the curtain that was drawn before the window, and as he flew up the steps and into the hall which was full of his own men who were conveying their booty hither, he heard Treslong's voice giving the toast—

"The Prince, the Beggars and the Independence of the Netherlands."

Just as he opened the door of the room from which the sound seemed to come, the toast received uproarious applause. It was a large room, magnificently furnished and lighted, and round a long square table some twenty men were standing with uplifted goblets, responding to the toast with enthusiasm. An ample repast was on the table. No sooner had Galama entered than he was perceived by some of the party, and a shout, of "Galama for ever," replaced their first cries. Not feeling in a mode to partake of their gaiety, he turned back to leave the room, but the men, among whom we find our acquaintance van Hagendorp, seized him, and carried him forcibly to the head of the table, where Treslong stood wondering what the noise might be.

"This is the man who had the first idea of it, gentlemen," cried van Hagendorp, "let us drink a bumper on his health and that of the beautiful nun he is looking for."

Karel who had put the cup to his lips almost against his will paused and looked at the speaker. A laughter from the assembled noblemen greeted him, but Treslong who understood his secret and pitiful look better, whispered to him, "She is safe."

The bumper was emptied in a moment, and another quickly followed it. The wine did him good, and the colour returned to his pale cheek.

"By all that's impudent," now cried one of the guests at the window, "here are our men plundering the church and we getting nothing of it." In a moment he opened the door, and ran outside followed by most of the others.

"I shall not let you wait any longer, Yonker," said Treslong, stepping to a door, "but I must say that for that fellow Peter Blink and myself, your mistress might have fared worse even than you expected. Here she is."

He opened the door and Karel entered the next room. On a kind of sofa two women and a man were conversing together, and one of the women as soon as she saw Galama's tall form enter the room, threw herself in his arms, regardless of Treslong or her two companions, who were none else than sister Anne, and Wouter Barends.

"And Maria?" asked Galama, after their first burst of joy was past.

"She is in heaven," answered Agnes, "she is happy now, and out of her troubles. She suffered a great deal."

"And have not you suffered a great deal?" asked her lover, looking tenderly at her thin and pale cheeks, for the treatment in the convent had at last robbed her of her roses.

"I suffered but little, my Karel," she answered, softly, "and most of *that* for you. What I underwent for Jesus' sake was to me no suffering ; for I bore it gladly. And I know that the heaviest part of Maria's suffering was the conviction within her that she had refused the cross, which God gave her to bear. She loved Him, and with her it was only a weakness of the flesh, but it haunted her so terribly, that I am certain had her denial gained her access to the greatest honours, wealth or pleasure, she would have revolted from their very sight."

"And is it not the same with us, Agnes?" said he. "Would not my life have been blighted had I offended you, and renounced you for aught in this world? You who have made me understand what it is to serve so great a Master. Ah, Agnes, these years have not been without use. They have served to develop within me the seed which you have sown, and," he added bending his head down to her, "they have strengthened our love towards each other, and towards Him."

Chapter Thirtieth.

THE CURTAIN FALLS.

"COME, Yonker," said Treslong next day, as he entered the same apartment where Galama was alone with Agnes, "we must be stirring. The admiral goes on like a madman. He wants to leave the city and return to sea, and leave the town as it is. We must induce him to remain, for I am certain that within a week we shall be besieged; and if we can keep the place for the Prince, it will be the greatest thing we have done yet. De la Marck has already been hanging several priests because they refused to show him their hidden treasures, which I do not suppose they possessed."

"I saw some priests ill-treated yesterday," said Galama, "and did I not hear you scream, Agnes?"

"I know I screamed," she answered, and then told him shortly how she had been released out of the clutches of that monster. "And to my great delight," she added, "I found Barends here, whom I prayed to go and look for Anne. He found her in the convent, nobody having troubled himself about her."

"Good Barends," said Treslong with a smile, "he actually prayed me to lend him some soldiers, that he might go to the house of van Alphen the corn-merchant, and defend it. Unfortunately van Alphen has left Brill these four years, it seems, so his services were not required. But as to your assailant, Mistress Vlossert, he has suffered for his insolence. It was that brute Herlijn. Thanks to Peter Blink, he is since dead."

At this moment, cries of "Sanglier! Orange!" were heard in the street, and a troop of Beggars rushed past the window. Fearing that something had gone wrong, Karel and Treslong snatched up their arms, ran into the street, and directed their steps to de la Marck's head-quarters. It was nothing, however, but a carouse of some intoxicated fellows.

They found de la Marck raving like a veritable wild boar. He would hang every Roman Catholic in the town, he would burn it, pull down the walls, and sail away. And as he stormed and swore, he pointed with a satisfied grin to the bodies of four priests, who had been hanged within his sight, dressed in all the pomp of their vocation. The same scene, which had been enacted in the house between the town and the shore, was enacted again with but little variation. At last the admiral gave in, and ordered all hands to join in strengthening the walls, and dragging guns out of the arsenal. Nor was this at all superfluous. Within a week, Bossu, a Spanish general, arrived before the town with ten companies of regular troops, and demanded the keys of the city.

On a part of the wall, not far from the northern gate, and almost at the back of the house of the late Baroness, we find de la Marck, Treslong, Galama and the principal officers in serious deliberation, for to judge by the number of ships which the enemy had brought

they numbered between one and two thousand men, and
the garrison of Brill was not more than five hundred. It is
true, immediately after it became known that the
Beggars of the Sea had taken Brill, many fugitives and
favourers of the Prince had joined them, and swelled
their number; still they had as yet but a small force.
Behind these officers we find a group of common
soldiers, who are looking at the Spanish ships,
gradually disembarking their men; and amongst them
we notice our old acquaintances, Hans, Peter Blink
and Dirk, the former servant of van Alphen.

"Dash it all," says Dirk, "I would not mind going out
to them."

"And get beaten," said Hans. "Do you not see that
there are about five times our number?"

"Bad job," growled Peter Blink, hacking the point of
his axe in a tree.

"Tell you what," says Dirk again, "if you will lend me
that axe of yours, Master Blink, I'll take and swim across
to the Niewland sluice yonder. I was one of the men
who made it, and I know I can get it loose in three
blows and all these Spaniards will be drowned."

It was a happy idea, and Hans at once communicated
it to Galama, who proposed it to the admiral. A few
moments later Dirk shouldered the axe, and plunging
into the moat swam across. Arrived at the other side
he ran to the sluice, and a few moments afterwards the
water poured through, almost carrying him along with it.
It was not long not the Spaniards found out what had
been done. That part of the land which lay between
the dyke on the Meuse, and the dyke which led to the

southern gate, was in a few minutes under water, which continued to rise every moment. The Spaniards retreated on the dyke and waited until all should have disembarked.

"They are following our example, my Lord," said Roobol, "we left nobody behind, and had no guns."

"Ay," said Galama, "and it struck me then, that we were acting very foolishly, for had there been a garrison, part of it could easily have cut the anchors of our ships and sent them adrift."

"Suppose we do it, now," said Treslong, "our boats are here." The three men looked at each other and smiled. The next moment, ever ready to execute a new idea, they had called their men, and were running to the harbour.

"A thousand ducats for the first boat that reaches them," cried Treslong.

"Come along, Peter," said Hans, dragging the dwarf behind him. They were followed by Dirk and four others, and leaping into their boat, so that it was almost swamped, they pushed off just as Galama, with a desperate leap, gained the back seat and took the helm.

"They cannot row against us, can they Peter?" said Hans, pulling at his oar.

"Right," growled Peter, pulling also. It was an exciting race of the four boats on the Meuse, rowing to do a daring deed, under a crossfire of jokes and laughter.

Galama's boat was the first to reach the vessels, some ten in number, on which but a few seamen had been left behind. Ten times their number would not have been able to oppose the rush of the Beggars as they climbed

c c

against the ships and immediately began cutting the anchors, the rigging and the sails. Suddenly a sharp report of muskets was heard from the city, and pausing in their work they saw the Spaniards led on to the walls by Bossu, where they were received by a murderous fire.

"To the boat, lads, at once," cried Galama rushing on deck from the cabin of the ship which they had reached. His orders were obeyed, and hardly had they left the vessel when with a fearful crash part of the deck flew off and a column of smoke and flames rose up in the air. Galama had followed Sextus's example and set fire to the powder. It was followed by the others, and in a little time half of the ships were on fire.

"To the boats, the Spaniards are coming back," cried Treslong. The boats were soon gained, and as they pulled away they could see the Spaniards wading along the dyke through the water which had meanwhile risen above it. The enemy had not bargained for so warm a reception and were completely staggered. After having been led on twice to the charge, and been defeated, they fled in disorder. The danger was surmounted, the city of Brill belonged to the Prince of Orange, and the first important exploit of the eighty years' war had been effected.

The effect which the taking of Brill had upon the people of the Netherlands was electric. It was as if the sun had suddenly shone in full lustre through a black and threatening cloud. City after city proclaimed for the Prince; town after town chased the Spanish garrison out of its walls. Treslong, at the head of a part of the men, set out for Flushing, and took it in name of the

Prince. Not long afterwards, an officer was sent by the Prince holding a commision as lieutenant-governor of the Island of Walcheren, the first nook where the standard of liberty was unfurled. How for a time the Spaniards almost crushed the renewed outburst of patriotism, how at last it triumphed, despite all the Spanish empire could do, how the Netherlands after a war of eighty years, became independent, and at last gained that freedom of worshipping God, which was their main desire, we leave hereafter to be related. For the present we take leave of our readers after giving them one little scene as farewell.

In the room of Treslong's house on the Maerlandt Square, where Galama had found Agnes, we find the couple, Barends, sister Anne, Treslong and Hans together. It is the evening of the day on which the Beggars of the Sea are going to depart.

"And are you really going to leave us?" asked Anne, as she looked at Galama.

"What else can I do, sweet nun?" answered he with a forced gaiety. "The real fight is only now beginning. But let Agnes decide."

Poor Agnes, who had been sitting motionless, here burst into tears, but forcing them back, she tried to smile, and said with a sob, "Go, Karel."

"I have another plan, Yonker," said Treslong kindly.

"You know I have just come from Flushing where I have seen the lieutenant-general, 't Zerearts. He asked me whom I could recommend as a good governor for Brill, and it struck me that you would not be a bad one—

"O my Lord!" here cried Agnes, falling before him, and kissing his hand.

"One moment, madam," said the seaman, smiling, " this is not all. You know your boat, Yonker, was first, and consequently I owe you one thousand ducats."

"That's my doing," whispered Hans, contentedly stroking his beard.

"As, however, I have but little ready money on hand-I thought I might give it to you in valuables. This house belongs to my family.   It was the residence and property of the old governor, my father, let it be so of the new. Let me congratulate you as the new governor of Brill, I know none more worthy to fill that post, as I never knew any one whom I loved and respected so much, and were it not that you have so great an attraction here I would never part with," and he bowed to Agnes.

Within a week of this scene Agnes and Karel were married in the Maerlandt Church by Wouter Barends and conducted in triumph to their new house by half the Beggars, whose departure had been purposely postponed though de la Marck had already sailed with the other half.

That their marriage was a happy one will scarcely be doubted; and their happiness was, all the greater because Wouter Barends lived with them and openly preached the reformed doctrines, no longer in the barn of van Alphen but in the cathedral.

FINIS.

APPENDIX.

———◆❖◆———

The Countess of Egmont. Page 41.

The interview between Alva and Egmont's noble and loving wife actually took place on the day before the execution. In reply to her supplications the Duke told her calmly that on the following day her husband would be released. She departed with hope in heart—but found out too soon the fatal meaning of the jest.—(*Motley.*)

Popular Superstitions of those days. Page 64.

The reader need not show any astonishment at the superstition of poor Gritta, when he remembers how the silliest tales were then believed by the lower, and indeed by many of the higher classes. Such for instance as that of a poor but pious woman, who prayed for a token, by which she might know that young children went to heaven. A child was born, and folding its hands immediately began to pray the Lord's prayer, after which it died, leaving the mother sorrowing, but not for the fate of her little one. Such also was that of the gay company, which chanced to make merry and dance on a Christmas evening, was cursed by the priest and continued dancing for three years without eating or drinking. After this strenuous exertion, they were no doubt glad to sit down and take some refreshment.—(*Vaernewyk.*)

Marnix de St. Aldegonde. Page 105.

This pious nobleman, the bosom friend of William, and the author of some beautiful verses and a translation of the Psalms had many political friends in England, ere he went, some years later, as ambassador to Queen Elizabeth.—(*Kok.*)

Count de Buren. Page 192.

After a sojourn of twenty years in Spain the Count de Buren once more visited his native land, native in name alone. His manners, his thoughts, and his language, were those of a Spaniard and the gloom and haughtiness with which he looked upon what were once his countrymen, convinced the King of Spain that what had been intended had been done. Not a single tie united him to the children of the Father of his people, William of. Orange.—(*Bor and others.*)

The fate of Spelle. Page 230.

The allusion of Hans to this personage was perfectly true. After Alva had allowed the miscreant to execute thousands of his own countrymen without warrant, he caused him to be imprisoned and beheaded for these very crimes. Such was Alva's gratitude.—(*Motley.*)

Blois de Treslong. Page 388.

The fortunes of this hero which are interesting enough to form by themselves the subject of a book, are too numerous to be given here. He, too, experienced that the greater part of man's life are " labours and sorrow." After the death of his illustrious friend and protector, the Prince, he was, in 1585 disgracefully imprisoned by the Governor of Middelburgh, his personal enemy, and it required the intereference of Leicester and his Queen to restore him to liberty. He never recovered from this blow, and, although he received many distinctions from Prince Maurice and other crowned heads, he retired to his country house and died there in 1594. His descendants, many of whom have since then filled prominent places in the history of the Republic, are still following their ancestor's illustrious example.—(*Kok.*)

Lumei, Count de la Marck. Page 388.

The end of this man's life strangely accords with the wild character which his deeds have given it. Soon after the capture of Brill, the Prince of Orange appointed him lieutenant of the province of Holland. His behaviour, however caused this appointment to be cancelled. After some vain attempts to raise an insurrection in his own favour, he retired to his property near Liege, where, having been bitten by a mad dog, he closed his life in fearful fits of hydrophobia.—(*Kok.*)

27, PATERNOSTER ROW,
LONDON, E.C.
June, 1868.

WORKS PUBLISHED BY

HODDER & STOUGHTON

(LATE JACKSON, WALFORD & HODDER.)

MARGARET HOWITT.

TWELVE MONTHS WITH FREDRIKA BREMER
in Sweden. By Margaret Howitt. In 2 vols., crown 8vo, with Portraits and Illustrations, 21s. cloth.

" Never was a pleasanter picture than that which Miss Howitt has painted for us."—*Literary Churchman.*

" Sketched with lively good humour, and brings out interesting details of Miss Bremer's domestic habits, benevolent character, and well-earned popularity."—*Morning Post.*

REV. E. PAXTON HOOD.

LAMPS, PITCHERS, AND TRUMPETS. Lectures
on the Vocation of the Preacher. Illustrated by Anecdotes—Biographical, Historical, and Elucidatory—of every Order of Pulpit Eloquence, from the Great Preachers of all Ages. Second Thousand. Crown 8vo. 10s. 6d. cloth.

" A book which we cordially recommend to all who take any interest in preaching. The book is a most valuable one—interesting as a romance, and quite unique in its kind."—*Dublin University Magazine.*

" For the treatment of this subject in a manner fitted at once to interest, to impress, and to improve his readers, Mr. Hood possesses peculiar qualifications. Himself a preacher of no mean order, with a genius in its own way, original, graphic, pictorial, with a mind teeming with ancient lore and modern literature, few men are more fitted to throw a charm over the whole theme."—*British and Foreign Evangelical Review.*

DARK SAYINGS ON A HARP, AND OTHER
Sermons. In crown 8vo., 6s. cloth.

" There is a remarkable originality throughout the volume, and great freshness and brilliancy of thought."—*Evangelical Magazine.*

ROBERT VAUGHAN, D.D.

THE DAILY PRAYER-BOOK, For the Use of Families. Square crown 8vo., 7s. 6d., cloth; or in morocco, 15s.

"He has written with good taste and right feeling, and his volume is well fitted to supply a want of heads of families."—*Daily News.*

THE CHURCH AND STATE QUESTION AS Settled by the Ministry of our Lord and of His Apostles. Small 8vo., 4s. cloth.

ENGLISH NONCONFORMITY. Second Thousand. 8vo., 7s. 6d. cloth.

COUNT DE GASPARIN.

THE FAMILY : Its Duties, Joys, and Sorrows. Crown 8vo., 7s. 6d. cloth.

"Since Isaac Taylor's ' Saturday Evening ' and ' Home Education ' we have had no book comparable to Count de Gasparin's on the Family. Indeed in many features we have no work to compare with it. So healthy and wise and beautiful a book has not come under our notice for years."—*Christian Work.*

E. DE PRESSENSE, D.D.

JESUS CHRIST : His Times, Life, and Work. New and cheaper edition, large crown 8vo., 9s., cloth. (Shortly).

"One of the most valuable additions to Christian literature which the present generation has seen."—*Contemporary Review.*

THE LAND OF THE GOSPEL : Notes of a Journey in the East. Crown 8vo., 5s., cloth.

"Brilliant life-like sketches of persons, places and events."—*British Quarterly Review.*

REV. Wm. TAYLOR, CALIFORNIA.

CHRISTIAN ADVENTURES IN SOUTH AFRICA. With Portrait and 15 Illustrations. Crown 8vo., 6s. 6d.

"His book is, in truth, full of adventures of all sorts ; revival scenes, practical suggestions in regard to missionary work, wilderness scenes, hunting stories, and social pictures, are strangely but effectively intermingled. The volume contains besides much solid and authentic information, and it is ornamented with sixteen telling woodcuts. It is a book to be obtained and prized by every man who cares earnestly for the conversion of the world."—*London Quarterly Review.*

"One of the most entertaining books of modern travel."—*City Press.*

CALIFORNIA LIFE ILLUSTRATED. New Edition, with 16 Illustrations. Crown 8vo., 4s., cloth.

REV. JOHN STOUGHTON.

ECCLESIASTICAL HISTORY. From the opening of the Long Parliament to the Death of Oliver Cromwell. In 2 vols. 28s., cloth.

"A markedly fair, charitable, large-minded, and honestly written history of of a period bristling with the very questions which sever Nonconformists from Churchmen to this very day."—*Guardian.*

CHURCH AND STATE TWO HUNDRED YEARS Ago: Being a History of Ecclesiastical Affairs from 1660 to 1663. Second Thousand. Crown 8vo., 7s. 6d. cloth.

REV. J. BALDWIN BROWN, B.A.

IDOLATRIES, OLD AND NEW ; Their Cause and Cure. Crown 8vo., 5s. cloth.

" A thoughtful, earnest, intelligent protest against the idolatry of the priest, of the sacrament, and of the Word ; written with manly vigour and much beauty."—*Freeman.*

THE DIVINE LIFE IN MAN. Second Edition. 7s. 6d.

THE DOCTRINE OF THE DIVINE FATHER-hood in Relation to the Atonement. Cloth limp, 1s. 6d.

THE LATE DR. LEIFCHILD.

REMARKABLE FACTS : Illustrative and Confirmatory of Different Portions of Holy Scripture. Crown 8vo., 5s., cloth.

"The narratives are admirably told, and many of them of the most singular character. A more impressive book, or a weightier testimony to the truth of the Bible principles, it would be difficult to find."—*Christian Work.*

REV. THOMAS W. AVELING.

MEMORIALS OF THE CLAYTON FAMILY. With Unpublished Letters of the Countess of Huntingdon, Lady Glenorchy, Rev. John Newton, &c., &c. In one Volume, 8vo., with Portraits. 12s. cloth.

" We have read this volume with unmingled satisfaction and untiring delight."—*British and Foreign Evangelical Review.*

O. DELL TRAVERS HILL F.R.G.S.

ENGLISH MONASTICISM : Its Rise and Influence. 8vo., 15s. cloth.

" Full of careful research and intelligent observation. He has written a highly interesting and thoroughly instructive book."—*Examiner.*

REV. T. BINNEY.

MICAH THE PRIEST-MAKER. A Handbook on
Ritualism. Second edition, enlarged. Post 8vo., 5s., cloth.

"It is surprising to see an outsider so thoroughly understanding the doctrine of different parties without his own community, or stating the whole case so emperately."—*Pall Mall Gazette.*

MONEY: A Popular Exposition in Rough Notes.
With Remarks on Stewardship and Systematic Beneficence. Third edition, crown 8vo, 5s., cloth.

THE PRACTICAL POWER OF FAITH. Illustrated
in a Series of Popular Discourses on the Eleventh Chapter of the Epistle to the Hebrews. Crown 8vo, 5s., cloth.

REV. R. W. DALE, M.A.

DISCOURSES DELIVERED ON SPECIAL OCCA-
sions. Crown 8vo., 6s., cloth.

"In Mr. Dale's 'Discourses on Special Occasions' we have some of the finest specimens of modern preaching."—*Contemporary Review.*

"It is long since we read sermons more full of stimulating thought, of catholic sympathies, of manly and noble eloquence."—*British Quarterly Review.*

THE JEWISH TEMPLE AND THE CHRISTIAN
Church. A Series of Discourses on the Epistle to the Hebrews. Crown 8vo., 7s. 6d., cloth.

MARIE SIBREE.

SERMONS FROM THE STUDIO. Crown 8vo.,
7s. 6d., elegantly bound, gilt edges.

"Six Art-sermons, each having for a text some great picture or statue, and consisting of a story connected therewith, mostly having an historical basis. Admirably conceived and exquisitely written."—*British Quarterly Review.*

"It is in every sense a beautiful book. Quiet, graceful, and effective in style, and very chastely got up, it ought to be a favourite book for presentation"—*Pulpit Analyst.*

REV. GEORGE GILFILLAN.

REMOTER STARS IN THE CHURCH SKY: A
Gallery of Uncelebrated Divines. In crown 8vo., 3s. 6d. cloth.

"The book is in every way worthy of the author of "The Gallery of Literary Portraits."—*North British Daily Mail.*

NIGHT: A Poem. In crown 8vo., 7s. 6d., cloth.

"A magnificent poem. The affluent imagery, the immense variety of allusions—historic, scientific, literary—the grand catholicity, and the reverend devoutedness of this poem will give it a permanent place amongst the choicest works of English bards."—*Homilist.*

S. R. PATTISON. F.G.S.

THE RISE AND PROGRESS OF RELIGIOUS
Life in England.   Post 8vo., 7s., cloth.

"Comprises a rich store of historic information of a very valuable kind."—*Homilist.*

REV. W. FROGGATT.

THE WORK OF GOD IN EVERY AGE. Crown
8vo., 6s., cloth.

"The present elaborate volume shows how deeply he has thought, how earnestly he has felt, and how wisely he has read on the subject. The book is unique, for it is employed entirely in tracing the history of great religious movements in the past, with the view of stimulating labour, strengthening faith, and encouraging hope in the present."—*English Independent.*

REV. CHARLES STANFORD.

SYMBOLS OF CHRIST. Crown 8vo., 7s., cloth. Contents: The Royal Priest of Salem—Shiloh—The Angel in the Burning Bush—Captain of the Lord's Host—The Shepherd of Souls—The Teacher of the Weary—The Refiner Watching the Crucible—The Healer—The Master of Life—The Wings of the Shekinah—The Advocate in the Court of Mercy—The Awakener.

"Cherished and familiar truths are presented in a great variety of aspects and with much richness of colouring, and the old words seem to glow with fresh life."—*Evangelical Christendom.*

CENTRAL TRUTHS.   Cheap edition, 3s. 6d., cloth.

"Mr. Stanford has an order of mind, and has acquired habits of study, eminently adapting him to be a teacher of wise and thoughtful men."—*Evangelical Magazine.*

INSTRUMENTAL STRENGTH.   Thoughts for
Students and Pastors.   Crown 8vo. cloth limp, 1s.

"The discourse is one from which every minister and student will learn something."—*Christian Work.*

POWER IN WEAKNESS.   Memorials of the REV.
WILLIAM RHODES.   Second edition, cloth limp, 2s.

"Mr. Rhodes's life was one of singular trial and affliction, and the remarkable development of mental power which he exhibited in the midst of great physical weakness forms the leading idea of the book."—*Record.*

JOSEPH ALLEINE: His Companions and Times.
Cheap issue. Second thousand, crown 8vo., 4s. 6d.

SECRET PRAYER.   Tenth Thousand.   2d.

FRIENDSHIP WITH GOD.   Eighth Thousand.   2d.

6

W. H. ALEXANDER.

THE BOOK OF PRAISES: Being the Book of Psalms according to the Authorised Version, with Notes, Original and Selected. In crown 8vo., 7s. 6d., cloth.

"Contains, in a condensed form, the best body of notes on the subject we have seen, abounding as they do in varied and valuable information and practical reflections."—*London Review.*

ISAAC TAYLOR.

THE FAMILY PEN. Memorials, Biographical and Literary, of the Taylor Family of Ongar. Edited by Isaac Taylor, M.A., Author of "Words and Places," &c. 2 vols., post 8vo., 15s., cloth.

"The Taylors of Ongar are a remarkable family, and for more than eighty years have been eminent for artistic skill, literary ability, and sincere piety. Of these characteristics the very interesting volumes now before us are the record, and we believe all readers will unite in commending the good taste displayed in their compilation."—*Record.*

THE HISTORY OF THE TRANSMISSION OF Ancient Books to Modern Times. Together with the Process of Historical Proof. Cloth. New Edition. Post 8vo. 7s. 6d.

CONSIDERATIONS ON THE PENTATEUCH. Third Edition, 8vo, 2s. 6d.

F. E. ANSTIE, M.D., F.R.C.P.

NOTES ON EPIDEMICS: for the Use of the Public. Fcap. 8vo. 4s., cloth.

" An important work, useful alike to the public and the practitioner, accurate in its facts, clear in its descriptions, and logical in its inferences, up to the most recent advance of medical science."—*Popular Science Review.*

EDWIN HODDER.

MEMORIES OF NEW ZEALAND LIFE. Second Edition, crown 8vo., 3s. 6d.

" A very graphic description of colonial society."—*Daily News.*

E. B. UNDERHILL, D.D., LL.D.

THE WEST INDIES: THEIR SOCIAL and Religious Condition. crown 8vo., 8s. 6d., cloth.

REV. JOSEPH PARKER, D.D.

THE PULPIT ANALYST. Designed for Preachers- Students, and Teachers. The First and Second Volumes. Edited by Joseph Parker, D.D.

REV. J. S. PEARSALL.

PUBLIC WORSHIP: the Best Method of Conducting
it. Second Edition, Enlarged.   Crown 8vo., 3s. cloth.

" A modest, wise, and catholic-minded book, on a great and difficult subject.   A volume full of good principles and of practical suggestions suited to
the present circumstances of the English churches."—*London* ~~Quarterly~~
Review.

THE
  Sec

MRS. BICKERSTAFFE.

ARAKI THE DAIMIO. A Japanese Story of the
Olden Time, crown 8vo., 5s. cloth.

"It exhibits in the writer a rare amount of information respecting the
customs and manners of the natives of Japan, and the tale is well told. The
book is not only very interesting, but very characteristic and instructive."—
Court Circular.

JOHN FOSTER.

THE IMPROVEMENT OF TIME. AN ESSAY,
with other Literary Remains. Edited by J. E. RYLAND,
M.A. Crown 8vo., 6s., cloth

"A really valuable production—it is fully worthy of Foster."—*Record.*

HANNAH MORE.

PIETAS PRIVATA : Prayers and Meditations. Chiefly
from the writings of Hannah More. With an Introductory
Essay on Prayer. Thirty-ninth Thousand, 32mo., 1s. 6d.,
cloth; 2s., roan, gilt edges.

J. E. RYLAND, M.A.

WHOLESOME WORDS; or, Choice Passages from old
Authors. Selected and Arranged by J. E. Ryland, M.A.
Fcap. 8vo., cloth, 3s. 6d., toned paper.

JOHN PYE SMITH, D.D. LL.D.

FIRST LINES OF CHRISTIAN THEOLOGY.
Edited by William Farrer, LL.B. Second Edition, 8vo.,
15s., cloth.

"The completest and safest guide in theological study to be found, as far as
we know, in any language."—*Eclectic Review.*

JOHN SHEPPARD.

THOUGHTS AT SEVENTY-NINE. By the Author
of "Thoughts on Devotion," &c. &c. Fcap. 8vo., 4s. 6d.

WORDS OF LIFE'S LAST YEARS. Fcap. 8vo., 3s.

THE FOREIGN SACRED LYRE. Fcap. 8vo., 5s. 6d.

THE CHRISTIAN HARP. Fcap. 8vo., 5s., cloth.

PRAYERS FOR TIMES OF TRIAL. Fcap. 8vo., 5s.

REV. CHARLES WILLIAMS.

THE FIRST WEEK OF TIME; or, Scripture in
Harmony with Science. Crown 8vo., 5s., cloth.

"Written in a fine spirit, with a noble reverence for the written word; and
the facts of science which are here gathered are fresh, and new, and striking."—
British and Foreign Evangelical Review.

7